The Mis-Education Against Homosexuality In The Bible

Rev. Gregory R. Smith, Harvestor

*All scripture is given by inspiration of God,
and is profitable for doctrine, for reproof, for correction,
for instruction in righteousness. That everyone may be perfect,
thoroughly furnished unto all good works.*
(2Timothy 3:16-17)

© 2010 New Points of View Publishing Group, LLC
"We Dare You To Write It"
Atlanta, Georgia

The Mis-Education Against Homosexuality in the Bible is designed to be a simple reference book from a black same gender loving perspective. The goal is assist Lesbian, Gays, Transgenders, and Same Gender Loving, friends and family members of the community in understanding biblical truths and untruths about homosexuality in the bible.

© 2010 Gregory R. Smith. Printed in the United States of America. All rights reserved. No part of this book may used or reproduced or transmitted in any form or by any means, electronic or mechanical, including photocopying, recording, or by an information storage and retrieval system—except by a reviewer who may quote brief passages in a review to be printed in a magazine, newspaper, or on the Web—without permission in writing from the publisher. For permission please contact:
New Points of View Publishing
P.O. Box 191754 Atlanta, GA 31119-1754
requests@newpointsofview.com

Although the author and publisher have made every effort to ensure the accuracy and completeness of information contained in the book, we assume no responsibility for errors, inaccuracies, omissions, or any inconsistency herein. Any slights of people, places or organizations are unintentional. First printing 2010

Unless otherwise noted scripture quotations are from the King James Version (KJV) of the bible.

FIRST EDITION
Library of Congress Control Number: 2010921882
Cataloging-in-Publication Data
    The Mis-Education Against Homosexuality In The Bible
    Rev. Gregory R. Smith, Harvestor 1ST Edition
    Includes bibliographical references
    Library of Congress Control Number: 2010921882
    1. Homosexuality – religious aspect –Christianity 2. Bible –Criticism, interpretation 3. Gay and Lesbian –United States—Religious Life
    ISBN: 1450569110   EAN-13: 9781450569118

Questions for the Author	author@newpointsofview.com
Book Orders, Permission, Speaking Request, New Authors	requests@newpointsofview.com
www.facebook.com/gregoryrsmith or greg smith	

ATTENTION WHOLESELLERS, UNIVERSITIES, COLLEGES, AND PROFESSIONAL ORGANIZATIONS: Quantity discounts are available on bulk purchases of this book for educational, gift purposes, or as premiums for increasing magazine subscriptions or renewals. Special books or book excerpts can also be created to fit specific needs. For more information, please contact New Points of View Publishing P.O. Box 191754 Atlanta, GA 31119-1754 or requests@newpointsofview.com

Dedicated To All The
Same Gender Loving Lesbians, Gay Men, Transgenders and Non-Identifying who have lived and died not knowing God loved them. You are not a mistake or an error; And will never be seen as a mistake or an error in the eyes of God. God's unconditional love supersedes human knowledge; We are manifestations of God's firm love. I dedicate this mission to you.

Special Thank you for their assistance and encouragement

Rev. Nancy Wilson - *My friend and Sista in the struggle who practices what she preaches.*
Bishop Tonyia Rawls - *An awesome woman of God appointed to me.*
Pastor Clay Allen - *An awesome Apostle for God. Our paths continue to cross as we celebrate our journeys and the anointed dialogue.*
Pastor Louis Holt Ph.D. - *You were never judgmental and I greatly appreciate it. You are an awesome Apostle for God.*
Tavarus Argas - *God has such great plans you. I thank you so much for all that you have done.*
Rashaan L. Nowell, M.Div. - *When this one accepts the assignment...watch out yawl.*
Oliver Sweeting - *This would not be possible without you.*
Rev. Ken Tennin - *My shoulder to lean on.*
Minister Paris Eley – *Always with loving words to share.*
Elder Claude Bowen - *Hellraiser, Agitator and Facilitator.*
Stanley McKinney - *Always loving and truthful with me.*
Cory Young – *You have been with me from the beginning when others would not listen. I am so grateful for your unconditional love.*
My Aunt Ella – *Your phone calls and voice messages always came when I was really feeling low and they always lifted me right back up.*

Table of Contents

Foreword		vii
Preface		xi
Introduction		xv
Terror Text Quick Reference Chart		xxiii

Chapter 1 — **The Mis-Education About The Bible** — 1
How we got the good book; Was King James a homosexual? Who were his lovers?

Chapter 2 — **The Mis-Education About Adam & Eve** — 15
Creation Story Challenges; Why are we being punished for the sin of Adam?

Chapter 3 — **The Mis-Education About The Rainbow** — 39
Noah's drunken decision; Cursing of Ham linked to slavery; Did Noah's son have sex with him?

Chapter 4 — **The Mis-Education About Sodom & Gomorrah** — 51
Was Abraham advocating for homosexuals? Desodomizing your minds; What Would Jesus Do?

Chapter 5 — **The Mis-Education About Being An Abomination** — 71
Abominations in the bible; Why Jesus challenged religious traditions? Why you are not an abomination?

Chapter 6 — **The Mis-Education About Gay Marriage** — 85
Does the church not know the scriptures; Marriage a social institution not a biblical solution; Civil Rights, No state elections for some marriages; Interracial and Slave Marriages.

Chapter 7 — **The Mis-Education About Present Day Gentiles (SGL)** — 109
Lesbianism in the bible; Practice what you preach; We are all guilty; LBGT connected to Civil Rights?

Chapter 8	**The Mis-Education About the Word Homosexuality**	131
	Effeminate & Homosexual Translation; Politics not homosexuality; First appearance of the word homosexual.	
Chapter 9	**The Mis-Education About Jesus & Homosexuality**	141
	What did Jesus say?; Love is the key; Misuse of Jesus and the Sodom scriptures	
Chapter 10	**The Mis-Education About Love In The Bible**	157
	Greek words for love; Ruth & Naomi; Jonathan & David; Robert Woods Theory; Our cultural vs. realities.	
Chapter 11	**The Mis-Education About Ten Words Used Against Homosexuality**	177
	Abomination, Anti-Christ, Curse, Devil/Satan, Evil, Hell, Immoral, Pervert, Repentance, Sinner	
Chapter 12	**The Mis-Education of Bible Topics & Homosexuality**	217
	Cross Dressing; Temple Prostitutes; Gay Clergy; Women To Be Silent; Book of Revelations	
Chapter 13	**The Mis-Education About Same Gender Loving Sexuality**	263
	Developing a healthy sexuality; Coming Out; Empowerment Networks; Dealing & Managing emotions; Avoiding Morality Utterances.	
Chapter 14	**The Rededication of Christians who happen to LBGT/SGL**	281
	Biblical scriptures to assist in building a stronger bible knowledge and insight into moving yourself to the next level.	
Appendix	A - Chapter Scripture References	349
Appendix	B - Charts & Figures	353
Appendix	C - Canada Marriage Bill Act	361
Appendix	D - Black SGL Survey	365
Bibliography		369
Index		373

Mission

First and foremost spread the love of God and the teachings of Christ Jesus Our Lord. Encourage our faith leaders to build ministries that meet our community where they are. Enlighten our community with perspectives that encourages them to begin having these conversations amongst themselves and within themselves.

FOREWORD

From My Sister In The Struggle

Rev. Greg Smith covers all the territory, and all the hot-button issues, as he "re-educates" us about mis-education. Rev. Greg roams all over the theological and biblical map, in a contemporary, engaging, conversation, that sounds like you could be having on someone's front porch.

He is provocative, imaginative and brings health and comfort and hope to so many. I know so many people who need this book, which is not intimidating, but inviting. His radically inclusive perspective, borne out of real-life experiences and ministry, is a refreshing take on the gospel of Jesus Christ.

The gay and lesbian movement in the United States has been largely perceived as a white male movement. This is at least in part because gay and lesbian white children, like other white children, are enculturated with sexism and white racism. Often, lesbian invisibility has meant that our specific issues as women get not attention in the "gay and lesbian" agenda. Likewise as with any movement, white people believe we have some divine right to rule, whether we acknowledge this or not.

This means that black gays and lesbians have had to walk a tightrope. To come out has often meant leaving home and family and culture behind. It has meant coming out into a white-dominated gay movement and having to work for change on both the outside and the inside of your movement. It has meant that black gay and lesbian people have often been asked to educate white leaders rather than being free to reach out to the black community. And in the black community, the movement for gay and lesbian rights has been seen as evidence of a "white man's disease." Racism in the U.S. has made overcoming homophobia in the black community more complex. In addition, the particular ways in which homophobia is related to sexism and the way that sexism and racism affect each other have made it hard for us to engage in dialogue about sexuality across racial lines.

Also, it is risky to compare oppression. Heterosexism and racism are not identical or equitable. I hear white gay and lesbian people express horror and disbelief that not all African-American politicians or church leaders support gay and lesbian rights, with the charge that the *"oppressed have become the oppressors."* Well, it isn't that simple. First of all, African-Americans do not have the power to reinforce their prejudices in our culture the way white people still do. Although anyone can have prejudices against persons of other races, in our world today, especially in the U.S., white people are more likely to have the power, wealth, and resources to make our prejudices count for something. White racism, as some have defined it, is the combination of personal prejudice with institutional privilege.

Secondly, there are many white gays and lesbians who have not really dealt at all with our racism (or sexism). We have not been willing to look at how we, as oppressed gays and lesbians, have often consciously or unconsciously perpetuated racism, sexism and classism. Why do we not also see ourselves as "the oppressed becoming the oppressor" when we do that?

I have also heard or seen African-American leaders act shocked or horrified when gay and lesbian people talk about oppression. This is made worse when the stereotype of gays and lesbians as a wealthy white minority is proffered by gay activist. The economic oppression of gays and of the black community is not equivalent, but it is also necessary to challenge the "white wealthy" stereotype of gays and lesbians.

Nevertheless, I want to be able to acknowledge and make use of the work that African-American biblical scholars and historians of African-American biblical interpretation have done, in order to help develop a gay and lesbian hermeneutic of the Bible.

Meanwhile, many black authors (starting with W.E.B. DuBois), sociologists, and linguist have written about the "double consciousness" that existed in the mind of black slaves in the United States, as they heard about and then eventually read the Bible for themselves. They wrote about how slaves heard and used the text to speak with a "double voice" about their experience. James Cone, in the *The Spirituals and the Blues*, wrote about how the words too many spirituals conveyed double meanings. Hymns that praised heaven were really about praising the freedom that could take place by traveling north. Many spirituals are filled with images of crossing over, crossing rivers, traveling on trains, being bound for glory, about destinations and a happier future, about the suffering and struggles of this life. "There's a meeting here tonight" was more about secret antislavery meetings and plans to escape than about church services. The slave had to develop this double consciousness: the public, and the private, almost double-entendre language that could even be spoken in the slave owner's presence without them understanding. This was an encoded language, shrouding feeling and intention.

In United Fellowship of Metropolitan Community Church, we have been compared to being in the closet to slavery. Sometimes we have done this in a way that does not take into account the real differences in these in these two experiences. This is similar to the way people today use the term closet generically to "anything kept secret or hidden." Sometimes that usage feels as though it trivializes the painful experience of gay and lesbian oppression. So, too comparing the closet with slavery can result in trivializing the horror of being owned by another human being, held captive against your will, beaten at whim, wrenched from your family, lynched, and murdered with no recourse for injustice.

Slavery is not just another form of oppression, and the closet is not just another secret. For gay and lesbian people, living in the closet, having to lie and cover up our sexuality has been soul killing and has often resulted in suicide, in lives of isolation, loneliness, and despair. It has been the source of enormous emotional, psychological, and spiritual pain. It has also been the cause of physical pain and discrimination. Gay people in the closet are more likely to engage in high risk sexual encounters and may be targets for extortion and other threats. They are at more risk for gay bashing and job discrimination.

Slavery, as an imperfect analogy, however, can help us understand our situation and our relationship to the biblical text. Gay and lesbian people, too, have had to have a kind of *double consciousness*, a secret vocabulary, an encoded language for public and private use. We, too, have tried to live in this double consciousness in a heterosexually dominated culture. We, too, have our "texts of terror" that have been used to justify the homophobia of the church and culture.

This analogy has helped me spiritually and emotionally to work through some of the insanity that has occurred over the years. As a church of "freed slaves," we are a living ecumenical witness to what a community for lesbian, gay, bisexual and transgendered folks (including our families and friends) looks like when homophobia is conquered (at least externally). We terrify those gays and lesbians church leaders and parishioner in the closet; we anger the liberals who want us to love them for privately supporting us while publicly betraying us; and we exasperate those conservatives who are convinced we can't be Christians when we pray, sing and testify of God's love for our community.

You can wander through the bible, its translations and commentaries, looking for hints and clues, debunking the traditional views of homosexuality and the bible. You can delight as we critique the critiquers. Or you can join us in the struggle. *"For this battle is not ours, it is the Lords."*

Rev. Nancy Wilson, Moderator & Author
Metropolitan Community Church Global Ministries
(Some of the foreword is excerpts from "OUR TRIBE: Queer Folks, God, Jesus and the Bible/African-American Lens on the Bible: Implications for a Gay and Lesbian Hermeneutics)

PREFACE

This book was commissioned to me more than twenty years ago. On the west coast many of my friends know me as Rev. Greg Smith but here in the southeast only a few of my friends know I was ordained in the Baptist Church. Yes, A Baptist Preacher. This book comes from years of self-discipline and a relentless pursuit to create an easy reference vehicle from a perceived complex subject.

These years have humbled me so, creating opportunities to build successful community programs, creating jobs, building networks, experiencing gay community physical assaults, public humiliation by gay rights activists, wrongful terminations, to meeting some of my dearest friends. I have learned from it all, but I am *"a better person not a bitter person"* about my life experiences. I learn from these experiences that there is a period in your life when bad people will let you go. There is a period in your life when you must let go of some good people. Letting go of the things of your past and pressing towards the mark is God shooting you towards your mark.

I was going crazy about the challenges with my sexuality and could not find any answers, so I had to study for myself. No one could understand the many times when I contemplated suicide, because I thought I was not worthy in the eyes of God. I had to free myself in addition to stop waiting for a preacher or someone to come out of seminary as my savior. I had to save myself.

I grew up in a bible-based church environment and within a black social consciousness movement. The bible was second nature to me but my understanding of homosexuality in

Preface

the bible was limited but had an inner yearning within me to seek a greater understanding of biblical truths. There were major challenges for me with homosexuality in the bible but my mental and spiritual freedom required me to address my inner challenges.

I have never been a supporter of outing Bible characters, but I understand and celebrate progressive theologian's critical analyses that have set the foundations before me. I have collaborated with some wonderful people across all spectrums of the LBGT/SGL community and the heterosexual religious community.

A few years ago one of my LBGT community activist colleagues asks me about my plans for the weekend. I told them I was working on this book about homosexuality in the bible. Their response was, *"I stay away from the discussion because it is so complicated."* Believe it or not this is a very common response but in spite of those responses; I refrained from telling some of my closest friends about this mission. This is the ark I have been asked to build in the middle of the desert.

I have witnessed countless noble attempts to teach on this subject matter. It was required to read and deconstruct a host of literature that would impress the noblest of scholars. This topic historically has been very conflict-ridden and controlled by a very segregated religious community. This is not limited to the heterosexual community but within the LBGT/SGL community.

In my commitment to provide knowledge to assist my community to becoming mentally free of the biblical institutionalized system of oppression. It is the Harriet Tubman syndrome embedded in my social consciousness, founded on the supposition of not waiting for your freedom but taking action to achieve your freedom. Ms. Tubman received a question from an interviewer, *(Modernization) "Harriet, you freed so many slaves. Ms. Tubman's response was, 'I could have freed* many *more if they knew they were slaves."*

If We Only Knew We Are Not Free.

If we only knew we are not free because we have houses, little dogs and fancy cars.
If we only knew we are not free because we can visit, bookstores, bathhouses and bars.

If we only knew we are not free, because seminaries will enroll us openly lesbian or gay.
If we only knew we are not free, when we are proselytizing in the same way.

If we only knew we are not free, when we have highest rate of suicide attempts amongst our youth.
If we only knew we are not free, when church folk attempt to legislate us and regulate us from the booth.

If we only knew we are not free, because we secure seats in a government office.
If we only knew we are not free, when we are still buried in a no name coffin.

If we only knew we are not free, because of a few celebrities on TV.
If we only knew we are not free, because our pastors don't talk about homosexuality.

If we only knew we are not free, when we live in fear of our discovery.
If we only knew we are not free, when deny ourselves spiritual recovery.

If we only know we are free, when never lose sight that there are many of our sista-z and brotha-z still operating in religious slavery.

Rev. Greg Smith, Harvestor

INTRODUCTION

You are not required to read this book in chronological order. Read the chapters that speak to you and can lead you and lead others to a fulfilling life with the teachings of Jesus Christ.

The book can be a tool to the biblically educated or uneducated with an interest to empower themselves and their LBGT/Same Gender Loving (SGL) friends, extended family members, parents and siblings.

The most important part for you is allowing yourself to listen to different points of view.

I would suspect a majority of you have no interest in arguing with people about the Bible. But if you wanted to facilitate a discussion, this book would equip you with some healthy dialogue information.

The Goals of This Book
(1) Provide a tool of reference to those seeking enlightenment.
(2) Creating a simple conversation on a believed complex topic.
(3) Provide a layperson's point of view.
(4) Encourage an exchange of ideas and thoughts.
(5) Encourage a genre of writings on this subject from a Kultural (LBGT/SGL) point of view.

What This Book Is Not Intended To Do

(1) Not intended to encourage people to leave their church.
(2) Not intended for the reader to bash *(disrespect)* the traditional church with this information.

(3) Not intended to make you question your belief in Jesus Christ.

(4) Not intended to be a weapon of truth or a platform of *"I know more than you"* point of view.

(5) Not intended to denounce the power and respect for the Bible.

This book's focus is not about convincing heterosexuals to embrace, love, and support or change their position on homosexuality. The focus is about developing empowering tools and images of our Kulture (LBGT/SGL) regardless of whether a person is Asian, Black, Caucasian, Latino, Jewish, Protestant, Catholic, Muslim, Atheist, Recovery Addict, Sex Worker, educated or spiritually misguided. It is important for you to learn how to embrace and love yourself and not be ashamed of who you are and to begin to develop healthy images of yourself.

The religious right wing groups, traditional black church and some of our closeted gay members in the black church will read or hear about this book and make the a case that the Kingdom of Heaven is under attack. That has been the religious platform of the Christian Church on gay marriage but it is nothing but *"love fighting back."* We love God so much, we going into the battle for our Lord. This not about the God who cannot but the God that has already won the battle.

Words You May Hear For The First Time

(1) "Same Gender Loving" is a phrase used instead of Lesbian, Gay, Bisexual and Transgender by some African Americans in the homosexual lifestyle. You will find many Africans Americans in the life that prefer this reference over Lesbian, Gay or queer *(you will not find queer used anywhere in this book)*. The phrase was

Introduction

originally introduced to the community by Mr. Cleo Manago, Founder of the AMASSI Centers. This term in some areas of the community is the politically correct reference for black homosexuals.

(2) "Brotha-z or Sista-z" - This is a phrase I established as a means to include all in our community regardless of how they self identify. Everyone is covered from *"a-z" sista-z or brotha-z.* **"BriSta-z"** is just a compound of the Brotha-z and Sista-z. This term is listed in alphabetical order not to imply the male takes precedence before female. The word Brista-z has its own evolution process evolving from "effeminate male or masculine female" or a collective way of referring to our Kulture.

(3) "Kulture" is a term I use to think outside of the stereotypical names of associated with the Lesbian, Gay, Bisexual, Transgender and Same Gender Loving. The purpose of spelling it with a **"K"** is to imply a relentless pursuit of knowledge. You may or may not fall under any of the stereotypical labels. In this Kulture, there is an evolution process of growing and understanding. You will find me using this word to stress in some areas the need for continually seeking of knowledge, understanding and the dangers of systematic labeling. You tell us how to refer to you.

Internalized Homophobia

"Never let anyone tell you that you cannot share your point of view on any subject."

On of the goals of this book is to encourage and embrace dialogue. There will be community debates about this book's point of view. Even some of my very close friends will have issues with various points of view. It will not be because our points of view are so different, but because the understanding and translations contradict what we may have been trained to believe. These conclusions will irritate and challenge many learned bible enthusiasts. In this part of the wilderness everything is open for discussion especially if it implies we are not worthy.

Our community dialogue is more than who is on the down low, what is the down low or a deluge of writings about our sexual escapes and fantasies. We celebrate all of it but we are much more that.

Our *"Institutionalized Homophobia"* is any system with a primary function to institute limitation, no hope, no change, fear, punishment, and superiority rooted in the insecurity of an individual and/or group of people. Institutionalized Homophobia has been built on the backs of others and has systematically programmed a negative image a community.

In Matthew 15:1-9

> *"Why do your disciples transgress the tradition of the elders? For they do not wash their hands when they eat bread."*
> *(Matthew15:2)*

The Pharisees' traditional belief system did not approve of the message Jesus Christ was sharing with the people. This was a threat to Pharisees' finances and power. If the people found out they received untrue information, the Pharisees could be stoned to death.

> *But and if we say, Of men;*
> *all the people will stone us:*
> *for they be persuaded that John was a*
> *prophet. (Luke 20:1-8)*

Introduction

We all have a right to share our point of view, but if people want to challenge it, there is a healthy and unhealthy way to present your positions. I have never run from a challenging conversation if it is facilitated in a healthy manner.

I am not a proponent of telling others what they should think. This is a toxic means of communication. In my pursuit for truth over the years I have listened to various healthy and unhealthy perspectives, in addition to attending speaking engagements with some very learned orators and even the ones I did not agree taught me what I did not know *"there perspectives."* When you journey on the lines of sister and brotherhood you are guaranteed to get different points of views *(i.e. lesbians, gay men, transgenders, down low, bisexuals, rich or poor gay folks, addicts in and out of recovery, gay rights activist, PLWA and preachers)*

I understand we all have a comfort zone and we address the issues that dramatically affect us emotionally and physically. Truth to one person may not be truth to another. I would encourage you to stay on a constant pursuit for the seeking of truth.

This will challenge us to view from four different points of view:

(1) LBGT/SGL Consciousness - Although you have experienced freedom to engage on sexual and social levels this is only the beginning to the liberation of your minds, body and souls.

(2) Black–On-Black Consciousness - Our own black family sees us as less than honorable in the community and is willing to advocate for the restriction and humiliation of their own black **sista-z** and **brotha-z.**

(3) Euro-centric Perspective - Very different value system rooted in a long history of imperialism, corporate thinking and incorporating systems of oppressive and controlling hierarchies (i.e. social groups, ethnic and gender). This is not about looking for bad or good but the residual affects of a dominant culture. It is healthy for European-Americans to utilize this method to assist them in developing a healthy working relationship with communities of color.

(4) Heterosexual Privileges – You have the right to be who you are, but the thought of losing this right and/or being challenged about who you are is not even a part of their conscious thought.

It is healthy for our Kulture (LBGT/SGL) to seek and understand the information from various perspectives to provide a level of knowledge that stimulates healthy dialogue and a decision making process, in addition to providing tools to manage the unhealthy thought process.

There is difference between *"institutionalized homophobia and internalized homophobia."* The residual affects of institutionalized homophobia is the root of internalized homophobia. Internalized homophobia is not just hating yourself but disregarding those who are trying to liberate you. The later is just as dangerous.

You are manifesting internalized homophobia when all the images and knowledge of liberation is given validation when a

Introduction

heterosexual perspective is presented but devaluing the perspectives of your own Kulture. It has manifested itself when you are invited to meet on the behalf of our people but yet instill you talk down to us as people but talk us up as a community to keep your seat in their system. When out of your mouth are condescending words *"sissy, faggot, dikes or you know how sissies are"* manifested from the institutionalized systems that gave breath them. You have manifested them when they are used as words of endearment.

I remember when Ms. Oprah Winfrey was interviewing Jay-Z and the topic of the word "nigga" was being discussed. They agreed to disagree on the impact of the word. I love her for taking a stance and accepting the criticism, at the same time I understand Jay-Z's challenge as well amongst his peers. For some within this black generation the consciousness is they have a right to use the word "nigga" because it has a different meaning to them today. In our Kulture many think on the same premise that the words sissy, faggot and dike are words they have removed negative images out of. This is what internalized homophobia breeds into our consciousness. The classes notion because I am out and use these words of oppression like a funny joke or to make ones self the life of the party. If one hundred million people, said something that was ridiculous that does not make it right, it is still ridiculous.

Internalized homophobia encompasses two primary dimensions from an outer and inner perspective. The inner is what you think on the inside manifested in self-hate, lack and limitation. The outer is what you express, your actions, your tone, your denial of truth, your lack of support for your own Kulture. This is a whole book within itself. Later!

The conversation of homosexuality in the bible is not complicated especially if we "desodomize" *(see Sodom & Gomorrah Chap.4)* these images in our consciousness. It is important to remove and/or manage the negative seed planting of superior and inferior perceptions. This limited thinking can grow into various degrees of internalized homophobia.

Excited About The Book

I am very excited about the conversation this book will generate and pray you find it to be an empowering and a good resource tool. I hope to meet you one day and hear your perceptive on life, scriptures and God's Love. Keep me in your prayers. *"The Harvestor"*

Terror Text
Quick Scripture Reference

Text	Scripture	Reference
Genesis 1:27, 2:21	Adam & Eve Creation Story	Chap 2
Genesis 9:20-24	Noah's & His Son-law	Chap 3
Genesis 19	Sodom & Gomorrah	Chap 4
Leviticus 18:22 & 20:13	Abomination	Chap 5
Deuteronomy 22:5	Cross Dressing	Chap 12.1
Deuteronomy 23:4-6	Laws of acceptance in the congregation	Chap 12.2
Deuteronomy 23:17-23	Whores, Sodom, Abomination	Chap 12.2
Judges 19:11-30	Tribal Immorality	Chap 12:15
1Kings 14:21-24	Sodomites in the land	Chap 12.3
1Kings 15:9-15	Temple Prostitutes	Chap 12.4
1Chronicles 21:1-4	Temptation by Satan	Chap 12.5
Job 1-2	Punished because of your sins	Chap 12.6
Ezekiel 16:49	Gods Punishment	Chap 12.7
Daniel 1:9 Acts 8:26-38	Eunuchs	Chap 12.14
Roman 1:26	Lesbianism	Chap 7
1Corinthians 6:9	Effeminate/Homosexual	Chap 8
1Cor 14:34 1Tim 2:11-12 1Peter 2:15	Sexist scriptures used against women and lesbian clergy	Chap 12.9
1Timothy 1:7-10	Defile themselves with mankind	Chap 12.8
James 1:14-15, 4:2-6	Source of Temptation	Chap 12.10
1Peter 1:22-25	Unfeigned love	Chap 12.11
2Peter 2:6	Condemned them to extinction	Chap 12.12
Jude 7	After strange flesh	Chapter 12:16
Revelations 11:8	Works of Destruction	Chap 12.13

Robert Goss, in Jesus Acted Up, first used the title of Phyllis Trible's book, Texts of Terror, to identify the six Bible passages quoted by fundamentalists and uninformed Christians to condemn homosexuality. These have become our "text of terror." Their existence, combined with millennia of misinterpretation, has formed a powerful wedge, keeping lesbians and gay men from any hope of being able to celebrate and experience the story and poetry of the Bible. (Our Tribe: Queer Folks, God, Jesus and the Bible, Rev. Nancy Wilson pg 65)

CHAPTER 1

The Mis-Education About The Bible

You do not need permission to read, write or share your thoughts about the bible, especially if the point of view is about your freedom. Stop guilt tripping yourself because you may not know your way around the bible. Just because someone grew in the church does not mean they grew up knowing God or their bible.

One way of looking at the bible is to think of it as a divine drama, with God as the chief character. It is not a spectacle for us to sit back and enjoy or criticize, however, for we are all taking part in the drama ourselves. The theme of the drama is the Acts of God---past, present, and future. It begins with a prologue; then come three acts, followed by an epilogue. The prologue, which contained in the first eleven chapters of Genesis, sets the stage for the whole drama. Act I is rest of the Old Testament. Act II is the gospels. Act III is the rest of the New Testament. The epilogue is the book of Revelations.

The bible is concerned with much more than with theology (study of God), that is, it is a book about God and his dealings with people (men and women). It does not speculate about the existence of God. That is something we can neither prove nor disapprove. God cannot be proven, God must revealed. It rather focuses our on certain aspects of life and the world around us, records certain things that have happened in history, claims to interpret their meaning, and then compels us to make a choice. It forces us to conclude that the interpretation of life which it offers is complete nonsense, or to accept that interpretation with all it's implications for ourselves.

The Bible does not stand or fall by the accuracy of its information, because it is not a textbook of science, or history or archaeology. It stands or falls by what it has to say about the purpose of life, the meaning of the world we live in, and the reality that lies beyond it. It claims to provide the clue to the mystery that surrounds our existence, to tell us who we really are, where we should be going, what we ought to be doing, and how we can do it.

There are professional bible pushers who would never change their oppressive way of thinking because it is not financially beneficial for them or operate under the false assumption they are saving The Kingdom of God.

I have grown very weary of the black church taking Anti-gay positions, because of what they think the bible says so. It was black folks and white allies who became "Sick N Tired" of groups using the Bible to justify the beating, humiliation and hanging of blacks in America. The KKK continues to use the Bible to teach hatred for Blacks, Jews and the LBGT/SGL community.

Now, the more this book circulates, people in the LBGT/SGL will also be critical for a host of reasons, especially those who have rationalize in their mind they are religious leaders and academic authorities for the LBGT/SGL community today.

They will convince themselves they must go out and protect the standard and accuracy of the bible book. I have the utmost respect for the institution of higher learning, but the institution must also respect all of the elders in this Kulture of nomads (wanderers).

Here is a little bible insight for you. In Romans 3:18 Paul pulls out from the Old Testament Psalms 36:1

"There is no fear of God before their eyes." (Ps 36:1)

The word *"fear"* is one of the most often misinterpreted words by church. You will read in Old Testament scriptures *"Thou shall feareth the Lord"* the word fear in Hebrew has several meanings in the traditional dictionary and bible dictionary.

Webster's defines the word:
1. a distressing emotion aroused by impending danger, evil, pain, etc., whether the threat is real or imagined; the feeling or condition of being afraid.
2. a specific instance and of or propensity for such a feeling
3. a concern or anxiety
4. *Reverential awe esp. toward God*

It was helpful to read through the four definitions before we arrived at the appropriate meaning. In Hebrew the word is translated as "believe and trust."

Here is a next level way of reading your Bible. When you read the "fear" in the bible (i.e. for thou shall fear the Lord) oftentimes if you replace it with *"believe and trust"* you see the reverence of God being spoken. *(Just a little Bible nugget for you; that was tasty, huh? :)*

As you read the Bible, you should look primarily at its religious and moral teaching, and only incidentally at background details. If you feel unworthy and/or ashamed, then the church has convinced you that God is limited and that is true "Blaspheme" on their part.

Old Testament - *For the commandment is a lamp; and the law is light; and reproofs of instruction are the way of life* *(Proverbs 6:23)*

New Testament - *All scripture is given by inspiration of God, and is profitable for doctrine, for reproof, for correction, for instruction in righteousness: That the person of God may be perfect, thoroughly furnished unto all good works. (2Timothy 3:16-17)*

When you study the life of Timothy, you learn about this young missionary worried himself sick dealing with the religious community. The church's role is to help you understand how Jesus can work in your life and why Christ's love is unconditional.

I understand for many it will be difficult to let go of the traditional thinking, especially when you have been programmed since you were a child to think of God divine love with limitation.

The Bible as the main source and standard of Christian teaching is not uniform. It does not present a simple unity of teaching but rather a multiplicity of different approaches which must be resolved by critical reflection, not necessarily but theologians. This may be considered to be the domain of biblical scholars rather than theologians. I conclude it is the mission of those who chose not be oppressed with faulty and in error biblical teachings. In black community we were in slaved due to some biblical scholars and theologians biblical interpretation.

The study of God serves faith through critical clarification, but there is a danger that the critical reflective

Chapter 1 The Mis-Education About The Bible

temper may replace rather than serve the humble openness and expectancy before God.

You Can Take The Red Pill or Blue Pill?

Remember in the movie *The Matrix*; Neo had a choice of the red pill or the blue pill. His choice required him to unplug himself from the master's programming and come discover life as it really was. Neo was a chosen one, but he questioned himself *"Are You The One"*.

There is famous story in Bible regarding John The Baptist. The Bible tells us that John had been jailed for doing God's work and was scheduled to die. John was scheduled to be beheaded the next day. John sent a question back through the disciples to Jesus: "Are You The One or Should I Look For Another?"

Morpheus in *The Matrix* was a parity of John The Baptist. It is probably time to unplug you. Which pill are you going to take: "red" or "blue?" Truth is always scary because it causes change and the shedding of old skin for new is very uncomfortable.

> *For God so loved the world, that he gave his only begotten Son, that whosoever believeth in him should not perish, but have everlasting life.17 For God sent not his Son into the world to condemn the world; but that the world through him might be saved. (John 3:16-17)*

Imagine yourself growing up and thinking that you are the only one. Growing up believing the thoughts you're having are nasty and dirty. You want so bad to get away but over time you believe this is how it is and there's no other way besides what you have been programmed. The processes of unplugging yourself is a conscious choice to question all that you know and all that you think you know. We know what we have been told not what we have yet to discover.

King James Version of the Bible

This translation was published in 1611 and very rapidly went through several editions, nearly all of which have some changes in the text. It took nearly fourteen years for the King James Version to replace the Geneva Bible in the affection of the people; once established, however, it became the Bible of English-speaking people for over 350 years, down to the present time.

King James was not really interested in the bible.

One area of the life of King James that for many years remained clouded in controversy was allegations that James was homosexual. When the Queen Elizabeth I, died, Prince James VI of Scotland became King James I of England. He was one of the most intelligent Kings to reign over England, but his personal life made him the most controversial since his relative, King Henry VIII.

Elizabeth was King; Now James Is Queen!

King James did father several children by Anne of Denmark; it is actually more accurate to say that he was allegedly a bi-sexual. While his close relationships with a number of men were noted, earlier historians questioned their sexual nature; however, few modern historians cast any doubt on the King's bisexuality and the fact that his sexuality and choice of male partners both as King of Scotland then later in London as King of England were the subject of gossip from the

Chapter 1 The Mis-Education About The Bible

city taverns to the Privy Council. People would write in Latin on the streets of England;

> *"Rex fuit Elizabeth nunc est regina Jacobas.*
> *Elizabeth was King now James is Queen."*

He was a flaming homosexual. His activities in that regard have been recorded in numerous books and public records; so much so, that there is no room for debate on the subject.

King James Male Relationships

His relationship as a teenager with fellow teenager Esmé Stuart, Earl of Lennox was criticized by Scottish Church leaders, who were part of a conspiracy to keep the young King and the young French courtier apart, as the relationship was improper, to say the least. Lennox, facing threats of death, was forced to leave Scotland. Esmé Stewart, 1st Duke of Lennox, 1st Earl of Lennox (1542–May 26, 1583) was the son of John Stewart, 5th Lord of Aubigny. Sir James Melville described him as "of nature, upright, just, and gentle".

Throughout his youth, James was praised for his chastity, since he showed little interest in women; and after the loss of Lennox, he continued to prefer male company.

In the 1580s, King James openly kissed Francis Stewart Hepburn, Earl of Bothwell. Contemporary sources clearly hinted their relationship was a sexual one. Robert Carr was considered to be his devoted lover.

If there is still any doubt, it should be noted that George Villiers also held an intimate relationship with King James about which King James himself was quite open. King James called Villiers his "wife" and called himself Villiers' "husband!" King James died in 1625 of gout and senility. He is buried in the Henry VII chapel in Westminster Abbey, with one of his favorite male suitors on his right, and another on his left. The church Bishops had issues with King James' sexuality, but they could not say anything. Why *"Off With Their Head."*

I know you want to fall out and laugh. But, whatever you do; do not under any circumstances use this information as a vehicle to discredit the church and its position on homosexuality. If you make this an issue at your church, you should probably start shopping for a new church home. They will be having a meeting about you and I don't think it will be about promoting you in the church, Brenda.

Feminist Interpretation of the Bible

From a feminist liberation perspective, feminist theory of interpretation begins with a different view of reality, asking what is appropriate in light of *"personally and politically reflected experience of oppression and liberation."* Interpretation does not begin with strict/narrow/harsh statements about the authority of scripture and principle.

There are similar issues that have been raised in areas of biblical authority, and reproduction of interpretation such as those expressed by writers within the Jewish, Black, Hispanic, and Asian community.

This feminist interpretation provides resources to develop healthy discussion in reference to Bible philosophy, lessons, and sermons in addition to individual pursuit of social consciousness. Feminism is a belief in the political, social, and economic equality of women.

The National Council of the Churches of Christ in the U.S.A. which holds the copyrights for the Revised Standard Version of the Bible.

The publication ignited a host of protest because it made substitutions for key biblical words and concepts:

God the Father [and Mother]; God the SOVEREIGN ONE.

New points of view are needed because of the growing consciousness of women requires them to challenge traditional biblical interpretations that reinforce patriarchal domination. From this point of view the liberation of women from a perspective of the traditional one-sided male dominated middle-class interpretation is moving women towards equal parity with biblical characters in concert while respecting the prophetic and liberating story of God's concern for the oppressed.

Inclusive Bible Language

In many religious communities today there is a lot of discussion about the word "he" being used in reference to God. Let us look at the understanding of the word "he" as we know it today. In our Kultural Faith Communities this word has challenged many collaborative relationships.

I am not taking a position for or against the usage of the word for God Is Spirit.

Webster's provides the following definition and history of the word "he";

> 1. The male person or animal being discussed or last mentioned; that male. *2. anyone (without reference to sex); that person(noun)* 3. any male person or animal; a man; he's

and she's. (adjective) Usage. Traditionally, the pronouns HE, HIS, AND HIM have been used generically to refer to indefinite pronouns like anyone, everyone, and someone and to singular nouns that do not indicate sex; *Every writer hopes he will produce a bestseller.* This generic use is often criticized as sexes, although many speakers and writers continue the practice.

Various approaches have been developed to avoid generic HE. One is to use plural forms entirely: *those who agree should raise their hands. All writers hope they will produce bestsellers.* Another is to use them as planned and the feminine singular pronouns together: he or she, she or he; he/she, she/he. For blending the feminine and masculine pronouns as she, have not been widely adopted.

"To define right and wrong is trained; to define healthy and unhealthy is a seeking of truth."

This new understanding of inclusive language in many circles has been harsh. It is healthy to keep in mind many in our Kulture are unfamiliar with this terminology and we should be sensitive to their lack of knowledge and not turn them off.

In this work we will have to repeat lessons over and over again. Then we will have to repeat the same lessons over and over again. If you are challenged with the role of repeating yourself; you should not accept the role of a teacher, pastor, minister, deacon, trustee, communicator, parent, or significant other.

Just because I have knowledge of something does not mean you should change your mind because of my new found knowledge. This is no different then fanatical Christian proselytizing.

Chapter 1 The Mis-Education About The Bible

| *I found Jesus and you need to come to Christ or you going to hell.* | *I have discovered a more inclusive way of spirituality and if you don't do it you are racist, sexist, religious fanatic or homophobic.* |

You see how we can repeat systematic oppressive ideologies. If we are not careful this issue will cause internal strife within our Kultural Faith Centers.

Inclusive interpretations have to do with imaging God as transcendent of male sexual characteristics or as inclusive of both male and female characteristics.

- ✓ · If you can see a woman you see God.
- ✓ · If you see a homeless person you see God.
- ✓ · If see an alcoholic you see God.
- ✓ · If you see a Same Gender Loving person you see God.
- ✓ · All are created in the likeness and image of God.

There is much to learn about the various models of power used to oppress various cultures. The African-American community is a healthy example of a culture; that re-examined the scriptures in concert with asking questions of masters (Pharaoh) teachings and about there suggestions or implications. While seeking the knowledge to liberate and engage in social movements of freeing the whole person mind, body and soul.

Use This Information With Caution

I would strongly recommend you do not use this information as a vehicle to discredit the church and its position on homosexuality. If you make this an issue at your church, you should probably start shopping for a new church home. In addition to being prepared for some if not all of the following:

    (1) They will attempt to humiliate you
    (2) They will question your education,
    (3) They will question your commitment to Christ,
    (4) They will question who you character,
    (5) They will go after your job,
    (6) They will passionate because they under the assumption they are protecting the Kingdom of God.
    (7) There will be gay folk in the church, taking the lead saying "Amen, Pastor."

This information is for you to understand a series of events that took place to put together a book that has been used a tool to empower many and oppress many others.

Moving Yourself To The Next Level

Chapter 1 The Mis-Education About The Bible

Each process question or thought can be viewed from the following perspectives: Same Gender Loving (SGL), Heterosexual (H) or Both (B). It is healthy to try and view from various perspectives to get insight into how others may process an issue. All perspectives are valid and should be respected and not condemned. In all thy getting; get understanding.

(1) (B) - During the black slavery period there were people with Ph.D.'s in Biblical Studies building academic platforms rationalizing slavery.
    a. What's the difference, if people with the same credentials rationalize the disapproval of persons in the LBGT/SGL community?

(2) (B) - If people of African-Descent did not reproof or challenge erroneous bible teachings for themselves.
    a. What do you think the historical black churches would look like?
    b. What does a slave message sound to you today?

(3) (B) - There is an African Proverb "We are who we are waiting for. No one is coming to save us but us."
    a. Who do you need to go and help?

(4) (SGL) - If the LBGT/SGL community does not build affirming churches for themselves.
    a. What do you think they will look like in the long run?
    b. If you were to attend one of these churches. What makes you uncomfortable?

(5) (B) - If you were taught how to cook a family dish but years later, learned the dish has been causing you major health problems.
   a. What healthy decisions do you need to make?

(6) (H) – If you were told by your spiritual guide that you are good heterosexual only if you are circumcised. How would you address this issue with your spiritual guide?

(7) (H) - The Holocaust was one of the greatest modern day tragedies to every happen. If you were Jewish what would you want to have known about your oppressors?

(8) (H) There is a young person in your church who may give the appearance of effeminate boy or masculine female.
   a. How should the church empower them to love themselves?
   b. What would be your challenges with addressing the need to empower all of God's children?
   c. If you were in a predominately white church and saw some of your friends treating a black member unfairly. What would you do and why?

CHAPTER 2

The Mis-Education About Adam & Eve

The story of Adam and Eve in the religious community has become one of the key arguments against homosexuality, *"for god created Adam & Eve not Adam and Steve."* Since, I am a same gender loving man; I have the right to question any arguments that would imply or attempts to justify me not only as being lesser than a man but also a mistake or an error in the eyes of God. For these reason alone I challenge the creation myths not as a disregard for the bible but the power of God that lives in me and affirms me one of God's Children made in the likeness and image of God.

Adam and Eve is one of the greatest stories ever told. In the story we learn about a spiritual creation and physical creation.

Spiritual Creation
"God created man in his own image
in the image of God created he him male
and female created he them."
(Genesis 1:27)

Physical Creation
And he went and put Adam to sleep
and took one of Adam's rib to make woman.
(Genesis 2:21)

God has the power to create all and is all.

We do not know how the universe started. Science has various theories about it, but no one knows for certain. We must not expect that the writer of the first chapter of Genesis, whose ideas were those of over two thousand years ago, thought any more scientifically about the origin of sun, moon, stars and of the earth itself, that did contemporaries. He is content to think of some kind of chaos or disorder as the first stage *"And the earth was without form, and void; and darkness was upon the face of the deep. And the Spirit of God moved upon the face of the waters." (Genesis. 1:2)*, out of which come an ordered and harmonious universe. The writer's chief is not in how this happened—which is what modern science is concerned with—but in making plain his conviction that it did not happen by accident.

We may disregard the various steps in the process. The writer divides it into six days. These do not mean "days" of twenty-four hours, or "years", or even "stages." This is a poem and not a timetable. The writer lets his imagination play upon the theme of the created world and its mysteries, which were as obscure to him as they are to us. He sees the orderly succession of night and day, the sequence of summer and winter. He scans the starry heavens, and the teeming life of land and sea. He contemplates man, with his purposeful control of the natural world. And he writes this great hymn of praise, because he sees behind it the entire mind and purpose of a Supreme Power, whom he has already, come to know in his own experience, and whose guiding hand he has seen in the movements of history.

The writer was a devout member of a community which regarded every seventh day as a day not only of rest but of recreation in the deepest sense. It was the day above all others when people gathered together to worship, pray and learn the will of God. It was the day when, above all, they acknowledged the sovereignty of God over their lives, when they confessed their failures, gave thanks for God's goodness, and sought his help. The seventh day was a real sense of the Lord's Day.

It is not surprising, therefore, that the writer of this magnificent hymn of Creation chooses to think of the ordinary creative working week of six days as a reflection of the great creative acts of God "in the beginning." The culminate in the seventh day, on which he pictures God resting and refreshing himself, and contemplating his work with satisfactions,

> *"And God saw everything that he had made, and, behold, it was very good. And the evening and the morning were the sixth day. Thus the heavens and the earth were finished, and all the host of them, And on the seventh day God ended his work which he had made; and he rested on the seventh day from all his work which he had made. And God blessed the seventh day, and sanctified it: because that in it he had rested from all his work which God created and made. "*
>
> *(Gen. 1:31-2:3)*

as a man, conscious of having done a good job for six days, would rest and recreate himself and commune with the Creator.

There is obviously nothing in this dramatic poem which conflicts with anything that biologists can tell us about the evolution of living creatures, or with what geologists have to say about the age of the earth, or with what astronomers may conjecture about an expanding universe. Science is looking at the problem from a different angle. It would not have alarmed the author of this chapter to be told that the earth was millions of years old, although it would no doubt have perturbed

Archbishop Ussher, who calculated in 1654 that the creation of the world had taken place in 4004 B.C.

Nor would this old writer have been greatly concerned to be told about the millions of galaxies, compared with which our solar system is very small fry. Indeed he was firmly of the opinion, like all his contemporaries, that the earth was a flat disc mounted on pillars, and the beneath the earth and above the solid dome of the sky were the waters of the great deep. But this kind of knowledge was incidental. He was much more interested in theology.

So we are right to see in the first four words of this chapter the really essential point in the biblical view of Creation. The Bible invites us to believe that the universe, by whatever process it has come into present state, and however long that process has taken, is not the result of chance or accident, or of some impersonal evolutionary development, or of some blind groping life force, but that it has its origin in the mind and purpose of the Supreme Being, whose nature an actions are disclosed in the drama that is to follow. Before there was a universe at all, the Bible tells us, there was God. Whatever is, is there because God willed it. He is the power behind and within everything that exists.

When we remember that the ancient Egyptians viewed Creation as an act of sexual self-abuse on the part of the Creator, and that the ancient Mesopotamians viewed it as the by-product of a conflict between numerous squabbling gods and goddesses, we cannot fail to recognize the profound insight which lies behind the Hebrew concept of Creation by divine command. The universe and all that it contains comes into being because: *"God said, Let there be..."* Here already the Bible introduces a theme which recurs again and again: the

Word of God. The created world is the product of the mind of God. He expresses his purpose in a rational way, a way that men understand. Later, the prophets of Israel declare the purpose of God for the world by using the same phrase: Thus saith the Lord. St. John, too, harks back to this creation story when he speaks of Jesus as the Word made flesh,

And the Word was made flesh, and dwell among us, (and we beheld his glory, the glory as of the begotten of the Father), full of grace and truth. (John 1:14)

the purpose of Creation summed up and expressed in a human life.

Now faith is the substance of things hoped for, the evidence of things not seen. For by it the elders obtained a good report. (Hebrews 11:1-2)

There are two other important assertions in this chapter. The first is that *"So God created man in his own image, in the image of created he him; male and female created he them" (Genesis 1:27).* The Bible sees man, as distinct from the other animals, in a special relationship to God. Whatever the word "image" implies, it certainly means that men in their own sphere are god-like. The psalmist speaks of man as the crown of creation (Psalms 8), controlling the forces of nature and controlling its natural resources. The author of this chapter sees man's status and function in the same way: privilege to run the world, but responsible and accountable to its Creator.

But if man alone is made in God's image, human personality has a value which is unique. Men and women may not be treated as goods and chattels, or as cogs in a machine, or as tools of the state. The Bible has high view of man because it has a high view of God. It sees man as capable of great things.

Above all, the idea of the image of God suggests that there is in man, unlike any other creature, the possibility of responding to God. He may do so or not, for man is free to choose. There is in any event a point of contact, an awareness of God, which St. Augustine has well expressed: *"Thou hast made us for thyself, and our hearts are restless till they find rest in thee."*

The other important claim that this Creation story makes is in Genesis 1:31:

> *[31] And God saw every thing that he had made, and, behold, it was very good. And the evening and the morning were the sixth day.(Genesis 1:31)*

This picture of the Creator gazing round on his handiwork with approval has great significance for our attitude to the world. If God made it, and delighted in it, it is not for us to spurn the material things of life, as if the Bible inculcated some kind of rarified spirituality which disdains the good things of this world. The Bible has certainly much to say about the wrong use of material things, but here we are reminded that this is God's world. If things have gone wrong in it that is no part of God's work or will.

Creation Story Challenges

Following the great liturgical hymn of Creation with which the book of Genesis opens comes, surprisingly enough, what seems to be a duplicate account of the same event. Quite clearly the second Creation story was not written by the author of the first. The style is quite different. In chapter one there is a magnificent restraint in the description of God's creative acts. The process is sketched rather than described in detail. God is pictured as the great Original, who utters the divine fiat and his will is done.

By contrast, the second Creation story reads like an old-fashioned fairy tale. God moulds man like a potter, *And the LORD God formed man of the dust of the ground, and breathed into his nostrils the breath of life; and man became a living soul. (Genesis 2:7),* plants a garden, *And the LORD God planted a garden eastward in Eden; and there he put the man whom he had formed. (Genesis 2:8),* strolls in it of an evening, *And they heard the voice of the LORD God walking in the garden in the cool of the day: and Adam and his wife hid themselves from the presence of the LORD God amongst the trees of the garden.(Genesis 3:8)* and makes clothes for Adam and Eve. *Unto Adam also and to his wife did the LORD God make coats of skins, and clothed them. (Genesis 3:21)*

The process of Creation is different, as is the order in which the various items appear. The first story begins with the creation of light *"And God said, Let there be light: and there was light."(Genesis. 1:3)* and ends with the creation of man *"And God said, Let us make man in our image, after our likeness: and let them have dominion over the fish of the sea, and over the fowl of the air, and over the cattle, and over all the earth, and over every creeping thing that creepeth upon the earth." (Genesis 1:26),* while the second begins with the creations of man *"[7]And the LORD God formed man of the dust of the ground, and breathed into his nostrils the breath of life; and man became a living soul." (Genesis 2:7)* and ends with the creation of woman *"[22]And the rib, which the LORD God had taken from man, made he a woman, and brought her unto the man."(Genesis 2:22)*

As long ago as 1753, Jean Astruc, physician to Louis XV, reached the conclusion that there were two separate narratives of Creation, from two different sources, and dating from two different periods. He further saw that these two elements were not confined to the Creation story, but that they could be traced right through the book of Genesis and beyond it. Since Astruc's day, scholars have consistently confirmed his theory and developed it. As we shall see, two further strands are added, one beginning at Genesis 15, and the other appearing in the book of Deuteronomy. There four strands, whether they were written documents or made up of fragments or oral tradition, were woven together to form the Pentateuch, the name given to the first five books of the Old Testament.

It is important to recognize that two of these strands are present in these early chapters Genesis. They account for the contradictions and inconsistencies in the stories of the Creation and the Flood and elsewhere. The older source, which refers to God's "the Lord", and can thus be easily detected, is responsible for the vivid lively narratives, while the younger source, which refers to God as "God", is more concerned with genealogies, details of ritual and ceremonial. The older source, probably dating from the ninth century B.C., is generally known as J or Jahwist, from the name it gives to God, Jahweh (Jehovah), blended in places after Genesis 15 with another version, the E or Elohist tradition, whereas the younger source is for obvious reasons called P or the Priestly source, and dates roughly from the fifth century B.C.

In the Creation story, then, the editors have incorporated two accounts: first, the liturgical poem in chapter one (P), and then the older traditional narrative in chapters two and three (J). That should help us to understand that we cannot dismiss the second Creation story as a fairy or merely as a primitive attempt to answer such questions as: Why the world? Why are there men and women? Why do we wear clothes?

The second story is clearly meant to be regarded as a sequel to the first, and not as a repetition of it. Its inclusion cannot be justified unless it has something to add. When we examine it, it emerges that far from this being rather naïve account of the origin of things, such as would b produced at primitive stage of civilization, it is in fact as highly theological and profound in its insights as is the first story. It is no more to be taken scientifically or literally than its predecessor, but it has certainly to be taken seriously. For having painted the picture in Genesis 1 of the world as God meant it to be, the Bible goes on now in Genesis 2-3 to paint a picture of the world as it is.

Adam and Eve are, of course, not intended to regarded as historical characters. This is not the story of the first man and the first woman and what happened to them, but the story of every man and every woman since human life began. The Hebrew words for Adam and Eve mean Man and Life, so perhaps if this wise old theologian had been writing today he might have entitled these two chapters: "The Story of Mr. and Mrs. Everyman." As we read these chapters, with their deep insights and profound understanding of human nature, let us remember that this is our story. Adam and Eve are you and I.

There are countless subtleties and nuances in this portrayal but the main lines are painted with a broad brush. We are shown God's good earth, the Creator's handiwork, with man charged with the task of developing it and keeping it in good order *"And the LORD God took the man, and put him into the garden of Eden to dress it and to keep it." (Genesis 2:15)*. At his side, as his companion and sharer of his life, is woman *"And Adam said, This is now bone of my bones, and flesh of my flesh: she shall be called Woman, because she was taken out of Man." (Genesis 2:23)*. The world and its resources lie open before them. Communion with God is theirs *(the tree of life Genesis 2:9) And out of the ground made the LORD God to grow every tree that is pleasant to the sight, and good for food; the tree of life also in the midst of the garden, and the tree of knowledge of good and evil."*, as also is the whole gamut of human experience.

Men and women many select from the field of experience what they will. Freedom of choice is open to them. But this freedom has its dangers. The ultimate standards of good and evil are not theirs to settle. They must recognize their limits as creatures under authority, and that it is God's prerogative to determine what is right or what is wrong. This is a function they must not usurp. If they attempt it, the consequences are fatal *"But of the tree of the knowledge of good and evil, thou shalt not eat of it: for in the day that thou eatest thereof thou shalt surely die."(Genesis 2:17).*

But this is the very thing that men and women try to do. The temptation to make their own standards of right and wrong, to flout God's authority, to run the world in their own way proves irresistible. Pride is their undoing, the pride that makes them want to be on a level with God *"For God doth know that in the day ye eat thereof, then your eyes shall be opened, and ye shall be as gods, knowing good and evil."(Genesis 3:5).* Inevitably disaster follows. Human relationships are tarnished *"And the eyes of them both were opened, and they knew that they were naked; and they sewed fig leaves together, and made themselves aprons." (Genesis 3:7)*; the world becomes a hostile place *"And unto Adam he said, Because thou hast hearkened unto the voice of thy wife, and hast eaten of the tree, of which I commanded thee, saying, Thou shalt not eat of it: cursed is the ground for thy sake; in sorrow shalt thou eat of it all the days of thy life; Thorns also and thistles shall it bring forth to thee; and thou shalt eat the herb of the field; In the sweat of thy face shalt thou eat bread, till thou return unto the ground; for out of it wast thou taken: for dust thou art, and unto dust shalt thou return."(Genesis 3:17-19);* worst of all, a barrier divides man from God *"So he drove out the man; and he placed at the east of the garden of Eden Cherubims, and a flaming sword which turned every way, to keep the way of the tree of life."(Genesis 3:24).*

Much ink has been split over the question of whether this picture is intended to represent that same point, early in the history of the human race, something went wrong and man took the downward path, which he ahs ever since followed. This is the traditional theological doctrine of the Fall. It assumes that man lived originally in a state of innocence and perfect communion with God, that the world was then in a fact a Paradise. Perhaps it is a not sufficient argument against this view that it is singularly difficult to do much more than assert it as a dogma to be accepted or rejected.

On the other hand, if we are not prepared to say that sin came into the world at the instigation of a talking serpent, in other words, if we recognize the poetic and symbolic nature of the whole story, it is not by any means clear that the Bible is talking about a historical or prehistorical event at all. Surely the truth that the Bible is conveying to us is much more that as long as there have been men and women on the earth they have used their freedom in the wrong way, by putting themselves as the center instead of God, by refusing to recognize that this is not their universe but God's and that it must be run in God's way not man's way.

Man, who is made in the image and of God, capable of making the right response to God, and living in the right relationship to him, consistently distorts the image o and frustrates God's purposes. The pride that makes Adam and Eve impatient of restraint and eager to be rid of any authority beyond their own, lies at the root of man's failure and perennial downfall. That is equally true today, and the Bible would tell us that it has always been so.

If we think of Creation as in one sense an even in time, in that nothing exists that has not bee brought into being by God, we may think of it in another sense as an eternal act, in that God is continuously creating new life and energy. Similarly the truth behind the Fall may be twofold. We repeat in our own lives every day the story of the Fall; our pride and our separation from God are too painfully real to allow us to forget them. But may we not also say that in the dim beginnings of man's evolution from the animal kingdom, there came the point when his behavior was no longer conditioned by reflexes or instinctive reactions, when he could in fact make rational choices. By choosing the lower way rather than the higher, the easier way rather than the harder, the selfish way rather than the unselfish, he began to follow the pathwhich all of us since then have followed, and stared off mankind on its rake's progress to destruction.

These two chapters (2-3) will repay careful and thoughtful study. They are a treasure house of insights into human nature, our relations with one another and with God. Notice how well the two sides of our being are reflected in Genesis 2:7. We are of the earth, earthy (in Hebrew, man—adam—comes from the ground—adamah *"The first man is of the earth, earthy; the second man is the Lord from heaven(spirit)." 1Corinthians 15:47)* but God breathed something of himself into us. The Garden of Eden is the symbol both of the beauty of God's created world and of our proper status in it as God's custodians, responsible to him for its care and maintenance *(Genesis 2:8-15)*. True marriage is beautifully described as an unselfconscious relationship *"[25]And they were both naked, the man and his wife, and were not ashamed." (Genesis 2:25)* where a man and a woman find that they become part of each other, almost as if they become a joint personality *"Therefore shall a man leave his father and his mother, and shall cleave unto his wife:*

and they shall be one flesh." (Genesis 2:24). Jesus set the seal of his approval *(Mark 10:2-12)* on this old writer's conception of marriage as a lifelong partnership, woven into the very basic fabric of society.

The serpent *"Now the serpent was more subtil than any beast of the field which the LORD God had made. And he said unto the woman, Yea, hath God said, Ye shall not eat of every tree of the garden?" (Genesis 3:1)* is the perfect symbol of temptation. It is not surprising that later, when the demonic character of evil was recognized, and personified in the symbol of Satan, the serpent in the Fall story should be thought of as Satan in disguise *"Nevertheless through envy of the devil came death into the world: and they that do hold of his side do find it." (Wisdom of Solomon 2:24).* Notice how he persuades the man and the woman that God's warning that violation of his laws will bring disaster cramps their freedom, preventing them from realizing their true greatness and form occupying their proper status in the universe *(Genesis 3:2-5).* "Glory to man in the highest" is a refrain as old as man himself.

It is sometimes thought that the Bible represents sin as primarily a matter of sex. This seems to be suggested by the emphasis on "nakedness" *(Genesis 2:25; 3:7),* but in a series of symbols such as we find in these chapters, fig leaves cannot be meant to be taken any more literally than serpents. The lesson surely is that failure to recognize the obedience of God as our highest obligation destroys the free and spontaneous relationship with one another which we ought to have. The sense of sin disrupts human society, separating us from one another's, as certainly as it separates us from God. The man and the woman are no longer as east inn each other's company, just as they feel out of harmony with God *"And he said, I heard thy voice in the garden, and I was afraid, because I was naked; and I hid myself."(Genesis 3:10)*

Note how cleverly our evasion of responsibility is characterized. The man blames the woman; the woman blames the serpent. Indeed the man practically accuses God: "It was you who gave me the woman in the first place" *(Genesis 3:12-13)*. Men have always tried to shuffle out of responsibility for their failures. We blame our instincts our environment, our partners, our wives or our neighbors, and if all else fails we can always blame God.

But the price has to be paid. The world is at war with itself. The joy has gone out of life, the harmony has been broken. Man's self-will has marred the Creator's fair design. It is unlikely that this old writer had any clearer idea than we ourselves as to shy there should b a tragic side to the beauty of the earth: the struggle for existence in the animal world, ruthlessness, torture and sudden death. But he maintains this is not in the purpose of the Creator. It is an intrusion into his plan. The plight of the serpent and its enmity with man *(Genesis 3:14-15)*, by which he symbolizes the whole mystery of man's relation to the natural world, the groaning and travailing of the whole creation as St. Paul puts it later *(Romans 8:22)*, is somehow the result of a cosmic breakdown. Not only mankind but nature itself is in constant rebellion against God. Pain and cruelty, disease and decay, are no part of a world which the Creator saw to be "very good." Once more the Bible offers not an explanation but a conviction.

An even deeper not is struck in 3:15. It may have been fanciful for early commentators to see in the words *"it shall bruise thy head"*, a promise of the coming of Christ, the seed of a woman, who would triumph over Satan and destroy the power of evil. But if the serpent symbolizes not merely the lower forms of animal life but the embodiment of cunning, temptation and guile, these words are at once recognition of the constant battle between mankind and his evil impulses, and a hope of ultimate victory for man. He may have to hobble along the way of life, bruised in the heel, hindered by evil, but evil itself is doomed to a worse fate, crushed to death under man's foot. Whatever was in the writer's mind this point we are right to think that with the coming of Christ and his victory over evil, the victory of Man as man was meant to be, these old words have come strangely and wonderfully true *(Romans 16:20)*.

Again, we are brought face to face with the mystery of pain in Genesis 3:16. Marriage and children are seen as part of the beneficent design of the Creator *(Genesis 1:27-28)* but the agonies of childbirth are no part of God's will. Why new life should come into the world at the cost of a mother's suffering, and sometimes her own life, we do not know, and the Bible does not tell us. But in this tale of Eve, the pains and subsequent cares of motherhood are regarded as is some way connected with the disorganization of the divine pattern which sin has occasioned.

Man pays the penalty for his disregard of God's laws in that his life becomes a burden. Work in the divine plan was to be creative and pleasurable *(Genesis 1:28-29; 2:15)* but as a result of man's pride his best efforts are labored and sorrowful. His problems multiply, his tasks loom menacingly over his head. His backbreaking toil brings him no more than enough to keep life in being, and at the end of it the earth from which he came received him back for ever. It we translate this picture into modern terms, its truth remains eve with a five-day week and automation. For the sweat of the brow substitute the monotony of mechanized industry, or the frustration of trivial occupations or the sense of futility and helplessness that makes so many question the whole trend and structure of modern society.

Modern man, in this atomic age, with all his ingenuity and resources, is still out of harmony with the world and with his neighbor. We do not need to look far in the international, social or economic fields to find the curse of Adam. We not only know from our own experience that the sin of Adam is our sin and that we pay the price, but we also find ourselves burdened with the legacy of wrong choices, pride and selfishness which the past has bequeathed to us, and which bedevils every attempt to put the world to rights.

So the picture would appear to be black indeed, though no more black than our knowledge of history and of the world today would confirm, and certainly no more black than we deserve. Man is given his opportunity; he is made in the image of God; but he abuses his freedom, flouts the laws of God, and brings upon himself disaster, pain and death. Thus, unerringly, this old biblical tale of the Fall illuminates the contemporary scene and speaks to our condition.

Yet, already we are given a hint that despite our stubbornness and folly God will not give us up. Man many have been in constant rebellion against God, but he still bears traces of the divine image. He is still potentially a child of God, with the breath of God's life in him. So, for the first time the characteristic pattern of God's attitude towards us is outlined, a pattern which we shall trace right through the Bible. God is Judge, and his judgment will not allow us to play fast and loose with the moral order of his universe. We must pay the price for our failure to live according to his will. But he is also the God of mercy and forgiveness, who will not forsake us or leave us to our deserts.

This pattern is revealed tellingly in the concluding versed of this Genesis story. Adam accepts God's judgment because he can do no other and knows it to be right, but something tells him that this is not God's last word—an empty future, futile endeavor and death to end it all. He still has hope, and signifies it by calling his wife Eve, a name implying the promise of motherhood and new life *(Genesis 3:20)*. In this we may perhaps see that element of hope in man at all stages of his existence, which has somehow refused to believe that despite his failure and the mystery that surrounds him of pain and decay and death, this world is nothing more than a meaningless chaos in an empty universe.

Adam's hope is well founded. The symbol of the coats of skins which God made for the man and the woman *(Genesis 3:21)* implies God's providential care for all mankind. Sinful, wayward, willful, ignorant though they be, all men everywhere are God's concern. He keeps them in life and shields them form the thrones and thistles *(Genesis 3:18)* which they have brought upon themselves. Paradise is not for us. We are unfit to live in full communion with God, which means to share his eternal life *(Genesis 3:22)*. We have godlike power which we cannot be trusted to use right. So man is banished to his joyless tasks and condemned to live estranged from God until death overtakes him. A barrier stands between him and the perfection that might have been his *(Genesis 3:24)*. But he has not been written off, for God still cares. It is o this fact that the whole story that the Bible records is founded.

Too much importance cannot be attributed to these three chapters of the prologue, which expound the theological doctrines of Creation and Fall. Their narrative form, replete with symbol and image, answers most perfectly than any doctrinal formulation the purpose in the mind of the writer. He is setting the stage for the drama that begins in Genesis 12, and while it is true that there are eight more chapters in the prologue, and that all have their contribution to make to the total picture, nonetheless the essential themes have already been stated: God's design and man's disorder, God's grace and man's sinfulness, God's judgment and man's punishment, man's hope and God's compassion.

In a sense it is a one-sided picture: a world without the Gospel and mankind without a Savior. As Christians we know that God does not leave man to reap the full consequences of his betrayal. He does not stop at compassion. He steps in to rescue man from his plight. He plans to save him from himself, because he is God and for no other cause, and beginning with Abraham, the plan for man's salvation comes into action. By the grace of God we live under the Gospel.

But the Bible pulls no punches. It insists that first of all we should see ourselves as we are and that we should recognize God as he is. We must see ourselves as stupid, twisted creatures, capable of every crime from simple folly through lechery and lust to murder. We must be shown that God is no benevolent cosmic sponge, prepared to wipe away our worst excesses and absorb them with genial tolerance.

We have to shown that a holy God hates sin and the he cannot gloss it over. He takes it seriously and expects us to do the same. Therefore, through these ancient stories of the prologue he lets us see ourselves as we are and the punishment we deserve. We are not under condemnation because once upon a time the first man and the first woman failed God, but

Chapter 2   The Mis-Education About Adam & Eve

because we ourselves are Adam and Eve and their failure is ours. What we deserve, we deserve, but for the love of God. We are to be shown what that love means in action, but first we must be told the full tale of our tragic human situation in the remaining chapters of the prologue.

Why Are We Being Punished For The Sin Of Adam?

Adam was the one who ate the forbidden fruit, so that's his problem not mines or my generation. The punishment resulting from the sin act conflicts with biblical scripture.

> *"the children shall not be punished for the sins of their fathers." (Deuteronomy 24:16)*

An often-used strategy of the church is to teach fear and damnation. If you question the word of God you are blaspheming. Blaspheming is not about questioning the bible but questioning the reverence, aweness and power of God. You blaspheme when you say, think or imply God cannot. There is no failure in God, with God, of God.

It is okay to believe in either the spiritual or physical creation. It is not okay to put limits on what God can do. We can do all things thru Christ that strengthens us and there is nothing to hard for God.

Cain & Abel: Who *"Dat"* Woman?

In Chapter 4, is the story Cain & Abel the two sons of Adam and Eve. This fascinating tale presents a variety of challenges. Cain harvested the fields, and Abel was a sheepherder.

The Mis-Education Against
Homosexuality In The Bible

There is an initial conflict between the two brothers Cain and Abel. In summary, Cain became angry with Abel because Cain thought Abel received more respect from God than he did. And the Bible says that Cain rose up against his brother and killed him. The writer says God asked Cain the question:

And the Lord said unto Cain, Where is Able thy brother? And he said, I know not: am'I my brother's keeper? (Genesis 4:9)

Cain is embarrassed and ashamed of what he did and he tries to run from God *(that's cute; run from God)* in this conversation between Cain and God, God places a mark on Cain so that no one would harm him.

Now, let us ask this question: if the only people on the earth are Adam and Eve, Cain and Abel then why would God be concerned about someone hurting Cain?

Now, we know we've got Adam and Eve, and Cain and Abel, right? So, we're not missing any characters, are we?

Stay with me here. In Genesis 4:16-17 it reads:
"and Cain went out from the presence of the Lord, and dwelt in the land of Nod, and the East of Eden; and Cain knew his wife and conceived, and bare Enoch: and he builded a city, and called the name of the city, after the name of his son, Enoch (Genesis 4:16-17)

Wait a minute! If you got Adam, Eve and Cain, right?
Who "dat" woman? Who are her people? Did we miss something?

Harpo who dat woman? Sorry folks I could not resist myself. I share that with you not as a mockery of the Bible but as visual example that we do not have all of the Bible's history.

Chapter 2   The Mis-Education About Adam & Eve

What else did the church take out, leave out or put in?

You Have God's DNA

You have "God's DNA". You are made in the likeness and image of God. You have DNA that links you to the Divine Creator starting from the beginning. Your genetic code is in the dust created by God and has been added to the creation formula. If God breath life into human life, you are extension of that human life.

Regardless of what church folks say, they cannot deny you're "DNA." Their opinion of you is not more important than the opinion you have of yourself.

Many in the SGL community's lives have been disrupted because they have been trained by the religious community to hate themselves because they believe they are a mistake, and/or the Bible says so.

Everything God created was good! (Genesis 1:1-2:3)
"I" have come to the conclusion there are three avenues into the development of a gay person:
 (1) A person is born gay
 (2) A person experiences negative events during same-sex encounters (i.e. molestation, rape) that may evolve into same-sex love.
 (3) An environment we are in may not be malicious, but there may be situations that create an opportunity for a person to begin to explore their sexuality.

We come out of our mothers naked;
everything else is just drag!"
RuPaul in her book "Letting It All Hang Out"

It is apparent that homosexuality does not have one particular "cause." It is not purely genetic in origin, for instance, because the very twin studies (Bailey and Pillard) that some interpreted as "proving" a purely genetic origin of homosexuality actually "disproved" it, because only 52% of identical twins of homosexual persons were also homosexual. If homosexuality were dependent on a particular "gay gene," both twins should have possessed that gene, and thus there should have been a 100% correspondence.

Most scientists researching this question are seeing their research pointing to at least a biological if not genetic origin of sexual orientation. This evidence is increasingly showing that sexual orientation, whether gay, straight, or bisexual, is probably set very early on if not in the womb or at conception. In other words, sexual orientation is inborn.

No one knows exactly how sexual orientation and gender identity determined. However, experts agree that it is a complicated matter of genetics, biology, psychological and social factors. For many people, sexual orientation and gender identity are shaped at any early age. While research has not determined a cause, homosexuality and gender variance are not the result of any one factor like parenting or past experiences.

In my experience in this lifestyle after listening too so many in our Kulture (LBGT/SGL). There are a lot of reasons, but I will stand firm on the above primary points.

Chapter 2   The Mis-Education About Adam & Eve

Moving Yourself To The Next Level

Chapter 2 The Mis-Education of Adam & Eve

Each process question or thought can be viewed from the following perspectives: Same Gender Loving (SGL), Heterosexual (H) or Both (B). It is healthy to try and view from various perspectives to get insight into how others may process an issue. All perspectives are valid and should be respected and not condemned. In all thy getting; get understanding.

(1) (B) - If you are made in the likeness and image of God.
    a. What positive images have you developed about your sexuality?
    b. What negative images have you developed about your sexuality?
    c. How can these images help one another for you?

(2) (B) - Have you ever stopped to think about why you love the way you do?
    a. If yes, write out your story. You will discover something about you they may shock you.
    b. If no, inquire within yourself as to why you choose not to discover you? If you are not ready to discover about you, then that's okay also.

(3) (B) - If God asked you do something that others may say you should not do.
    a. How would you way out your consequences?
    b. What could do for God that would shock you?

CHAPTER 3

The Mis-Education About The Rainbow

The Rainbow Is A Promise Not A Curse. In this chapter you learn no one has the right to curse your vision, assignment, relationships and dreams. No Archbishop, Pastor, Evangelist, Deacon or Bible fanatic has the right to curse anything in your life.

I use the story of Noah and the Ark for two reasons. This story has been used in the past to rationalize slavery and to give explanation that homosexuality is a sin as a result of this act.

In the LBGT/SGL community the rainbow is a commonly used sign of equality, freedom and pride. The rainbow was a sign God gave Noah as a reminder that I have an agreement/promise with you, to never bring harm onto God's people. The rainbow was a promise not a curse.

God promises to bless your visions, bless your assignments, bless your relationships, and bless dreams. God promised to love and protect you even when others hate you.

Jesus says, Blessed are ye, when men shall revile you, and persecute you, and shall say all manner of evil against you falsely, for my sake
(Matthew 5:11)

What happens when people you have respected, brakes their promise to represent God without judgment.

> *Judge not, that ye be not judged.*
> *For with what judgment ye judge, ye shall be*
> *judged; and with what measure ye condemn,*
> *it shall be measured to you again.*
> *(Matthew 7:1-2)*

If you curse someone, you curse yourself. In the church, many have been curse by people who are not operating under God's guidance but out of the learned behaviors and inferiority complexes.

No one has a right to curse anything in your life. Regardless of their title or what they have done for gone in the past.

In Genesis 6:8-9:29 is the story of Noah and the Ark. God assigns Noah the task of building an ark that would protect Noah, his family, and every manner of animal from an impending deluge that would annihilate all other creatures living on the Earth. When God's destruction was complete, Noah and his family would repopulate the Earth, and from Noah's sons all races that we see today would be born. Genesis 9:22 describes how Noah cursed his youngest son Ham and Ham's descendents, generally believed to be all black (indigenous) Africans. The nature of Ham's transgression against his father is not clear and is highly debated

Ham is one of Noah's three sons, the brother of Shem and Japheth, and father of Canaan. He is described as helping Noah to build the ark. That this curse was the result of seeing his father's nakedness may be an attempt to explain the later restraint of the Canaanites to Israel as resulting from Canaanite sexual perversion.

Chapter 3   The Mis-Education About The Rainbow

Some modern interpretations mean Ham molested his father Noah while he was asleep and was then cursed by Noah for his deed. The same passage was used to justify the enslavement of black people.

New International Version
> *19 These were the three sons of Noah, and from them came the people who were scattered over the earth. 20 Noah, a man of the soil, proceeded to plant a vineyard. 21* **When he drank some of its wine, he became drunk and lay uncovered inside his tent. 22 Ham, the father of Canaan, saw his father's nakedness and told his two brothers outside.** *23 But Shem and Japheth took a garment and laid it across their shoulders; then they walked in backward and covered their father's nakedness. Their faces were turned the other way so that they would not see their father's nakedness.* **24 When Noah awoke from his wine and found out what his youngest son had done to him, 25 he said, "Cursed be Canaan! The lowest of slaves will he be to his brothers."** *26 He also said, "Blessed be the LORD, the God of Shem! May Canaan be the slave of Shem. 27 May God extend the territory of Japheth; may Japheth live in the tents of Shem, and may Canaan be his slave." 28 After the flood Noah lived 350 years.*

The text reveals to us when Noah realized what his son had done, he cursed him and his descendants for the next 350years of his life, and he lived to be 960 years old. Talk about losing your temper!

Noah was a good person that did a great and mighty deed for God but made long term negative decision that affected the lives many generations to come. He cursed his grandchildren and their children. It hurts when you are being judged by something you have nothing to do with.

Remember our text from above Matthew 7:1-2, "Judge not that you be not judged." Noah cursed generations that did not even exist.

If you are mad at someone in your life; try to let it go the best way you know how. The longer you stay mad or disappointed with them, the longer you measure against yourself.

Noah's Task

The Bible says Noah found grace in the eyes of the Lord. These are the generations of Noah: Noah was a just man and perfect man in his generations and Noah begot three sons Sham, Ham and Japheth.

Noah was given a charge by God to build an Ark in the middle of the desert. There was no CNN, Fox or 24 hour Weather Channel for Noah to verify any potential rain coming. Instructed to build an ark in the middle of the desert, even to the most learned, the task sounded crazy.

In the instructions, Noah was to collect a group of goats and ducks and chickens and bring them into the ark. The TV version shows him bringing them in two by two, but when you read the Bible, you will discover in Genesis 7:2 of every clean beast thou shalt be taken by sevens, the male and female: and the beast that are not clean by two, the male and female.

The Bible tells us that God informed Noah upon completing the Ark within seven days he will rain upon the earth 40 days and 40 nights. In Hebrew, the word "40 (forty)" means "a lot of."

Chapter 3   *The Mis-Education About The Rainbow*

Noah was 600 when the rain began. Now Noah entered with Shem, Ham, and Japheth, the sons of Noah, Noah's wife and three wives of Noah's sons.

You know the story; he sends out a dove after 40 days and 40 nights with an olive leaf; which today is a symbol of peace.

And God blessed Noah and his sons, and said unto them, be fruitful, and multiply, and replenish the earth. The Lord said;

> *"I do set my bow in the cloud, and it shall be a token of the covenant between me and the earth and it shall come to pass, when I bring a cloud over the earth that the bow shall be seen in the cloud: and I will remember my covenant, which is between me and you and every living creature of all flesh; and the waters chef no more become a flood to destroy all flesh"*

Chapter 9:18 and the sons of Noah, that when fourth of the ark, where Shem, and Ham, and Japheth: and Ham is the father of Canaan. These three sons of Noah: and of them was the whole earth populated. Now we're clear that it is only Noah, his wife, his 3 sons and 3 daughter in-laws.

So now we know God promised never to destroy the earth again. This puts Noah in a position of authority that comes with public humiliation and an assignment and did not make any sense.

This is challenging to me; one would assume if Noah was harvesting grapes, it would be safe to say he has celebrated with wine in the past. This story could suggest he has probably been drunk before. The text says he found favor with God and it appears alcohol and drunkenness was not the issue for God. It is quite funny to see over and over again how God uses people that do not meet the church's social picture of perfection. I love God.

Noah's Drunken Decision

The Bible tells us Ham went to his brothers and told them what he had done. The brothers moved into action to cover their father before he awoke, but when Noah woke up, he realized what his son had done.

We must ask ourselves a few questions here? If the son only removed the covers over Noah's naked body and his brothers walked in backwards and replaced the covers, one would have to ask the following: how would a drunken person know about covers being moved?

If Ham did something to Noah and he went back and told the brothers that he saw Noah's nakedness it does not appear there was a sexual act. Did the brothers not care about Ham's same-sex desire? The Bible says,*"And Noah awoke from his wine, and knew what his younger son had done unto him" (Genesis 9:24).* In verse 21 it says, "he was uncovered within this tent" and in verse 22 it says, *"saw the nakedness of his father " (Genesis 9:23)*

Noah cursed his son and the children of generations to come not even born yet? But what life experience could be so powerful you would for 350 years outcast your son and grandchildren?

What life experience have you had that allows you to carry anger towards the person or group for the rest of your life?

The most challenging spiritual growth paths we all experience is forgiveness. Our ability to let go of negative life experiences is key to our spiritual development.

Cursing Of Ham Linked To Slavery

The Bible was used during a period of time justify *black* slavery. When Noah discovered what his son had done Noah cursed Ham and his descendants: *"the lowest of slaves shall he be to his brothers"* (Genesis 9:25). Since the black Africans are generally believed to be the descendents of Ham (Genesis 10:6-20), this was interpreted to mean the enslavement of Africans is a *natural* result of this curse.

> *I realize that gay people have put me on a pedestal, and I love it. Of all the oppressed minorities, they have to be the most oppressed.*
> Sylvester, Disco Artist

Today, we are referred to as African Americans, but in the past we were called *less than, property, n_ _ _a (dirty word)*, but we were not considered Children of God.

When theologians of this modern time rationalize and justify the oppression of Same Gender Loving folks, our response should be: *"Noah, you have no right to curse me."* Noah overstepped his authority. His God-given task was to get those lions, tigers, bears and sheep on that boat. Noah had no right to curse anyone.

People can take the Bible and use it against you and we will carry generations of baggage due to someone losing their temper, applying traditional thinking, preaching hatred to a culture of people.

There are churches today that teach the idea that black people are descendants of the Canaanites and are not worthy as Children of God. Today we have church people teaching hatred for Same Gender Loving people with the Bible. In the past, we had people with these same credentials rationalizing slavery, so the initials behind a person's name should not justify their ignorance and or oppression of any group of people. There are young SGL's who have been programmed with hate themselves. You may have been infected yourself.

The Christian church's assignment is to bring people to Christ and they have overstepped their authority.

Did Noah's son really have relations with him?

Second, some translations state, Genesis 9:22 *"He had relations with him (sex)."* So, let's have this conversation. If God destroyed all of the earth because of the evil and this was supposedly including the homosexuals?

> *and God saw that the wickedness of man was great in the earth, and that every imagination of the thoughts of his heart was only the evil continually.(Genesis 6:5)*

Now the text tells us that God saw the heart of man. Am I right? In Genesis 7:7, the text tells us,

Noah went in, and his sons, and his wife, and his sons' wives with him, into the ark, because of the waters of the flood. Why did God not stop Noah from bringing Ham onto the Ark? It would be safe to assume that if there was so much homosexuality going on, God knew what Ham felt in his heart and had forty days and forty nights to address Ham's homosexual thoughts. Many theologians are under the assumption, based on the Bible translations, that Ham had sexual relations with Noah.

Now, supposedly, Ham had sex with Noah, and the reason God destroyed the earth was because of the evil thoughts, which the church likes to translate into homosexuality. Uh Huh!

Now, if God has killed all the goats and the ducks and the chickens and the bears and the cows and all the evil people, God supposedly killed all the homosexuals also.

But, if Noah's son had sex with him and they departed from the Ark, they harvested the land, they were celebrating; well, at least Noah was. If God, who is all-knowing (omniscient), knew the heart of Ham, then you would think that he knew Ham had a same-sex attraction all along. I would think that the all-knowing God knew about these feelings; he just destroyed everybody else.

A Point of View on the Ham Scenario

"IF" we were to believe this was a homosexual act, it would be logical to conclude God knew of Ham's same sex attraction. This logic *"could be"* supported from the book of Jeremiah

> *Before I formed thee in the belly I knew thee; and before thou camest forth out of the womb I sanctified thee, and I ordained thee a prophet unto the nations.* *(Jeremiah 1:5)*

Jeremiah had a calling on his life and God assigned the mission in the belly of his mother's womb. God knows what you are in the belly of your mother's womb, so it is no surprise to God but it is a surprise to you and those around you. God is omnipresent (everywhere), omniscient (all knowing) and omnipotent (powerful) and can not be surprised. You are made in the likeness and image of God and God has specifically designed you to do the will of God to share unconditional love.

The arguments that will probably come up is are you born gay. There is no 100% of anything if this is the struggle for you begin to the process to identify that for yourself. Everyone has a very different journey. In my opinion without any scientific support there are three origins of development into this Kulture(LBGT/SGL): (1) Some are born gay (2) Some have environments that allow them to explore their sexuality and they may choose their direction (3) Some have negative experiences and their transition becomes the result of this series of events. Everyone can discover their transitions for themselves.

Chapter 3   The Mis-Education About The Rainbow

Moving Yourself To The Next Level

Each process question or thought can be viewed from the following perspectives: Same Gender Loving (SGL), Heterosexual (H) or Both (B). It is healthy to try and view from various perspectives to get insight into how others may process an issue. All perspectives are valid and should be respected and not condemned. In all thy getting; get understanding.

Chapter 3 The Mis-Education About The Rainbow.

1. (B) - A curse can be seen as a negative life experiences that we replay over and over again in our thoughts.
    a. What negative life experience cursed you?
    b. What are you going to do about it?
    c. Who have you cursed and what are you going to do about it?

2. (B) - What tools do you need to put in place to prevent others from hurting you in the future?

3. (B) - Who can you help with their inner struggle?

4. (B) - What does your agreement with God look like?

5. (SGL) - How do you feel the racial tension in the LBGT/SGL community should be address?

CHAPTER 4

The Mis-Education About Sodom & Gomorrah

How the church got us focused on homosexuality is astounding. Sodom and Gomorrah is one of the greatest Biblical manipulations executed against a culture of people.

The story of Sodom and Gomorrah told in Genesis Chapter 19 is the granddaddy of all the Bible stories that speak about homosexuality. Generations of children have been forsaken by their parent's house and rejected by family, friends, co-workers and church members as a result of the misrepresentation of this Bible story.

Later in this chapter, I introduce the "desodomization" of your mind - the deconstruction of the negative images about your sexuality and reconstruction of your thoughts about your sexuality with positive and affirming images.

In many progressive religious circles you will hear it the story of Sodom and Gomorrah was not about homosexuality but hospitality. Although this is charming verbiage, it does not reveal the primary biblical truths from the story.

Some biblical scholars believe these twin cities on the plain of the Dead Sea must have suffered a dramatic and sudden disaster, in all probability, as the story suggests, as result of earth movement coupled with volcanic activity.

When we study Genesis 19, the meat of the message is located in Genesis 18. The two angels came into the city looking for *"Ten Righteous In The City"*. Hospitality not homosexuality it is charismatic but *"Are There Ten Righteous In The City?"*

> *the two angels arrived at Sodom in the evening and Lot was sitting in the gateway of the city. When he saw them, he got up to meet them and bowed down with his face to the ground. 2 "My lords," he said, "please turn aside to your servant's house. You can wash your feet and spend the night and then go on your way early in the morning." "No," they answered, "we will spend the night in the square." 3 But he insisted so strongly that they did go with him and entered his house. He prepared a meal for them, baking bread without yeast, and they ate.(Genesis 19:1)*

During this ancient period when strangers entered a city the traditional custom was to provide acts of hospitality: *(1) A place to rest   (2) A place to wash   (3) Something to eat*

Lot was sitting at the front gate and greeted two Angels, offering his hospitality to these two strangers.

God to the citizens of the city was no different or no more special than any other God that was worshiped in this Pre-Christ period. Just as with any other religious beliefs, the citizens of Sodom worshiped as they believed or how they were taught to worship. Obviously, **apparently though** ritual sex **still** disturbed the sensibilities of other religious authorities, probably in much the way homosexuality offends the religious and political authorities today. Sacrificing animals *(e.g., goats, chickens)* in the name of God was normal for many during this Pre-Christ period.

Chapter 4 — *The Mis-Education About Sodom & Gomorrah*

Sodom and Gomorrah was an active city diverse in culture. You may have heard some preachers refer to many big cities (e.g., San Francisco, Los Angeles, and Atlanta) as places of the Sodomites. The preachers in these large cities often reference many smaller communities within the city as home of the Sodomites (e.g. West Hollywood, California; the Castro District of San Francisco; Midtown Atlanta; and Boystown, Chicago).

In this Bible story, the term sodomite is translated to mean male prostitution associated with places of worship. It is important to note the text addresses male prostitution not because they engage in **sexual relationships** with other males; they, like the female prostitutes, are addressed because they serve alien Gods. **The present day culture has wrongly referred to this biblical reference of Sodom as an exclusive association with men who have sex with men.**

God to the citizens of the city was no different or no more special than any other God that was worshiped in this Pre-Christ period. Just as **with** any other religious **beliefs**, the citizens of Sodom worshiped as they believed or how they were taught to worship. Obviously, **apparently though** ritual sex still disturbed the sensibilities of other religious authorities, probably in much the way homosexuality offends the religious and political authorities today. Sacrificing animals *(e.g., goats, chickens)* in the name of God was normal for many during this Pre-Christ period.

I know that members of the LGBT community are sometimes considered to be a little to the left, or experimental, when it comes to sex acts and rituals" but having sex in the church "I most certainly think not." You let me walk up in a church and they bring a goat or chicken in the sanctuary to the altar and cut the animals' throat. Lord, Help! And if I, or probably any homosexual for that matter, walked into a church where they were sacrificing animals or engaging in prostitution, Lord help me I would high tail it out of there and as I'm doing so, probably place a call to the police.

Nowadays, many progressive scholars have built their careers on the story of Sodom and Gomorrah being about *hospitality not homosexuality* and in my studies as well, I find that hospitality was most likely the straw that broke the camel's back when the final decision was made to destroy the city. I will talk more about that later in this chapter and how the destruction of Sodom was not about changing sexuality but about hospitality and temple worship and who do you choose to put before your God.

Is Abraham Advocating To Save The Homosexuals?

Was Abraham an advocating to save the city and its citizens?

If a person argues the city was destroyed because of homosexuality, it would be logical to assume Abraham was an advocate for the safety and salvation of all that sinned within the city whether they be homosexual, bi-sexual, adulterous or what have you. Because most would agree that in Sodom heterosexuality, homosexuality, bi-sexuality and even "tri-sexuality" were all present and going on in the city, not just homosexuality.

The missing link to the Sodom and Gomorrah story is in Genesis Chapter 18. In the chapter, you will read Abraham is negotiating with the angels who passed through to fulfill the promise that his wife would bear a child. During their visit, they informed Abraham they were on their way to destroy the City of Sodom and Gomorrah.

I love this text because there is more here than what is on the page. In Genesis 18-19, the scriptures tells us Abraham and Lot negotiated with representatives of God, and Abraham passionately advocated for them not to destroy the city.

Abraham knew what was going on in the city, but Abraham saw the human value of everyone in the city. He had no judgment of the people in Sodom, but compassionately advocated they were worth saving. Abraham did not make any of the

"love the sinner but hate the sin"
(Note: This is not a scripturally sound quote)

quotes; he did not use any demeaning words of this biblical period to single out any particular group.

How does the religious community justify Abraham as a righteous man, who happened to be an advocate on behalf of the salvation of Sodom and Gomorrah and the homosexuality present there, if homosexuality was really the issue? And then turn around and use the same text to justify hatred and destruction of homosexuals and their communities?

To better understand this, it would help to research angels and you will see how the religious community loves to create higher and lower level ways of thinking. In one Pentecostal denomination they have created and distributed information that angels have different positions or offices with God. Man is so vain.

The concept states there are five different offices or positions of authority among the angels: (1) thrones, (2) dominions, (3) principalities, (4) authorities and (5) powers.

The religious community is rooted in higher and lower level thinking. The commitment to understanding the text would require us to do more critical thinking of the angels and/or the ranking system.

In Chapter 18, Abraham was approached by three angels, yet in Chapter 19 there are only two. What ranking of angels are we dealing with here? Are they the low-ranking angels or are they working for promotion? **This entire ranking system is yet another display of man's subtle but apparent displays of vanity.**

Abraham offers the angels a place to rest, wash up and food to eat. They share their intentions to destroy the City of Sodom and Gomorrah. Abraham is aware of the pagan rituals and prostitution but he advocates for the safety of the city. Abraham was a great person of faith. He was respected by others and courageous in defending his family at all costs.

It is helpful to have an understanding of the word "righteousness" as spoken of by Abraham. The word *"righteousness"* means *"adhering to commitment to God."* Morality in various cultures has a tolerance level normally related to social, economic and religious practices.

Hospitality Not Homosexuality Appeared To Be The Issue But It Really Is Not

Lot is well aware of the acts in the city but he pleads with angels to come to his house and *"wash their feet, rest*

Chapter 4   *The Mis-Education About Sodom & Gomorrah*

themselves, and gets something to eat"(Genesis 19:2-3) and he would not accept *"no"* as an answer.

When I was growing up, I remember my grandmother and mother embracing and welcoming everyone that came into our home. I remember a time when it was an honor to have someone come into your home. We called it *"breaking bread and sipping soup."* There used to be a time when people would visit from out of town and **certain families would insist they come and stay at their house. This was real hospitality. Nowadays though your very own church members don't even want you to know where they live.** (don't like the use of the word folk. Sounds like slang)

In Genesis 19:4-7, it tells us of the conversation Lot is having with the people of the city who have come to his house in search of the two strangers:

> *4 Before they had gone to bed, all the men from every part of the city of Sodom--both young and old--surrounded the house.*
> *5 they called to Lot, "Where are the men who came to you tonight? Bring them out to us so that we can have sex with them."*
> *6 Lot went outside to meet them and shut the door behind him*
> *7 and said, "No, my friends. Don't do this wicked thing.*
> *(Genesis 19:4-7)*

When Lot appealed to the men at his doorstep, Lot responded with respect not condemnation, **because they were all sinners of a different nature. He responded with respect to his brothers for the safety** of his guests.

It was very common during this biblical period that people would become curious of strangers who were sometimes scouts sent into the city to identify its internal weaknesses to develop plans to capture a city.

The scriptures read

Genesis 19:5

King James Version	New International Version
"Where are the men who to you tonight came into thee this night? Bring them out unto us, that we may know them."	*"Where are the men who came to you tonight? Bring them out to us so that we can have sex with them."*

The latter provides us with a more sexual reference. There are Biblical scholars that interpret this scripture being more of a case of rape than it was homosexuality. **During this biblical period, "rape" was considered a means of conquering a person and/or demeaning them to a lower level.** However, The Bible says all the males of the city were at Lot's house, which would be logical because their role during this time was to protect the city.

The majority of the men may not have been homosexual and the New International Version may have this completely wrong. Maybe they were just suspicious of newcomers entering their city and perhaps wanted to know and greet them.

The focus of the story was has historically been about homosexuality when that is really furthest from the truth.

Are There Ten Righteous In The City?

The angels that were visiting the city ultimately decided to sleep in the street because the agreement was made with Abraham to find ten righteous in the city to spare the city from destruction. If homosexuality was the issue, why would the angels of God sleep in the streets with homosexuals all around them? The angels were **not concerned with** the homosexuals; they were looking for "Ten Righteous In The City?"

Many biblical scholars believe that hospitality was not the primary reason the angels came to the city. If you look behind the scriptures, you will find the angels had no expectation of the people of Sodom in reference to hospitality.

Hospitality is a custom. This custom was broken but the act of harming another child of God **would probably have been deemed by** the angels as unforgivable. They were not looking for a place to sleep, eat or rest. The angels after talking with Abraham were looking for ten righteous in the city. If hospitality was the issue, then many cities and churches would be destroyed ten times over.

Additionally, in the scriptures the angels inquired with Lot about the whereabouts of his family. If Lot's son-in-laws were out in the city where there are homosexuals, one could "assume" the angels did not inquire into the sexuality of the son in-laws. I stand firm on the position that homosexuality was not the issue.

It was not about who lived in the city of Sodom & Gomorrah but who in the city Loved the Lord with their whole heart, mind and soul.

In Genesis 19:8-10, the scripture illustrates Lot offers his two daughters as a sacrifice to protect the visiting angels. The angels pulled Lot back into the house after his confrontation with the men of the city. It is not necessary for Lot to sacrifice his daughters for angels on the behalf of God. In our critical thinking one would have to inquire, if all the men were suppose to be homosexuals. Why would Lot offer his daughters? God does not need nor does he want parents to put their children at risk for physical and emotional abuse.

Many of young homosexuals have experienced negative situations with their parents because your parents thought they were pleasing God, when really, they were just following church traditions and teachings. In their traditional thinking, they still think they are pleasing God.

Many of us have a lot of old tapes about a God of condemnation and paths to internal hell that have been programmed in our head based on negative perceptions of who we are. Our challenge is with people we love and embrace and we have the highest degree of respect for. They continue to pick and choose what oppressive religious traditions they want to hold onto and pass them onto other generations. It is time to "evict" these old tapes out of our ideas and thoughts.

I believe a major area that deserves more critical thinking in this story is the roles of the angels. They did not come into the city asking with whom you were sleeping; they came into city searching for "Ten Righteous" people. They did not come into the city asking if you were lesbian, gay, transsexual, bisexual or heterosexual. They were looking for "Ten Righteous" people who loved God with their whole heart, mind and soul.

In today's society, religious organizations have established entire platforms based on their anti-gay positions. The black clergy has bought into this platform utilizing the religious fear tactics out of Sodom and Gomorrah. These religious platforms are rooted in a systematic belief they must protect the Kingdom of Heaven and the church, especially the black church, has bought it hook, line and sinker.

Why would God destroy a city when he promised in the covenant with Noah that life would never be destroyed? (Genesis 9:13-16)

Are there ten righteous in the city?

- ✓ Are there ten lesbians who love God?
- ✓ Are there ten gay men who love God?
- ✓ Are there ten transgenders who love God?
- ✓ Are there ten bisexuals who love God?
- ✓ Are there ten heterosexuals who love God?
- ✓ Who love the Lord with their whole heart, mind and soul? Just need "Ten."

The angels did not care what sexual orientation the ten righteous were, they just wanted to find the ten.

Sodom and Gomorrah

"(WWJD) What Would Jesus Do?"

We know the angels decided to destroy the city if they could not find ten righteous people in the city.

In the Christian community today one of their favorite cliché terms is *"What Would Jesus Do? (WWJD)"* as a stock answer to all the dilemmas they face. Rather than using sound teaching principles or commissions from scriptures on the various topics they just say, *"What Would Jesus Do?."*

Let's us review the statement using a scriptural cross reference of Sodom and Gomorrah and Jesus rejected by the Samaritans *(Luke 9:51-56).*

Dr. John Caputo, one of the leading philosophers of religion in America and a leading voice on religion and postmodernism. Argues that in his own way Jesus himself was a deconstructionist and that applying deconstruction to the church can be a positive move toward renewal.

Deconstruction is not *destruction* but rather a breaking down of the object in question so as to open it up to its own future and make it more loyal to itself. This is because in deconstructing, the undeconstructible is revealed, in this case, the eternal truth of God revealed in the gospel.

Note: I do not know of Dr. Caputo's ideology pertaining to our LBGT/SGL community but since he has presented such a logical form of reviewing biblical text we will use this as tool to review the following the text of Luke 9:51-56.

City of Samaria Rejects Jesus

In Luke 9:51-56 is the story of Jesus as is preparing to visit the city of Samaria, while on his way to a very hostile environment in Jerusalem were he would face false persecution and death. He sends some messengers to prepare for his arrival but the city rejects the appearance of Christ or to provide sleeping accommodations. *(Sounds familiar).*

After Assyria invaded the Northern Kingdom of Israel, and resettled it with its own people (2Kings 17:24-41), the mixed race that developed became known as the Samaritans and they in turn grew to hate the dominant Jewish religious system. So many tensions arose between the Samaritans and southern Judaea most Jewish travelers often walked around rather than through Samaritan territory, even though this lengthen their trip considerably. Jesus held no such prejudices or fears of Samaritans, and he sent messengers ahead to get rooms in the Samaritan village. But the village refused to welcome these Jews travelers.

Jesus illustrates in the preceding verses *"And whosoever will not receive you, when ye go out of that city, shake off the very dust from your feet for a testimony against them." (Luke 9:5)*. When the disciples were rejected by the Samaritan village, they did not desire to stop at shaking the dust from their feet *(Luke 9:5)*. The disciple's responds to Jesus was *"And when the disciples James and John saw this, they said, Lord, wilt thou that we command fire to come down from heaven, and consume them, even as Elias did? (Luke 9:54)*

1. Feeling rejected the disciples assumed destruction of the city was an option.
2. Jesus understood why the Samaritans were resisting with their arrival. There was a long history of condemnation and unfairness by the dominant religious culture.
3. Jesus had walked thru the city before when he met the woman at the well *"And he must needs go through Samaria." (John 4:4)*.
4. The woman at the well was a Samaritan *"Then saith the woman of Samaria unto him, How is it that thou, being a Jew, askest drink of me, which am a woman of Samaria? for the Jews have no dealings with the Samaritans. (John 4:9)*

In Luke 9:55-56 *9:55 But he turned, and rebuked them, and said, Ye know not what manner of spirit ye are of. 9:56 For the Son of man is not come to destroy men's lives, but to save them.*
1. Jesus challenged their spiritual hearts.
2. Jesus did not destroy the city but he took the longer route.
3. Jesus is not a rejecter of God's children *"For I and my Father are one" (John 10:30).*
4. We are one family with God not with the church. Jesus says; *"I in them, and thou in me, that they may be made perfect in one; and that the world may know that thou hast sent me, and hast loved them, as thou hast loved me."(John 17:23)*

In the bible version illustration below are the verses Luke 9:54-56. If we were to compare Old Testament about the series of events involving the City of Sodom with Lot and the Angels to New Testament story of Jesus and the rejection of the City of Samaria, I think it is very healthy dialogue.

| **Should The City Be Destroyed?** ||
Sodom & Gomorrah (Genesis 19)	**City of Samarians** (Luke 9:51-56)
Outcast because of worship practices	Outcast because of mixed race
Visited by Angels	Visited by messengers from Jesus
Lot showed hospitality with a place to sleep	City refused to provide a place to sleep
Destroy with fire from heaven	Threaten to be destroyed by fire from heaven
Chose not to shake off the dust from their feet	Jesus chose to shake off the dust from his feet
Seeking Righteousness	Unrighteous Spirit
Destroyed life	Jesus Saved Lives

Charts &Figures 4.1

Chapter 4   The Mis-Education About Sodom & Gomorrah

City Samaria Rejects Christ And He Does Not Destroy The City (Luke 9:51-56)

New American Standard Bible (NASB)	The Bible in Basic English	New International Version (NIV)	King James Version (KJV)
9:54 When His disciples James and John saw this, they said, "Lord, do You want us to command fire to come down from heaven and consume them?"	**9:54** And when his disciples, James and John, saw this, they said, Lord, may we send fire from heaven and put an end to them?	**9:54** When the disciples James and John saw this, they asked, "Lord, do you want us to call fire down from heaven to destroy them?"	**9:54** And when his disciples James and John saw this, they said, Lord, wilt thou that we command fire to come down from heaven, and consume
9:55 But He turned and rebuked them, [and said, "You do not know what kind of spirit you are of;	**9:55** But turning round he said sharp words to them.	**9:55** But Jesus turned and rebuked them,	**9:55** But he turned, and rebuked them, and said, Ye know not what manner of of spirit ye are of.
9:56 for the Son of Man did not come to destroy men's lives, but to save them."] And they went on to another village.	**9:56** And they went to another small town.	**9:56** and they went to another village.	**9:56** For the Son of man is not come to destroy men's lives, but to save them. And they went to another village.

Charts/Maps/Figures 4.2

"Desodomizing" Your Minds

We have many in our Kulture that have been spiritually wounded because of the misinterpretation of the story of Sodom and Gomorrah.

In the same gender loving culture there is an extremely high rate of teenage suicides, development of unhealthy co-dependency behaviors, relationships challenges and self-hate (internalized homophobia).

"Desodomizing" the mind is an imperative step to developing healthy decision making about yourself and how you perceive others in the same gender loving culture.

"Desodomization" is the deconstruction of the negative images about your sexuality and reconstruction of your thoughts about your sexuality with positive and affirming images.

What makes your sexuality dirty is because you have put it in the gutter. Coming out to be sexually free is not coming out. Coming out and being mentally free is truly being out.

Mentally free is about not repeating the oppressive behaviors of the oppressor. You are not mentally free if you support bashing other same gender loving persons because they are effeminate or masculine. You are not mentality free if you limit yourself to interact with opposite sex within the same gender loving community. You are not mentally free if you continue to hide pictures of you and your lover in your house when your family visits. Desodomization begins with a question for the individual or groups with the purpose of

Chapter 4 The Mis-Education About Sodom & Gomorrah

seeking enlightenment that empowers and nurtures their consciousness.

The pursuit for enlightenment is not about right or wrong. It is about addressing issues from a healthy or unhealthy perspective of oneself, partners, neighbors, authority, institutions and various social networks (i.e. houses, elders, chat rooms). It is deconstructing the traditional teachings and establishing a more critical way of reviewing and managing our religious challenges; in concert with implementing healthy models to empower the mind, body, and soul.

If your family does not approve of your lifestyle it is healthy for you to forgive them first.

Jesus was asked; "How many times should thou forgive? His response was Seven times Seventy."
(Matthew 7:7)

In most cases ones parents did the best they could with the information they were working with. Many of today's churches have clergy that have limited or no knowledge base about this issue and are not open to hearing anything different, and that is their loss. More importantly, what do you hear?

If you have experienced this with your parents, it might be healthy to recognize and/or understand that this experience was not normal. Our parents are our first identification with unconditional love and to have this love taken away for many is a devastating and horrible thought.

That negative experience with your parents was not normal. It is healthy not to try and rationalize this oppressive behavior. You are beautiful and made in the likeness and image of God.

If any negative experience hurt you, try to acknowledge the hurt. Do not let the pain, shame, and guilt manage you. You manage it, but you cannot manage what you do not acknowledge. If you are challenged with addressing these issues, this increases the odds the issues will not manage you. Find friends and have open conversations and listen to one another. We are who we are waiting for.

Have you ever cried yourself to sleep at night because you thought that you were the only one and you were going to hell? Let's change that image. Begin imagining your parents walking into your room and embracing you with unconditional love.

> *Sometimes you need to cry;*
> *To make it to the other side*
> Hari Williams

If your parents were exposed to a teacher who taught unconditional love, this too would have been your experience.

Your parents were only working with the information that was provided to them. Forgive them first if this has been your challenge. It is now in your control.

Since you have now recognized your attraction for the same sex, it is not mandatory to change your parent's points of view; it is healthy for you to change the negative perceptions of yourself.

"Change Is Mandatory, Growth Is Optional"

Like Abraham, having faith in other believers, that they may change is crucial. Realizing that your individual actions may be contagious and could possibly be hurting the community as a whole, are you holding on to negative images of yourself that were passed down can hurt your relationships, career decisions, friendships and ministry.

Desodomizing your mind is a necessary step to developing healthy decision making of yourself and how you perceive others and they perceive you in the same gender loving community.

Moving Yourself To The Next Level

Chapter 4 The Mis-Education About Sodom & Gomorrah

Each process question or thought can be viewed from the following perspectives: Same Gender Loving (SGL), Heterosexual (H) or Both (B). It is healthy to try and view from various perspectives to get insight into how others may process an issue. All perspectives are valid and should be respected and not condemned. In all thy getting; get understanding.

(1) (B) - Discover building a positive image of you.

(2) (B) - What does it feel like being a stranger amongst people you love (i.e. family, friends, church members)?
   a. What are your next steps to addressing those feelings?

(3) (B) - Do you treat people in the LBGT/SGL community differently, if they do not look or possess the societal behavioral norms?
   a. Effeminate men or Masculine females – Why or you or your friends challenge with their behavior?
   b. Transgenders – What makes you uncomfortable with them?

(4) (B) - Discover what will help you change those negatives images about yourself and other people in the LBGT/SGL.

(5) (B) - Discover how to build a closer relationship with God.

(6) (SGL) - Search for a good faith-based worship center that affirms all of you and your family configuration.

CHAPTER 5

The Mis-Education About Being An Abomination

How many times have we heard this scripture?

> "'Do not lie with a man as one lies with a woman;
> that is an abomination. *(Leviticus 18:22)*

Most Christians could not find this scripture in the Bible if their life depended on it. Their response is normally,

> *"I know it is in there, but I don't know where;
> but it is in the Bible."*

You are been mislead or better yet operated under the "The Mis-education of God's Love for Homosexuals." Homosexuality is not an abomination in the eyes of God. In the eyes of the Levite priest it was, in the eyes of the modern day church it is, but in the eyes of God; you just an expression of God's love.

In our Kulture many have committed suicide in addition to having of the highest LBGT/SGL teen suicide rates. We experience hate crimes against us because we are same gender loving.

In public arenas people refer to using as punks, sissies and faggots. In our Kulture, these words should be placed on the same levels as, "nigga." It is morally wrong students to use these names as a way of spreading hatred and dislike towards another student who appears to have feminine and/or masculine behaviors or identifies as bisexual, gay, lesbian, transgender or same gender loving.

The reality is a majority of the hatred is acquired from the misguiding teaching of the religious community. If the church would show God's unconditional love; we would not have these challenges but instead they teach of about a God with limited love against a Kulture(LBGT/SGL) of people. Well, they are wrong and we stand on the word of God and show them how wrong but the LBGT/SGL we must most not see themselves as wrong in the eyes of God..

The church has blood on their hands because of these misinterpretations.

> **Dr. Martin Luther King Jr** in an interview responded to question presented by the reporter. In your statement you assert that our actions, even though peaceful, must be condemned because they precipitate violence. But is this a logical assertion? Isn't this like condemning a robbed man because his possession of money precipitated the evil act of robbery? Isn't this like condemning **Socrates** because his unswerving commitment to truth and his philosophical inquiries precipitated the act by the misguided populace in which they made him drink hemlock? Isn't this like condemning **Jesus** because his unique God-consciousness and never-ceasing devotion to God's will precipitated the evil act of crucifixion? We must come to see that, as the federal courts have consistently affirmed, it is wrong to urge an individual to cease his efforts to gain his basic constitutional rights because the quest may precipitate violence. Society must protect the robbed and punish the robber.

There are writings that suggest that one of the main reasons the tribes had a problem with homosexuality was about economics; there were male-to-male encounters within the

Chapter 5   The Mis-Education About Being An Abomination

twelve tribes of Israel, and it was a threat to the growth of the twelve tribes of Israel.

They lived in a foreign land and the priests wanted to keep the Jews separate from the growing interest in other cultures.

We have people today making millions of dollars promoting anti-gay agendas because they think we are a threat to the growth and prosperity of the family. There are religious groups raising millions of dollars with two primary religious trigger words *"gay marriage and abortion."* It is good business for the religious communities to keep you confused.

If you are LBGT/SGL or non-labeling accepting your net worth is not justified by your sexual behavior; your net worth is justified by the love you have for yourself.

Homosexuality in the bible is not complicated.

Parents Don't Sacrifice Your Children

In the book of Leviticus 20:1-5, it talks about the penalties of worshipping the god of Molech. In the Molech religious system, children were given as a living sacrifice over a fiery pit.

Now, Jesus had to confront himself when approached by this Syro-Phoenician (Canaanite) woman because the Syro-Phoenicians worshipped the god of Molech.

Read the story out of Matthew 15:21-29.

> *21 Jesus left that place and went away to the district of Tyre and Sidon. 22 Just then a Canaanite woman from*

that region came out and started shouting, "Have mercy on me, Lord, Son of David; my daughter is tormented by a demon."23 But he did not answer her at all. And his disciples came and urged him, saying, "Send her away, for she keeps shouting after us."24 He answered, "I was sent only to the lost sheep of the house of Israel."25 But she came and knelt before him, saying, "Lord, help me."26 He answered, "It is not fair to take the children's food and throw it to the dogs."27 She said, "Yes, Lord, yet even the dogs eat the crumbs that fall from their masters' table."28 Then Jesus answered her, "Woman, great is your faith! Let it be done for you as you wish." And her daughter was healed instantly. NRSV

Jesus knew about the Molech traditions and did not approve of this woman kneeling at his feet. The "sista" was crying out for help for her daughter. She set a trigger off *(negative feelings from the past)* in Jesus and he relapsed back to traditional thinking and responds in a rather harsh manner toward the woman:

"It is not fair to take the children's food and throw it to the dogs." (Matthew 15:26)

Oh, my! Jesus refers to this sister in the context of a "dog." It was a harsh response, because he despised the practice of harming your children in the name of God. But the sista would not leave his feet, even when the disciples asked him to send her away. Jesus heard something deeper in her outcry; he heard "faith."

The illustration above is an example of a physical sacrifice hidden with the hope of spiritual benefits. Today the physical sacrifice is hidden the language with "saving the kingdom of god" or "it is a sin unto to God.

Many parents have sacrificed their children due to negative religious teachings. In the form or out casting, spoken evil of the children and letting people in authority speak evil about their children. This parents are under the assumption they are pleasing God. This is no different than what the Syro-Phoenician woman was trained to believe bring a sacrifice of God.

Your parents were trained in a tradition rooted in limitation and based on someone's misinterpretation of God. If their teachers (i.e. Bishop, Pastors, Evangelist, Prophets, and Respected Family Member) taught the true Love of Christ they would understand sacrificing their children is not honorable unto God and is incorrect life saving teachings of Jesus' Christ.

Is it the parent's fault if their child is gay? It is never anyone's "fault" if they or their loved one grows up to be gay, lesbian, bisexual or transgender. If you are asking yourself why you or your loved one is LGBTQ, consider asking yourself another question: Why ask why? Does your response to a LGBT/SGL person depend on knowing why they are LGBT/SGL?

If you see homosexuality in the Bible, then this means it existed. If you only see negative images of yourself, that is what the church wanted you to see by systematically harboring shame and guilt using the language they were taught to believe as the sovereign word of God.

The Concern with Homosexuality

"Wherever it has been established that it is shameful to be involved with sexual relationships with men, that is due to evil on the part of the rulers, and to cowardice on the part of the governed." Plato

In the book of Leviticus, the high priests responsibility was to establish the laws governing the twelve tribes of Israel. In Chapter 18, they deal with the *"Laws of Sexual Sin."* In this chapter you will find laws pertaining to incest (18:6-17), women's menstrual period (18:19), adultery (18:20), and bestiality (18:23).

The "Holiness Code" is a comprehensive series of ethical and ritual laws found in Leviticus chapters 17- 26. Holiness in Hebrew means separate from the ordinary or profane.

There are two passages in the "Holiness Code" of Leviticus, at 18:22 and 20:13-14, which appear to be fairly clear-cut condemnations of same-gender sexual relations among males. Sexual relations between females is not mentioned here, or anywhere else in the Old Testament (Review Chapter 10 Ruth & Naomi).

The seriousness of this practice in the Hebrew eyes was compounded by the belief that *"to lie with a man as with a woman"* violated the dignity of the male and female sex. Women were property, but men were the direct image of God. To treat a man the way a woman was treated was to reduce him to property, and, thereby, to violate the image of God.

Every society develops sexual taboos to regulate marriage practices, adultery and other acceptable sexual practices.

These restrictions are often transferred from one culture to another, but they are all designed to reflect the economic and moral values of their society during their period of time.

Abominations in the Bible

> *The Bible contains 6 admonishments to homosexuals and 362 to heterosexuals. This doesn't mean that God doesn't love heterosexuals; it's just that they need more supervision.* (Lynn Lavner)

Daily Wages
"You shall not defraud your neighbor; you shall not steal; and you shall not keep for yourself the wages of a laborer until morning." (Leviticus 19:13)

When you read the scripture, it says at the end of the day you were to be paid your wages. It did not say at the end of the week, biweekly, bimonthly, or monthly. Society and the church are guilty of an abomination. You know if we were paid at the end of every day, bills would be all screwed up. This is an abomination, per the Bible!

Love Thy Neighbor
"'Do not hate your brother in your heart. Rebuke your neighbor frankly so you will not share in his guilt.'" Do not seek revenge or bear a grudge against one of your people, but love your neighbor as yourself. I am the LORD" (Leviticus 19:17-18)

When you look at the scriptures it says, *"Hate not thy brother or rebuke thy neighbor, no more any grudge against the children of the people."* My sisters and brothers, are we not neighbors to church folks? This is an abomination, per the Bible.

Do Not Mix Materials
"Keep my decree.
Do not mate different kinds of animals.
Do not plant your field with two kinds of seed.
Do not wear clothing woven of
two kinds of material." (Leviticus 19:19)

Now the fashion folks love this one. The Bible says that you should not "mingle" material; this means, not to mix linen with wools or rayon with cotton. So, if we went to Wal-Mart *(by the way I love the store)*, do you think we would find an abomination on the racks? Wal-Mart has taken pride in making affordable clothes for the everyday person and their largest customer base is the religious community. This is an abomination, per the Bible.

No Rare Steaks
"'Do not eat any meat with the blood still in it.'" Do not practice divination or sorcery." (Leviticus 19:26)

The Bible says you should not eat any meat that still has blood in it. When you see the next Longhorn Steakhouse or Black Angus commercial, you see steaks with blood just oozing out. How many folks like a medium rare or rare steak? Well, you are guilty of an abomination.

Do not get me wrong—I am not trying to imply by no means that you should not eat steak. Hell, I have one in the refrigerator marinating now, and it's going to be lovely when I cook that it. Yes, lovely, but it will be "well done." I prefer mine all the way dead ☺. I know you vegetarians/vegans are thinking that I should not be eating beef anyway; *"Go eat a tofu cookie."* ☺ This is an abomination, per the Bible.

Men No Hair Trims
*27"Do not cut the hair at the sides of your head
or clip off the edges of your beard."*
(Leviticus 19:27)

The Bible says that you should not cut the corners of your head or the corners of you beard. This would mean a haircut and/or trim (depending on your hairstylist) is an abomination. How many folks are in church every Sunday with fresh haircuts even the preachers has a fresh hair cut. This is an abomination, per the Bible.

No Tattoos
*"Do not cut your bodies for the dead
or put tattoo marks on yourselves. I am the LORD."*
(Leviticus 19:28)

The Bible says that you should not have any markings on your body. Need I say any more? This is an abomination, per the Bible.

I visited one of the Mega Churches to hear the "Word." If you did not know by now I love the Lord and love to hear a good old preacher just bring the "Word." While in the church, the men were walking around in t-shirts just rolled up with fresh tattoos, and the Pastor was denouncing Gay Marriage. I was just so tickled. This is an abomination per the Bible.

Oh, yeah, and to my gay family cynics who are probably thinking, *"Why would you go to a church like that anyway,"* my response is *"learn how to listen beyond someone else's ignorance and you will continue to grow while they remain the same."*

Sabbath Laws

Observe my Sabbaths and have reverence for my sanctuary. I am the LORD. Do not turn to mediums or seek out spirits, for you will be defiled by them. I am the LORD your God. (Leviticus 19:30)

The Bible says you shall keep the Sabbath, meaning that you should not work on the seventh day. In some religious circles, the Day of Sabbath (i.e. Seventh Day Adventist) would be Saturday; in other religious circles, that day would be Sunday. When you study the scripture, you find it was an abomination to heal someone on the Sabbath. The religious community used this text as part of the plot to kill Jesus. This is an abomination, per the Bible.

Jesus would have challenging conversations with the religious leaders.

Jesus Challenges Religious Traditions

12:1 At that time Jesus went through the grain fields on the Sabbath; his disciples were hungry, and they began to pluck heads of grain and to eat. 2 When the Pharisees saw it, they said to him, "Look, your disciples are doing what is not lawful to do on the Sabbath."3 He said to them, "Have you not read what David did when he and his companions were hungry? 4 He entered the house of God and ate the bread of the Presence, which it was not lawful for him or his companions to eat, but only for the priests.5 Or have you not read in the law that on the Sabbath the priests in the temple break the Sabbath and yet are guiltless? 6 I tell you, something greater than the temple is here.7 But if you had known what this means, 'I desire mercy and not sacrifice,' you

Chapter 5   The Mis-Education About Being An Abomination

> *would not have condemned the guiltless. 8 For the*
> *Son of Man is lord of the Sabbath."*
> *(Matthew 12:1-8)*

In the New Testament, you will find in the scriptures Jesus is being questioned about breaking the Old Testament Sabbath Laws (i.e. Matthew 12:1-8). Jesus knows what the religious leaders are attempting to do by using friendly Bible discussion as a catalyst for their plot.

Jesus says, if you really knew the scriptures, you would not be asking me these kinds of questions. How can you have somebody hungry and there is food for them to eat and not allow them to eat the food? Remember when your great-grandfather David went out into the fields (storehouse) when his people were hungry and he took what he needed to feed his people.

Remember the issue with Jesus is not really about violation of the "Sabbath"; it is his universal appeal that challenges old traditions that hinder people's relationship with God.

Jesus mission was to share a universal love for all Gods Children. In no way would anyone be an outcast. This is the true love of God.

We are called to challenge any tradition that prevents us from loving God with our whole heart, mind and soul. In addition we should love our neighbors as ourselves. We should question the thoughts or systematic theologies (teachings) of anyone being left out of the family of God.

In our Kulture (LBGT/SGL), if you do not challenge the teachings of limitations with God, who is in Christ Jesus our Lord. Then you blaspheme, because you have allowed them to convince you God is not able.

Never put anyone, group or anything above God, "Seek ye first the kingdom of God and thy righteousness and all these things shall be added unto you" (Matt 6:33). With God all things are possible and God is able to do all things.

Jesus Accused of Blasphemy

Jesus questions traditional laws:
> *9 He left that place and entered their synagogue; 10 a man was there with a withered hand, and they asked him, "Is it lawful to cure on the Sabbath?" so that they might accuse him. 11 He said to them, "Suppose one of you has only one sheep and it falls into a pit on the Sabbath; will you not lay hold of it and lift it out? 12 How much more valuable is a human being than a sheep! So it is lawful to do good on the Sabbath." 13 Then he said to the man, "Stretch out your hand." He stretched it out, and it was restored, as sound as the other (Matthew 12:9-13)*

Jesus was addressing arguments over Biblical interpretation. Jesus' guiding rule was "love"; their guiding rule was "law." When a person(s) is trained in a strict legalistic way of thinking, it is extremely difficult to present new insight to their systematic way of thinking. The thinker has a science mentality; I must have evidence (lawyer talk) in order for this to be right or wrong. Jesus says love is the law.

The religious communities are plotting to kill Jesus because he was challenging religious traditions.

As you continue your biblical studies on the New Testament, you will observe the religious communities were major players in various community challenges, but they always found a way to keep themselves on the sidelines so they would not appear to have blood on their hands.

The blood of Matthew Shepherd and countless silent voices in our Kulture are on the hands of the church. These were spiritual hate crimes.

You Are Not An Abomination

As open-minded as many of us think we are, we can relapse into our old ways of thinking. We can be out of a negative environment for a long time, but if we are approached and/or presented with something that is a reflection of a past negative experience, it can set off a "trigger." Our reactions are usually with a negative verbal, physical and/or emotional response.

Jesus was placed in a similar situation with a Syro-Phoenician woman that required him to address some of his own traditional thinking about a culture of people, and he challenged himself about how he viewed someone. I love Jesus because he shows the human aspect of himself when dealing with people.

You are not an abomination unto God. The Levite priest taught what they believe was ordained by God. Jesus is challenging all of our trained belief systems. In your challenges be like Jesus and question whatever you believe is causing a conflict between you and your relationship with God.

Jesus does not see you as abomination. Never have and never will. Love is not complicated, but the business of religion is an ongoing calculus problem.

Moving Yourself To The Next Level

Chapter 5 The Mis-Education About Being An Abomination

Each process question or thought can be viewed from the following perspectives: Same Gender Loving (SGL), Heterosexual (H) or Both (B). It is healthy to try and view from various perspectives to get insight into how others may process an issue. All perspectives are valid and should be respected and not condemned. In all thy getting; get understanding.

(1) (B) - Where did your teachings of homosexuality being an abominations originate from?
    a. How will you address these erroneous teachings?

(2) (B) - What person, place or group do you need to disempower in your mind?

(3) (B) - Are you challenged with effeminate men or masculine females? Why,
    a. If no. How would you help those who do have that challenge?

(4) (SGL) - If your parents disapprove of you being same gender loving.
    a. What are your next steps to addressing this challenge for you?
    b. If you have addressed this issue in your life. How would you help someone who is challenged with this issue?

(5) (SGL) What image do you have of yourself?

CHAPTER 6

The Mis-Education About Gay Marriage

<u>Inclusive Definition of Marriage</u>
The love between two people who have decided to make a lifetime commitment to each other.

Does The Church Not Know The Scriptures?

In the past few years, the conversation about gay marriage
has been very divisive. We have the traditional church telling us God did not commission for two people of the same sex to marry. In the gay community, you have gay people who have convinced themselves it is wrong for two people of the same sex to marry.

I have witnessed some remarkable work facilitated by the Human Rights Campaign, National Gay and Lesbian Task Force, Marriage Equality USA and the Victory Fund.

These organizations deserve our support and whatever resources (i.e. finances, time, and connections) we can provide. I support their missions; we must have voices in all branches of government, provide training and organize our constituent base. Yes, I am very political. A negative church statement of which you may have heard:

"Adam and Eve, not Adam and Steve or Alice and Eve"

We have many in the religious community quoting this type of phrase and this is the extent of their knowledge about homosexuality in the bible.

There Is Neither Male nor Female In Heaven

In **Matthew 22:23-33**, you will find an historical account of the conflict with Jesus and the Sadducees.

> *22:29 Jesus answered and said unto them, Ye do err, not knowing the scriptures, nor the power of God.*
> *22:30 For in the resurrection they neither marry, nor are given in marriage, but are as the angels of God in heaven.*
> *22:31 But as touching the resurrection of the dead, have ye not read that which was spoken unto you by God, saying,*
> *22:32 I am the God of Abraham, and the God of Isaac, and the God of Jacob? God is not the God of the dead, but of the living.*
> *22:33 And when the multitude heard this, they were astonished at his doctrine.*

In this Biblical reading you will find Jesus having conversations with a group of religious folks, the Sadducees, who are a rival religion with the Pharisees. These groups would attempt to have conversations in public with Jesus as a way to accuse Jesus of being a false teacher because he did not obey the law.

Sadducees and Pharisees were competing religious groups, but plotted together to kill Jesus. It is amazing how enemies can come together when they find a threat to their finances or power!

Chapter 6   *The Mis-Education About Gay Marriage*

Jesus answered and said unto them, You do err,
Nor knowing the scriptures, nor the power of God.
For in the resurrection they neither marry, nor given
marriage, but are as the angels of God in heaven.
(Matthew 22:23-33)

The church has convinced themselves that in heaven, they will be segregated: The Smith Family, The Jones Family, The Gonzalez Family, The Ying Family, and The Roberts Family. Jesus makes it clear that when we get to heaven there is no separation; there is no hierarchy; we are one with God. I love me some Jesus.

The religious community has convinced themselves they know God better than anybody else. No one fully knows God and to believe we fully understand all of the thoughts of God is arrogant on the part of the believer. How do you fully understand God's love?

Marriage is a social institution not a biblical solution

"Homosexuality Is Not Unnatural"

"Homosexuality is assuredly no advantage, but it is nothing to be ashamed of, no vice, no degradation, it cannot be classified as an illness." Sigmund Freud, letter to an American mother's plea to cure her son's homosexuality, 1935

Homosexual behavior is condemned *by the church* based on the foundation that two people of the same sex who love each other cannot procreate, so it is not blessed by God. They are firm that a heterosexual relationship was God's primary intention for a man and woman.
Is this lifestyle really unnatural? The definition of "unnatural" is defined as: contrary to laws of nature.

Mary Miraculously Conceives (Luke 1:34-37)

Then said Mary unto the angel, how shall this be, seeing I know not a man? And the angel answered and said unto to her, The Holy Ghost shall come upon thee, and the power of the Highest shall overshadow thee: therefore also that holy the thing which shall be born of thee shall be called the Son of God. And, behold, thy cousin Elizabeth, she has also conceived a son in her old age: and this is the sixth month with her, who was called barren: For with God nothing shall be impossible.

Could this be considered "unnatural?"

You be a "sista" and go to the church house talking about you a virgin and you pregnant with child. The first thing they will do is look at you real funny and, depending on the church, they will probably take you to the altar and start throwing holy water on you and rebuke you in the name of Jesus. Coming in here talking about you pregnant without sexual relations with a man. That ain't nothing but the devil. Ya'll know how church folk get.

The story tells us the Holy Ghost fell upon Mary without man's help. That was not "procreation"; with Mary, it was an unnatural event by ancient and modern-day standards. God shows the ability to operate outside of what we see as the social norm.

The Civil Rights Act

Historically, many issues were passed via the legislative process due to the dominant popular opinion weighing heavily against equality. There were equality issues *(i.e. civil rights, women's right to vote),* if put to a vote before the general

Chapter 6   *The Mis-Education About Gay Marriage*

public on a state level they would have never passed in the general election. In addition, many state legislative branches were not showing judicial fairness if the issues remained in their control. President Abraham Lincoln who ran on a platform to maintain slavery signed the Emancipation

These issues were not delegated to the states because of their consistent judicial unfairness. There was a gross violation U.S. Citizens' rights as stated in the 14th Amendment of United States Constitution.

> **Fourteenth Amendment (Amendment XIV)**
> *Section 1. All persons born or naturalized in the United States, and subject to the jurisdiction thereof, are citizens of the United States and of the State wherein they reside. No State shall make or enforce any law which shall abridge the privileges or immunities of citizens of the United States; nor shall any State deprive any person of life, liberty, or property, without due process of the law; nor deny to any person within its jurisdiction the equal protection of the laws.*

Charts & Figures 6.1

No State Elections For Some Marriages

There was no public vote. The Proclamation to abolish slavery, known as the Emancipation Proclamation consisted of two executive orders issued by President Lincoln during the American Civil War. The first one, issued September 22, 1862, declared the freedom of all slaves in any state of the Confederate States of America that did not return to Union control by January 1, 1863. The second order, issued January 1, 1863, named the specific states where it applied.

Booker T. Washington (*American educator, orator, author and leader of the African-American community*) while at the age of 9, remembered the day in early 1865

> *As the great day drew nearer, there was more singing in the slave quarters than usual. It was bolder, had more ring, and lasted later into the night. Most of the verses of the plantation songs had some reference to freedom.... Some man who seemed to be a stranger (a United States officer, I presume) made a little speech and then read a rather long paper—the Emancipation Proclamation, I think. After the reading we were told that we were all free, and could go when and where we pleased. My mother, who was standing by my side, leaned over and kissed her children, while tears of joy ran down her cheeks. She explained to us what it all meant, that this was the day for which she had been so long praying, but fearing that she would never live to see.*

The feelings a young Booker T experienced are similar to what was felt by many African-Americans all over the world when President-elect Barack Obama was voted the 44th President of the United States of America. *In this lifetime.*

The Emancipation Proclamation took place without violence by masters or ex-slaves. It represented a major step toward the ultimate abolition of slavery in the United States and a *"new birth of freedom".*

The Civil Rights Act of 1964

(July 2, 1964) was legislation outlawing racial segregation in schools, public places, and employment. Written

Chapter 6   The Mis-Education About Gay Marriage

to assist African Americans, before being passed the bill was amended to protect women, specifically Caucasian women for the first time. It also created the Equal Employment Opportunity Commission. President

John F. Kennedy introduced the bill in his civil rights speech on June 11, 1963, he asked for *legislation "giving all Americans the right to be served in facilities which are open to the public—hotels, restaurants, theaters, retail stores, and similar establishments," as well as "greater protection for the right to vote."*

Racial Equality In The Military

President Harry S. Truman, Executive Order 9981 expanded on Executive Order 8802 by establishing equality of treatment and opportunity in the Armed Services for people of all races. The operative statement is:

> *It is hereby declared to be the policy of the President that there shall be equality of treatment and opportunity for all persons in the armed services without regard to race, color, religion or national origin. This policy shall be put into effect as rapidly as possible, having due regard to the time required to effectuate any necessary changes without impairing efficiency or morale.*

The idea of same sex marriage being placed in the hands of the dominant oppressive voters is no different than during the slavery period when black citizens were being oppressed by very hostile dominant white community.

There were issues that could not be placed on a ballot in the general public or assigned to the state legislators.

Historically with the issues of race and gender issues many states were not willing to provide the neighboring states citizen's legal protections.

It is not justice when you advocate having citizens rights removed or modified to lessen their freedom of expression or protect themselves and their families.

"An injustice anywhere is a threat to justice everywhere"
Dr. Martin Luther King Jr.

Marriage Vs. Civil Union

To my surprise many people in the black LBGT/SGL community are challenged with same-sex marriage.

The systematic s thinking programmed into the minds slaves, cause many to have no hope of seeing in their lifetime the signing of the Emancipation Proclamation, a Civil Rights Bill or a Black man being elected President of the United States.

There were slaves who believed in their hearts master (pharaoh) had been good to them and the freedom fighters were asking for too much too fast.

They cannot:
1. ·See this is not about them as an individual but we as a Kulture.
2. ·See the legal protection for their friends in committed long term relationship.
3. ·See there was probably a time in the life when they met someone very special and if the circumstances were right they would have married them.
4. See being happy with one person.

Chapter 6   The Mis-Education About Gay Marriage

5. ·See committed couples working hard but having the fear of their families challenging their assets if their partner were to get sick or pass away.
6. ·See advocating their disapproval for same-sex marriage makes them a part of their own problem.
7. · See it is dysfunctional to advocate against their right to legally protect their relationships.

Marriage is when people marry for reasons of love and commitment. But marriage is also a legal status, which comes with rights and responsibilities. Marriage establishes a legal relationship between you and your spouse. It is a relationship that is recognized across cultures, countries and religions. One state does not have the right to deny your rights because of the religious belief or lack of understanding.

Civil Unions exist in only a handful of places: Civil unions were created in 2000 to provide legal protections to gays and lesbians in relationships in that because gay marriage is not a popular option based on social opinion. The protections do not extend beyond many state borders and no federal protections are included with a Civil Union. Civil Unions offer some of the same rights and responsibilities as marriage, but only on a state level.

Conservative Christian Coalitions

Black Church –
You've been hoodwinked;
You've been bamboozled!

The black church has taken on an agenda from groups that historically have been their oppressors. Moving from

*The Mis-Education Against
Homosexuality In The Bible*

During the later years of the Clinton administration a lot of black faith leaders partnered with many of the Christian Coalition groups. These groups experience a tremendous amount growth during the George W. Bush administration.

Their goals were to push mainstream agendas via their faith-based congregations. The Christian Coalition was founded by Rev. Pat Robertson, who served as the organizations President from its founding until February 2001.

Mr. Robertson has been known for making some very candid statements.

> *Just like what Nazi Germany did to the Jews, so liberal America is now doing to the evangelical Christians. It's no different. It is the same thing. It is happening all over again. It is the Democratic Congress, the liberal-based media and the homosexuals who want to destroy the Christians. Wholesale abuse and discrimination and the worst bigotry directed toward any group in America today. More terrible than anything suffered by any minority in history." –Pat Robertson*

> *"I would warn Orlando that you're right in the way of some serious hurricanes, and I don't think I'd be waving those flags in God's face if I was you, this is not a message of hate -- this is a message of redemption. But a condition like this will bring about the destruction of your nation. It'll bring about terrorist bombs; it'll bring earthquakes, tornadoes, and possibly a meteor." –Pat Robertson, on "gay days" at Disneyworld*

> *"The feminist agenda is not about equal rights for women. It is about a socialist, antifamily political movement that encourages women to leave their husbands, kill their children, practice witchcraft, destroy capitalism and become lesbians." – Pat Robertson*

Chapter 6   The Mis-Education About Gay Marriage

> *"I know this is painful for the ladies to hear, but if you get married, you have accepted the headship of a man, your husband. Christ is the head of the household and the husband is the head of the wife, and that's the way it is, period."* –Pat Robertson

The Christian Coalition of America values are consistent with those of the Christian Right. On the coalition website it states: Christian Coalition of America is a political organization, made up of pro-family Americans who care deeply about becoming active citizens for the purpose of guaranteeing that government acts in ways that strengthen, rather than threaten, families. As such, we work together with Christians of all denominations, as well as with other Americans who agree with our mission and with our ideals.

The Christian Coalition consisted of many groups that took off the "white sheets" and put on "white collars" and hid under the umbrella of Conservative Christians.

There were many mainstream black church preachers excited about being apart of these religious good ole boy clubs. Many of the mainstream black preachers wanted Cable network access to help them to build a their membership base and donor pipeline.

The Promise Keepers movement was a wakeup call for many of the black Christian believers and leaders. It is only fair to mention that not all members of this group have this active or passive aggressive racist mentality and are guilty only by association. We all have experienced being guilty by association in our faith centers and social environments.

These types of groups created networks that developed church doctrines and white papers on the issues of gay marriage, abortion and immigration reform.

If you research the network associations you find many of these groups can be linked to many of the State Constitutional Amendments, Three Strike Laws, Anti-Abortion Issues, and Abolishment of Affirmative Action Initiatives.

Millions of dollars have been raised via books, video, conferences and church donations to fight what the morality midgets promote as a threat to the Kingdom of Heaven.

These anti-gay issues have become a major donor pipeline for many church denominations and evangelist with no church congregations. The moral midgets like to get their members riled up and then request their financial support.

This is more about money than it is about saving the Kingdom of Heaven. The sad reality is there are people who **truly want to serve the Lord but have been led to believe God will not receive our Kulture in Heaven**

Re-Addressing The Marriage Definition

Our goal is not to redefine family traditions for most families have various cultural differences. Our goal is to redefine the definition of the word marriage without linking it to a groups specific religious beliefs.

The Definition of Marriage

"The love between two people
who have decided to
make a lifetime commitment to each other."

In this commitment they desire to establish the legal protections under the law. History reminds us this morality

Chapter 6   The Mis-Education About Gay Marriage

argument was used against interracial marriages and the marriages of slaves.

> *Neither shalt thou make marriages with them; thy daughter thou shalt not give unto his son, nor his daughter shalt thou take unto thy son (Deuteronomy 7:3)*

It was consider as redefining marriage. Marriage is not just for white people, black people or Patriots. The religious fundamentalists have used the fear of God as a platform since biblical times to oppress various groups.

Marriage is a social institution not a biblical solution!

Deuteronomy 25:5

King James Version	Bible In Basic English
If brethren dwell together, and one of them die, and have no child, the wife of the dead shall not marry without unto a stranger: her husband's brother shall go in unto her, and take her to him to wife, and perform the duty of an husband's brother unto her.	If brothers are living together and one of them, at his death, has no son, the wife of the dead man is not to be married outside the family to another man: let her husband's brother go in to her and make her his wife, doing as it is right for a brother-in-law to do.

Charts & Figures 6.2

Historically various biblical passages have played a significant role in shaping the ideas of our social consciousness and political systems.

*The Mis-Education Against
Homosexuality In The Bible*

The passage above is an example of how over a period of time our socially acceptable point of view on family has changed.

In our Kulture, transcending how we see family will be a process that we can no longer afford to avoid. In the heterosexual community it is a struggle with their traditional teachings. In The LBGT/SGL defining our traditions is our responsibility.

2008 State Ballot Initiatives	
Arizona Proposition 102: Ban on Gay Marriage	Passed
Arizona Proposition 202: Hiring Illegal Immigrants	Passed
Arkansas Initiative 1: Ban on Gay Couples Adopting Children	Passed
California Proposition 8: Ban on Gay Marriage	Passed
California Proposition 4: Abortion Limits	Failed
Colorado Amendment 46: End Affirmative Action	Failed
Colorado Amendment 48: Human Life from Moment of Conception	Failed
Florida Amendment 2: Ban on Gay Marriage	Passed
Nebraska Initiative 424: End Affirmative Action	Passed
South Dakota Initiative 11: Abortion Limits	Failed

Charts &Figures 6.3

Chapter 6   The Mis-Education About Gay Marriage

Canada Legalized Marriage

In 1999 the Parliament of Canada reaffirmed the historic definition of marriage by a vote of 216 to 55. In 2001 the first same-sex marriage judgment was delivered by the British Columbia Supreme Court. It decided against the applicants. It argued that marriage served unique social purposes and concluded that it could not be redefined without a constitutional amendment.

In July 2002 the Ontario Superior Court declared that the existing legal framework was discriminatory and gave the federal government 2 years to explore other legal options: a) redefining marriage, b) civil unions, or c) having the state step back from marriage. In Sept. 2002 the Quebec Superior Court produced a similar judgment. In response the federal government inaugurated public hearings across Canada.

Almost five hundred presentations were made to the Standing Committee on Human Rights and Justice. After the public hearings the parliamentary committee began to prepare its report.

On June 10th 2003, the Ontario Court of Appeal dismissed the two year period for Parliamentary deliberation, abolished the traditional definition of marriage, and redefined marriage as a union of two persons. The federal government immediately terminated the work of the parliamentary committee, decided not to appeal the Ontario judgment, and on June 17th, 2003, it announced that it would introduce legislation to redefine marriage.

In July 2003, the government put forward a series of reference questions for the Supreme to seek its opinion on whether the government has the constitutional authority to redefine marriage.

On Dec.9, 2004 the Supreme Court of Canada rendered its opinion on the constitutionality of the proposed legislation.

On Feb.1, 2005 Bill C-38 was tabled in the House of Commons. **See Appendix D for Bill Language (information source www.marriageinstitute.ca)**

Marriage is a social institution not a biblical solution!

South Africa Legalized Same Sex Marriage

On November 30, 2006 Same-sex marriage became legal in South Africa when the *Civil Unions Bill* was enacted after having been passed by the South African Parliament. South Africa became the fifth country, and the first in Africa, to legalize same-sex marriage.

Three laws currently provide for the status of marriage in South Africa. These are the Marriage Act (Act 25 of 1961), the Customary Marriages Act (Act 120 of 1998), which provides for the civil registration of marriages solemnized according to the traditions of indigenous tribes, and the Civil Union Act (Act 17 of 2006). South Africans may choose in terms of which of these laws they wish to be married, but may be married in terms of only one at a given time.

Same-sex marriages are only allowed in terms of the Civil Union Act. Couples marrying in terms of the Civil Union Act may choose whether their union is called a civil partnership or a marriage partnership. Couples joined in a marriage partnership in terms of that act enjoy the same privileges as couples married in terms of the Marriage Act.

Chapter 6   The Mis-Education About Gay Marriage

If it can be proven that a couple is married in terms of any of these three acts, that marriage is legally valid and may not be regarded as an invalid marriage or a non-marriage by anyone or any organization. It is therefore illegal for any organization to treat any such married persons as if they were unmarried.

A person who is a marriage officer in terms of the Marriage Act, and who has an objection of conscience, religion or belief to marrying same-sex couples, may object to the government in writing, after which he or she will be granted exemption from having to perform such marriages. A person who is a marriage officer in terms of the Civil Union Act will not be exempted from performing same-sex marriages.

Such an objector may, however, give up their office as marriage officer altogether by resigning from whichever organization they belong to by virtue of which they are a marriage officer, or if said organization as a whole requests from the government that their members no longer be recognized as marriage officers by virtue of their membership to that organization.

Marriage is a social institution not a biblical solution!

Interracial Marriages

In the landmark case of Loving v. Virginia, 388 U.S. 1 (1967) in which the United States Supreme Court declared Virginia's anti-miscegenation (inter-racial marriage) statute, the "Racial Integrity Act of 1924", unconstitutional, thereby overturning *Pace v. Alabama* (1883) and ending all race based legal restrictions on marriage in the United States.

The plaintiffs, Mildred Loving, a black woman and Richard Perry Loving, a white man, were both residents of the Commonwealth of Virginia were married in June 1958 in the District of Columbia, deciding to leave Virginia due to the unfairness of Racial Integrity Act, a state law banning marriages between any white person and any non-white person.

The local law enforce in Virginia coordinated a surprise visit one night at their home while sleeping because this married couple was found sleeping in their bed by these officers. There were additional crimes on the books that prohibited interracial couples from having sex.

They provided the police officers an original copy of their marriage certificate hanging in the bedroom. The judicial system used this evidence to bring criminal charge because they were married in another state. They were charged under Section 20-58 of the Virginia Code, which prohibited interracial couples from being married out of state and then returning to Virginia, and Section 20-59, which classified "inter-racial marriages" as a felony punishable by a prison sentence of between one and five years.

On January 6, 1959, the coupled was forced to plead guilty to the charges and could receive a one year prison sentence. They in turn had the option of leaving the State of Virginia on the condition they would not return for at least twenty-five years.

The trial judge in the case was Leon Bazile, and he quoted Johann Friedrich Blumenbach, a German doctor and physiologist, one of the first to explore the study of mankind as an aspect of natural history

Chapter 6   The Mis-Education About Gay Marriage

Almighty God created the races white, black, yellow, Malay and red, and He placed them on separate continents. And but for the interference with His arrangement there would be no cause for such marriages. The fact that He separated the races shows that He did not intend for the races to mix.

There is an historical reflection here. It is imperative we do not let these moral midgets transfer their racist, sexist and homophobic attitudes into our consciousness as if they have the keys to marriage.

Marriage is a social institution not a biblical solution!

Slave Marriages

Leslie Howard Owens, author of "This Species of Property:
Slave Life and Culture in the Old South" provides a fascinating study exploring the personality and behavior of the slave within the context of what it meant to be a slave.

Based on a variety of plantation records, diaries, slave narratives, travelers' accounts, and other items bearing on the slave's experiences in his relationships to slaveholders, it concentrates on the years between 1770 and 1865.

The Freedmen's Bureau was established as an agency to rebuild the African-American family structure. The Bureau attempted to provide two services
(1) the right to education
(2) the right to choose one's employment.

These were commonly thought of as the two most important rights that were denied to slaves. However, the cruelest aspect of slavery may have been the denial of a slave's right to a secure family structure.

Current social theorists emphasize strong family relationships as being paramount for an individual's emotional and mental health. A stable family was almost impossible to maintain under slavery. Marriage between slaves was not legally recognized. Slaves requested permission from their masters to be allowed to marry and the recognition of the union only came from within the slave community. The slave marriage ceremony, if one was held at all, varied from the couple jumping over a broomstick together to exchanging vows in front of a white minister.

Whatever the nature of the wedding ceremony, slave marriages ultimately depended on the will of the masters. Some slaves were forced into "marriage" for breeding purposes. Husbands, wives, and children were often separated when sold. To many whites, the slave family consisted of transient members who could be easily exchanged emotionally by the slave as they could physically by the master. Because of this, slaves obtained a reputation among whites as being immoral and devoid of family values.

The black church has forgotten its roots. It needs to be reminded how they see us is how many European-American Christians viewed the black race and their negative perception of the black family.

Recently CNN reported on a story about a church out in Kansas that placed this quote on their marquee

America_We_Have_A_Muslim_President._
It_Is_A_Sin_Against_The_Lord.

(Exodus 20:3)

I know you're wondering what does Exodus 20:3 say.
"You shall have no other Gods before Me"

Yep, that is the foundation of their belief. Although President-elect Obama has repeatedly said he is Christian. There are some who have decided to keep many believers confused. In the event he was Muslim, so what. There is an American-Muslim who one day wants to be president.

Believe it or not there are many Black Churches that would have a problem of with a Muslim/Moslem (person of Islamic faith) being the President of the United States.

People in our LBGT/SGL community must realize in the black church, we have black clergy preaching the same hatred. If your pastor is silent on the matter then they are just as bad as the fanatic preaching the hatred or disapproval of two people trying to love each other. They have an opportunity to empower and inform but they have taken the safe route "silence." When black preachers use the pulpit to promote their social bigotry, in addition those in our Kulture repeating their verbal madness as a reality. It just adds on to the community challenges of achieving equal rights.

Marriage is a social institution not a biblical solution!

New Understanding of Jumping The Broom

During the slavery period, the laws did not allow the slaves to get married. The slaves did not let this stop them; they created their own form of matrimony known as "Jumping The Broom." Eventually the courts recognized the marriages.

We do not wait for legislation to say "I Do." We go to the courthouse and lawyers and put together the "seven" legal documents that all LBGT/SGL couples should have notarized.

(1) *General Power of Attorney*
(2) *Power of Attorney of Healthcare Matters*
(3) *Power of Attorney of Financial Matters*
(4) *Power of Attorney for Hosp. Visitation Rights*
(5) *Living Will*
(6) *Living Trust*
(7) *Will*
(8) *Guardianship (if you share joint child custody)*

NOTE: I listed these from memory so I apologize if I did not get them all correctly but you get my point. Powers Of Attorney's are void upon death of the person. You should seek legal counsel to protect you and loved ones. In case one of you were in need of emergency assistance or were to pass away. If you are in a committed relationship I do not recommend you leaving these matters up to your biological family. If something happens to you our families can be real Jekyll and Hyde's.

The time has come now for Same-Gender-Loving, Lesbians, Gays and Transgender to create a more inclusive form of matrimony. We do not need to wait on the courts while continuing to advocate in the courts.

Our ceremonies should celebrate being equal in the relationships, not based on the roles we play in the bedroom. Our ceremonies should incorporate walking together. Our ceremonies should not require our fathers as the primary person to give one of the partners away. If daddy does not approve, it is our responsibility to create alternatives and the view with an understanding of normal.

It's not just our time; it's our turn.

Chapter 6   The Mis-Education About Gay Marriage

Moving Yourself To The Next Level

Chapter 6 The Mis-Education About Gay Marriage

Each process question or thought can be viewed from the following perspectives: Same Gender Loving (SGL), Heterosexual (H) or Both (B). It is healthy to try and view from various perspectives to get insight into how others may process an issue. All perspectives are valid and should be respected and not condemned. In all thy getting; get understanding.

(1) (B) - If we are all spirit and shall be one with God. Why does the concept of death after life language haunt you?

(2) (B) - When do you think God becomes aware of a persons same-sex attraction?

(3) (SGL) - What do you think surprises people when they realize someone they know have same sex attractions?

(4) (B) - Have you ever been in a relationship and realized you were the only one in love in the relationship?
   a. If yes, How did you manage that experience?
   b. If no, Have you ever lead someone along with the faulty assumption you were in love with them?

(5) (SGL) - Do you plan on being single the rest of your life?
a. If yes or no, Why?

(6) (B) - If you are in a relationship. What have you learned about yourself?

(7) (B) - If you are in a long term relationship. What could you teach others?

CHAPTER 7

The Mis-Education About Present Day Gentiles (same gender loving)

In the New Testament of the bible we discover one of Paul's greatest challenges was sharing this new found life with Jesus Christ and convince the Gentiles they could have a relationship with Jesus Christ. The Gentiles were suspicious of the new religion and that only a certain types of people could have a relationship with Jesus Christ.

In LBGT/SGL we face similar challenges of being taught only a specific group or type of people could have a relationship with Jesus Christ. This is logical when you have been programmed or trained since you were a child that something is wrong with you. It is the same type of negative programming a young child in one culture would receive about another culture of people. They grew up believing the negative image was truth, until they challenge the traditional teachings and images of people and a god with conditional love.

A Gentile in the bible is defined as a non-Jew. **A non-Jew anyone not born of Jewish mother or father also known as the uncircumcised.** Christianity is derived from Jews (Israelites) who saw Jesus Christ as the coming messiah. This is where we get the term Judeo-Christianity (Jewish Christians).

The challenge was people would bring various rituals or laws (aka traditions) from their old religious practice to their new religious practice. The religious people were bringing in tradition but traditions have no place in the church. The Judaizers still wanted to hold on to traditions. Women in the church are not going to look like women in the 50's. If all you sing is songs from the church you were brought up in then you are bringing your family traditions. If men were brought up in a culture where women could not sit in the pulpit and implement this practice in the new church it is traditions, holding onto traditions of the men or male dominated practices. There was a time women could not preach in the church. In the Catholic church women cannot be priest. The "spirit of exclusive" is when you separate from one group but exclude another group.

The founder of the Apostolic Faith Movement Bro. Charles Parham a white southern preacher could not let go of traditions when he denounced the move of the Holy Spirit during the Azusa Street experience because he saw Blacks and Whites worshipping together and speaking in tongues. It was lead by one of his black students Bro. William J. Seymour. Bro. Seymour could not sit in the classroom with the other white students so his seat was outside the window and when it rained they would let him sit in the hallway. The connection between Seymour and Parham was broken, however, in October 1906. Bro. Seymour had invited Bro. Parham, his "father in the gospel," to preach in Azusa Street, but Parham's negative messages and attempts to correct what he saw as abuses lead to expulsion from the church. From that period on there was a complete rupture between Seymour and Parham that never healed.

Bro. Seymour would become the bridge and laying on of hands for great people of God to launch their Pentecostal movements. From Gaston Sarnabus Cashwell of the Pentecostal Holiness Churches, they would burn crucifixes in front of his church. Cashwell lead several holiness denominations (i.e. The Pentecostal Holiness Church, The Church of God, The United Holy Church of America).

In November 1906, C. H. Mason, head of The Church of God In Christ, came to Azusa and received the Pentecostal experience. In Birmingham, Alabama, M.M. Pinson and H.G. Rogers, pillars in the Assemblies of God and predominately white denomination with a challenging racial history.

Protestantism (Protest) was a break off from the Catholic Church. Under Protestantism you would find various denominations (i.e. Church of God In Christ, Assemblies of God, Four Square, Baptist, Pentecostal, and Seventh Day Adventist).

In each group they saw themselves and not totally accepted and decided to break away for a multitude of reasons but still brought traditions. We have the black church in part because many white churches did not accept blacks as fully equal in the eyes of God. So they built their own church denominations.

Today, many white and black churches do not accept Same Gender Loving Christians This has creating the birthing ministries like Metropolitan Community Church, Unity Fellowship Church of Christ, non-denominational LBGT/SGL ministries. In our developing ministries there is challenging with each group wanting to bring their worship styles (traditions) as a rule of this is how it is done because "when I grew up". Yes, grew up with traditions. The gentiles and the LBGT/SGL had to seek a relationship for themselves and re-evaluate church traditions and cultural biases.

In the LBGT/SGL we must seek a relationship with Jesus Christ for ourselves and question the teachings of these denominational traditions.

Gentile Mentalities

Holding a bible certificate and/or degree in religion does not give anyone the right to teach oppressive or exclusive thinking to you. They may have passed the test of the oppressive system but they failed the test of Agape Love (God Unconditional Love).

You do not have to justify homosexuality in the bible; you are justified by God's Unconditional Love (Agape). **The religious community will manipulate the teachings by implementing exclusiveness hidden in their traditions.** Paul was about establishing a personal relationship with God and it is wrong for any group to question who God loves.

You've been hoodwinked, you've been bamboozled!!!!

God loves you just the way you are and if you do not like what you see and/or feel uncomfortable about yourself. **Then seek some additional empowerment resources.** Do your homework this is really about you.

In your bible studies you will learn Paul's greatest challenge was trying to convince the Gentile's they could have an unconditional relationship with God. One of our greatest challenges today is trying to educate our Kulture (LBGT/SGL) that God loves them just the way that they are.

This is not about telling the religious community they should embrace our community. Your assignment is to encourage yourself and others the LBGT/SGL community to

Chapter 7   The Mis-Education About Present Day Gentiles
(same gender loving)

embrace who they are. Encouraging the each other not to give any person, place or groups more power than their Divine Creator.

This is not about trying to prove the church wrong or proselytizing to our own community. We do not want to replicate the traditional behavior of the oppressor, but be respectful of the religious community but not condone their exclusive behaviors. Some of our sisters and brothers will continue to believe these misguided lessons rooted in traditions and exclusiveness.

I Am Not Ashamed of the Gospel

The scriptures in the Book of Romans are the easiest of the negative text used against our Kulture (LBGT/SGL). This is a not a complicated issue.

In the Book of Romans, the scriptures have been used and abused for centuries. An area of bible study that usually causes a misunderstanding of the scripture is when people read one verse and not any preceding (before) or succeeding (after) verses *(old school Bible preachers love that kind of talk)*.

Romans could be seen as probably the easiest of the terror texts to review because it is so plain. When people tell you this is a complicated issue, what should you do? Run like your sanity is depending on it.

Romans is considered to be one Paul's greatest writings. In the book he describes some of the challenges in the city of Rome. He questions the competing religious systems because most of them humanize God and imply and/or create a belief that *"man can fix everything"* without God's help.

Romans is also known in many religious circles as the "Sin" book, partially because Paul speaks about this hot topic during this ancient time—it is the same today in reference to the issues of gay marriage and abortion rights in the church. There are many modern-day books that provide Hebrew and Greek interpretations of unnatural, ungodliness, wickedness, and impurities about lesbians. Times have surely changed, during this biblical period if a woman sin in adultery she could be stoned. Jesus says, "Let them who is without sin, cast the first stone" (John 8:7).

In Romans Chapter One, we find the "Introduction of the letter to the Christians of Rome." Paul is familiar with the customs of Rome and provides the readers with knowledge of their common interest: "Jesus Christ." He celebrates their commitment in living a life with Christ and he affirms it with his walk with Christ. He concludes with

I am not ashamed of the gospel of Christ;
For just shall live by faith (Romans 1:16-17)

Paul begins to speak to them about the reasons and challenges for Gentile Guilt.

The word "*gentile* " means " *nation* ", non-Jewish, according to several traditions, the Israelites were required to maintain strict separation from them in matters of religion, marriage housing, socialism and politics. Paul was teaching that we are not separate under the eyes of God.

The development of Christianity, which began as a Jewish movement, was profoundly affected by the success of the Gentile mission undertaken by Apostle Paul and others. Paul had a directive from God but was sent to the people he thought he was better than, if Paul would have had his choice

Chapter 7   The Mis-Education About Present Day Gentiles
(same gender loving)

he would have went to the Jews. There was controversy over the role of Gentiles in the church.

Christianity during this post-Christ resurrection ancient period for the most part consisted of Jewish people. So many Judeo-Christians (Jewish Christians) brought some Jewish traditions into this new Christian community (aka Judaizers). It is often times very difficult for people to transform or leave behind their religious organized ways of thinking and operating.

Jesus taught two lessons from the parable of the marriage feast (Luke 14:7-14). First, not to seek places of honor in the temple. Service is more important in God's Kingdom than status. Secondly, not be exclusive about whom you invite. God's Kingdom is open to everyone.

We know this all too well, every time a new church or denomination is started it is oftentimes the domino effect of someone or group identifying another purpose to serving or worshipping God. In most cases they have chosen a different way of operating within the traditional system and this oftentimes caused internal church conflict with their religious traditions. Some will translate the change as the Lord has given them a calling to start their own ministry. **People were breaking away from the traditions. (i.e. Mormons did not include blacks until recently).** In truth they have a different way they want to worship or are "Sick N Tired" of the church pastor and or church representatives.

Lesbianism In The Bible

I love Paul's writings, especially the way he communicates to sustain the attention of the readers and hearers of his letters.

For this cause God gave them up unto vile affections: for even their women did change the natural use into that which is against nature: And likewise also the men, leaving the natural use of the woman, burned in their lust one toward another; men with men working that which is unseemly, and receiving in themselves that recompense of their error which was meet.(Romans 1:26-27)

Now before you start condemning yourself or lesbians, let us undress this specific scripture and review it thru the entire text housed in Romans chapters one, two and three.

Paul's written engagement is more a conversation style of philosophical writing, challenging them with an imaginary opponent and thereby demolishing possible objections to his position in a dramatic manner. In other words he did not single out one individual he spoke in the contexts of groups.

Paul speaks, as we know it today, about behaviors that are occurring in the religious community. This scripture topic of Roman 1:26-27 is where "women same sex attractions aka lesbianism" is mentioned for the first time in the Bible.

This is the only scripture that, apparently, talks about homosexual behavior among women as well as men. Paul is referring to fertility cult worship that is prevalent in Rome. The homosexual activity, which he refers to as idolatrous, gives us the impression all of the cult worshippers engaged in idolatrous behaviors. The interpretation written about homosexual behavior in general would lead us to believe that all idolatrous people were homosexual--an obviously loose interpretation. In some pagan worship rituals same sex attractions were common practice. The challenge came when this sex acts were performed during religious ceremonies and was not limited to heterosexual or homosexual. It was part of pagan religious worship rituals.

Rome during this time is a major metropolitan city of *(i.e. New York, Johannesburg, London, Atlanta, San Francisco)* commerce and diverse cultures. You have various religions in the city but this is the beginning of the Christian movement. Paul writes about idolatrous people who place worldly things or concerns over their devotion to God. The church historically loves to take these scriptures to build their anti-gay position but Paul masterfully writes in this letter a list of citywide challenges.

In the end of verse Romans 1:27, this specific reference to fertility cult worship cannot be construed to condemn homosexual behavior in general. Again traditions, homosexuality was considered normal in many cultures but the Judeo-Christians traditions were still holding on to Old Testament teachings found in Leviticus 18:22 and 20:13. Many LBGT/SGL persons have been trained out of these traditions that their sexual orientation is not normal. This is an incorrect traditional teaching. It was in the eyes of Jewish traditions to be an abomination unto God but was practices in other pagan religions. Christianity had not formed during this biblical period.

In the early years of the AIDS epidemic religious leaders concluded, this scripture is why we have "AIDS," but the truth of matter is we have "AIDS" because of man's hatred and greed. This hatred has killed countless babies, hemophiliacs, sickle cell patients. In the early years of AIDS many were condemned as this was a punishment from God.

For God sent not his Son into the world to condemn the world; but that the world through him might be saved. (John 3:17)

God does not put sickness on his people. Some of the best people in the world get sick with Pneumonia, Cancer, Alzheimer's, diabetes, and some have died.

Practice What We Preach

We are called to question the traditions that exclude people from having a relationship with God.

Then came to Jesus scribes and Pharisees, which were of Jerusalem, saying, Why do thy disciples transgress the tradition of the elders? For they was not their hands whey they eat bread. But he answered and said unto them, Why do ye also transgress the commandment of God by your tradition? (Matt 15:1-3)

We are called to practice what we preached. We are hypocrites when we tell people they are very special but we do not treat them like they are very special.

Practice what we preach, and if the teachers of the good news is not practicing what they preach. You have the right to call to question into their human actions regardless of what their title or position of authority.

You do it everyday with our government, parents, partners, friends and family. Our gentile mentalities cause to refrain from questioning people of faith. Love does not mean silence. There are times in life when you have to address "good

Chapter 7   The Mis-Education About Present Day Gentiles
(same gender loving)

people". Just because they are nice person does not mean do not "miss the mark".

In the book of Galatians 2:11-20 Paul gets in the face of Peter because he refuses to be seen sitting and eating with the Gentiles.

When Peter came to Antioch, I opposed him to his face, because he was clearly in the wrong.   (Galatians 2:11)

Peter was good people. He was in the Upper Room with Jesus but that did not stop Paul from addressing his behavior. Peter saw himself as better than the gentiles. He wanted to preach to them but not eat with them. Others who followed him begin to do the same. Paul was not about works, he was about faith in Jesus Christ. Now many would find this challenging since they learn in James that "faith without works is dead" but James but the true translation is are you working your faith. Your faith results in good works. True faith transforms our thoughts of Christ love for us and love for all Gods children. You can have a great preacher who has people screaming and shouting in the isle but behind closed doors they are raging, manipulative and egoistical. There works does not superseded their faith which is the foundation of love.

In Chapter 2 of the Book of Romans, Paul writes about the religious community being judged according to the truth. He is addressing the Judeo-Christians and masterfully challenges the thought process in his references about not having the right to "judge" anyone. And they disguise it with the truth and/or a person's commitment to Christ.

He continues on about the religious community being judged by their works. He emphasizes the importance of works and the need to know the truth and the unloving deed of condemning groups by disguising it as God's Work.

In Romans 2:11-16, he talks about the religious community being judged with impartiality. Paul makes the statements, "God has no respect of persons," and "it's **not about the hearers of the law who are just** before God, but the doers of the law shall be justified." The hearers of the law were men who studied the law. The tradition did not allow women to study the law. To have respect of persons was to show favoritism to some people over others. God views all people as equals.

In Romans 2:17-29, Paul talks about how the religious community does not obey the law. He is challenging them on the premise that they keep teaching the law as the measuring stick, but the Gentiles continue to be segregated from temple worship and teachings. He stresses this is about the heart and spirit, not about the praise of men, but of God. Read Galatians 4:21-31 "Law and Grace Cannot Coexist".

In Romans 3:1-8, the religious community does not believe the writings. Paul at this point is being very firm and he uses himself as an example. He talks about being just a man and emphasizes that his role is not to judge anyone's belief, and he concludes in the last verse here:

> *"And not rather, (as we be slanderously reported,*
> *and as some affirm that we say),*
> *Let us do evil, that good may come?*
> *Whose damnation is just?" What then? Are we better*
> *than they? No, in no wise: for we have before proved*
> *both Jews and Gentiles, that they are all under sin;*
> *(Romans 3:8-9)*

Chapter 7   The Mis-Education About Present Day Gentiles
(same gender loving)

Paul is speaking to them, if they promote negative images about the Gentiles, then what good are they? And if we are to be judged by God, not by man, then we are required to make sure we do not believe our own lies or forget our issues. We have all missed the mark and are guilty of the sins of omissions (denial you have ever sinned). There is no such thing as a little sin or a big sin. An example, if someone asked you to pray for them and you don't "you sinned." If a person in an interracial relationship walk in the room with their partner and just for a moment or a second your thoughts are negative "you sinned." When you attempt to condemn some one to hell "you sinned." Sorry the Jesus says

> *Judge not, that ye be not judge,*
> *For with what judgment ye judge,*
> *ye shall be judged:*
> *And with what ye measure by ye shall also be*
> *measured. And why beholdest thou the mote that*
> *is in thy brother's eye, but considerest not the*
> *beam that is in thine own eye? (Matthew 7:1-3)*

Just because a person is in authority does not mean they are voice of God on every issue in someone's life. In ministry every preacher is not learned in all areas of biblical teachings. Just as a doctor, lawyer or psychologist are not experts in all aspects of their profession. Another example is if you take a Baptist Preacher and replant them in a Catholic Church the traditions are dramatically different.

We Are All Guilty

In Romans 3:9-31 Paul concludes *"All are guilty before God."* But because of justification it's like it never happened. Jesus brings justification and acquittal for all. Paul concludes using scriptures from the Old Testament and he writes in Romans 3:9-10;

What then? Are we better than they?
No, in no wise: for we have before proved both
Jews and Gentiles that they are all under sin; as
it is written, there is none righteous, no, not one.

In Romans 3:21, Paul is stressing in this letter that all of us are guilty and not one of us is free of sin (disobedience to God's will ...Love).

Description of Righteousness, *For all have sin, and come short of the glory of God. (Romans 3:21)*

Paul did not leave out the Bishop
Paul did not leave out the Evangelist
Paul did not leave out the Deacon
Paul did not leave out the Assistant Pastor
Paul did not leave out your parents
Paul did not leave out "you."

Paul addresses the hypocrisy with people who were educated in the law or assigned to lead all people to a relationship with Jesus Christ. The teachings of Jesus Christ do not deny unconditional love.

God so loved the world that he gave his only begotten
son, that whosoever believeth in him should not perish,
but have everlasting life. For God sent not his Son into
the world to condemn the world; but that the world
through him might be saved. (John 3:16-17)

Our call is to question traditional teachings that are exclusive. In developing ministries to address the multitude of

Chapter 7   *The Mis-Education About Present Day Gentiles*
(same gender loving)

needs in the LBGT/SGL communities, we must be careful of replicating the oppressive systems we came out of. It is dangerous when our evangelical platforms become a reflection of the behaviors of our oppressors. Just because you use the new political correct language of "inclusivity" does not mean you are being inclusive. Be careful you may deny some access to you because they do not speak the same spiritual language. This would make you exclusive.

We are not a White, Black, Latino or Asian church. We are not all Catholic, Apostolic, Baptist, Methodist or Lutheran. We do not all speak in tongues. We are not all charismatic or didactic. We are not all believers in the entire teaching of the bible. But what we are, is a community of people searching for peace, love and happiness.

In your spiritual journey, you may have to get in the face of some good people as Paul did with Peter. You may conclude within yourself that you have become exclusive and are more concerned about how others see you.

We all have missed the mark. Your spiritual journey is not about walking down the beach or thru the woods barefoot. Your spiritual should inspire you reach out not just for yourself but on the behalf of others. This is faith to address something that appears bigger than you or irrelevant to others.

The gentiles had to challenge the tradition of their Gentile elders, Jewish communities and Jewish Christians. Today we are called to challenge the mainstream traditional white church, black church and openly LBGT/SGL ministries who mocked these traditional systems (i.e. Apostolic, Methodist, Baptist, Catholic etc).

In additional to addressing our internal fighting that develop in the LBGT/SGL community, related to the many mix races congregations. These are traditional issues that we are often carrying.

Black LGBT/SGL "Blood Line" Connected To Civil Rights History.

Our Kulture (LBGT/SGL) should speak to the "black moral midgets" who think we cannot reflect on slavery and the civil rights movement as a comparison to gay liberation. They are greatly mistaken. Not only can we use it, but we also have a right to use it, transferred from generation to generation, it is called "blood line."

Regardless of what anyone says, the civil rights is our history. *Coretta Scott King, the First Lady of the Civil Rights Movement, said,*

> *For many years now, I have been an outspoken supporter of civil and human rights for gay and lesbian people. Gays and lesbians stood up for civil rights in Montgomery, Selma, in Albany, Ga. and St. Augustine, Fla., and many other campaigns of the Civil Rights Movement. Many of these courageous men and women were fighting for my freedom at a time when they could find few voices for their own, and I salute their contributions.*

Our blood line gives us the right to every part of the civil right history. No one person or group can take that away from us and we do not plan on giving it to them. We have kept silent

Chapter 7   The Mis-Education About Present Day Gentiles
(same gender loving)

in their homes, churches, schools and the court rooms of injustice.

There is some of our blood also in the·
- ✓ Streets of Montgomery, Detroit, Charlotte
- ✓ ·Jails of Birmingham, Atlanta, Salem, Memphis
- ✓ ·Bombed churches
- ✓ ·Hanging on trees throughout this great nation

The black community is in our "blood" and we are not ashamed of it and neither are we going to offer or give it back. Freedom is in our blood. We will see you at the mountain top.

Our African-American Kulture (LBGT/SGL) has an obligation to itself to begin writing from our perspectives. We are a very loving community, but we are not naïve; *well, some of us are not.* Our history has provided us with countless examples of people who have overcome difficult situations. Your freedom is not complicated.

During the black slave trade period, there were many black slaves introduced to the bible by Caucasian Christians. This slavery process over the years took many shapes and systematic applications of inferior thinking and institutionalized racism. Slaves were not educated in hermeneutics *(art and science of interpretation, esp. of the scriptures,)* but homiletics *(the art of preaching)* spoke to the slaves about freedom.

Now there were many slaves who could barely read and write, so Bible interpretation did not mean a thing to them.

The slaves knew they were "Sick N Tired" of master's physical and emotional imprisonment and they did not need a new Bible translation, Biblical interpretation, academic approval or some Negro with a goal to write a thesis and do a "focus group" on the plight of the slave. They knew in their mind, body and spirit change was mandatory.

Did the South Africans wait on white Bible scholars to advocate for their freedom? I think not! Clergy, black and white, collaborated with the people (i.e., Steven Biko, Nelson Mandela, and Desmond Tutu) on the liberation of all South African people. Since the ending of apartheid, the government of South Africa has enacted into law the right for Same Gender Loving citizens in their country to marry. It is in our blood to be totally free.

Systematically during the slavery period in order to control any of the emerging "leaders," the slave owners realized their power and control over the slaves were dependent upon the absence of any indigenous leadership among the slaves.

Any slave, who began to emerge as a natural leader, was identified early and was limited, isolated, killed, or ridiculed.

In their place was put a leader that had been carefully picked, trained, and tested to stand only for the master's welfare. In other words, unnatural heads were attached to the slave communities. They furthered the cause of the master and frustrated the cry for freedom.

The slaves were taught to view with suspicion naturally those who emerged from among themselves. Such aides were defined as "uppity" or/and were branded as troublemakers who were destined to bring trouble to the entire slave community.

Generation after generation of being conditioned to reject natural and strong leadership had not only stifled the

Chapter 7   The Mis-Education About Present Day Gentiles
(same gender loving)

development of such leaders, but African-Americans still respond by rejecting such leaders.

Below is an illustration of past and present day slavery in our Kulture (LBGT/SGL).

Slavery and **LBGT/SGL Comparison**	
Slave	**Our Kulture(LBGT/SGL)**
Slave Master (Oppressor)	Pastors with Anti Gay Position
Slave Master (Liberator)	Love and Accepting Ministry—teach how to read for ourselves, sacrificed family, potential financial gain and alienation from peers.
Field Negro	Out and acknowledges same gender attraction.
House Negro	"House Homo" will not talk with master, even though they have a prominent position in his house *(i.e. Church Clergy, Media Personalities, Entertainers, Executives).*
Abolitionist	Heterosexuals who speak about the inclusion of LBGT/SGL community
Freedom Fighters	LBGT/SGL Activists

Charts & Figures 7.1

Our history tells us that Dr. King was condemned in the early days of his civil rights campaigns as a "troublemaker." Dr. King and many of the young ministers who spearheaded the civil rights movement had to leave National Baptist USA and established the

Progressive National Baptist Convention along with Southern Christian Leadership Conference (SCLC) to escape the criticism of their traditional colleagues who saw the social activism as troublesome because it was not welcomed by the white dominant culture. Only after receiving recognition from an increasing numbers of "liberal" European Americans was he accepted as a leader.

Our leaders will come out of the places were many noble activist would never visit and have developed a very negative image of *"Why does your master eat with the publicans and the sinners?" (Matthew 9:11)*.

Chapter 7 The Mis-Education About Present Day Gentiles
(same gender loving)

Moving Yourself To The Next Level

Chapter 7 The Mis-Education About Present Day Gentiles (SGL)

Each process question or comment can be viewed from a Same Gender Loving (SGL) perspective, Heterosexual (H) perspective or Both (B) perspectives.

1. (B) - Who have you given more power than God? Why?

2. (B) - What traditional teachings hold you mentally hostage? Why?

3. (B) - In life sometimes we are called to question some good people in our lives.
    a. What good person in your life do you feel you must address? Why?
    b. What do you fear will happen? Why

4. (SGL) - Why are you not addressing the self-hate programming?

5. (B) - Are you challenged with masculine females or effeminate males? If yes. Why?
    a. How would you enlighten the person that is challenged with this issue?

CHAPTER 8

The Mis-Education About the Word Homosexuality

You have been hoodwinked, bamboozled, lie on, talk about and mistreated for all the wrong reasons. The word effeminate in the bible is a mistranslation and the word actually does not mean homosexual and has not to do with gender in the bible.

In this chapter, it is about the mis-education of the word "effeminate" in the bible and how we must address this mistranslation with ourselves, friends, family, church leadership and members.

There are countless same gender loving men who live everyday thinking they are not loved by God. It saddens me that so many have died with the same belief.

I would recommend you read the following materials that will provide you some detail background information on the origins of the word homosexual from various points of view.

1. *Peter Gomes: The Good Book, pgs 155-162*
2. *What The Bible Says About Homosexuality: Dr. Daniel Helminiak pgs 117-130*

The content provided in these books is more academic but both writings provide a very clear and easy to understand overview.

Effeminate and Homosexual Translations

In First Corinthians 6:9, *"Effeminate and Homosexual"* are two words that continue to be mistranslated by bible translators. In the original translations of word effeminate and homosexual you will be amazed at how the church has manipulated us for so long.

Various religious translators provide a homosexual meaning of the words. There are writings that reveal a more proper meaning of malakoi (effeminate) which means *"morally weak".*

The religious community loves to start their verbal madness with *"the Bible says"* jargon. In our Gentile Kulture, the challenge with those negative tapes stored in our thoughts, they take up to positive thoughts.

When the Bible reads, "Nor effeminate?" in reference to *"not being able to inherit the kingdom of heaven,"* the question we would ask is: Does the word *"effeminate"* mean a male who has female characteristics? Or a homosexual man? Does this remove lesbians from the scripture?

The scriptures provide us with working knowledge of "effeminate," of which the meaning of the word is "wantons," as the Geneva Bible did accurately translate Paul masterfully points out in the language knowing the scholars were well versed in the current language on the streets. The word

"wanton"*(aka effeminate) refers to people who live delicately, wantonly, lavishly and excessively, women and men alike, who would not inherit the kingdom of heaven.*

Chapter 8   The Mis-Education About the Word Homosexuality

It has nothing to do with sexual orientation, and everything to do with the love for worldly possessions and the pleasure those possessions bring.

> *"Where your treasure is, there will your heart be also."*
> *(Matthew 6:21)*

> *"No man can serve two masters: for either he*
> *will hate the one, and love the other; or else*
> *he will hold to the one, and despise the other,*
> *Ye cannot serve God and mammon (riches)*
> *(Matthew 6:24)*

Often "Bible scholars" do not accurately study the Word of God and translate it correctly, The Thomas Nelson Publishers of Bible versions, illustrates that only "effeminate homosexuals"—that is, those who live wantonly – are excluded from heaven.

Well, isn't that interesting? Now, heterosexuals can live "wantonly" all they want. *Riiiiggght!:)* The Bible scholars continue to teach this mistranslation.

We have the word homosexual in Tyndale's New Testament translation of 1526 "weaklings" and the Geneva Bible of 1560 says "wantons." The King James Version was printed in 1611 and says "effeminate." Even John Wesley's commentary on First Corinthians says this:

> *"Nor the effeminate - who live in an easy, indolent way;*
> *taking up no cross, enduring no hardship."*

Even as late as the 18th century it was understood that King James' substitution of "wantons" for "effeminate" meant a soft life brought about by wealth and lack of hard work -- which makes one weak spiritually (and thus a "weakling").

Somewhere within the last two centuries, however, some "Bible scholars" decided effeminate meant homosexual.

And, of course, our current "Bible scholars" are sticking with this decision. How many preachers are guilty of "wantonness?"

They just collect money from the faithful and they spend it wantonly on a worldly lifestyle: expensive homes, luxury cars, lavish vacations, designer labels, and five-star restaurants:

> *"Ungodly men which turn the grace of our God into wantonness."* (Jude 1:4)

Modern-day Bible revisionists would like us to believe various words are linked to homosexuality. Go to your Bible and review these verses: (1) Deuteronomy 28:54, 56, (2) Isaiah 3:15-24

The word "tender" used in the scriptures means persons who does not have a strong will. Hebrew translation (1) to be tender, be soft; be weak (of heart). In addition review 2Kings 22:19, Job 23:16, Psalms 55:21, Isaiah 7:4.

In our community many men were labeled as tender because they were not trying to over power people (alpha male), gentlemen who did not talk loudly, slow to speak and very friendly to strangers.

Alpha male is a term used in describing any group or society of animals that live closely together and have a dominant leader.

Chapter 8   The Mis-Education About the Word Homosexuality

The Primary Issue Was Politics Not About Homosexuality

In Chapter 6, Paul argues for the need of church courts in society and also addresses sexual offenses. It is possible that the legalism Romans 6:1-8 are the effects of Romans 5:1-2; if so, such legal matters would clearly be displaying the church's dirty laundry before the world.

In the city Corinth was one of the major urban centers of the ancient Mediterranean and one of the most culturally diverse cities in the Roman Empire. Roles during these ancient times were determined by social status. The people with wealth and power preferred religious, philosophical and political ideologies that supported their positions of power. The Corinthian Christians were like most Christians today they had their own social interest, which seemed natural from their perspective.

Religious communities in the Mediterranean world had their own courts in the cities. Bringing internal disputes (church confusion) of the Jewish or Christian communities before secular judges was the luxury these minority religions could ill afford; there was already too much slander against them in the broader society.

Like modern-day courts, Rome's society was extremely legalistic. Cases began to be heard at dawn and sometimes could be argued as late as sunset. Judges were always chosen from the wealthy community, and most legal disputes revolved around money. Members of the upper class received better treatment in the law courts. Further, social inferiors could not sue members of the upper class. But for Paul, even the lowliest believers were qualified to judge cases.

The religious communities outside Palestine were very conscious of their minority status and did not wish to reinforce negative questions of their morality. Consequently, they were use to dealing with Jewish problems within their own community. Christians were an even smaller minority at this time. Paul questioned the Jewish method of setting disputes within the community.

> *"The unrighteous just would not inherent God's kingdom,"* *(1Corinthians 6:9)*

They would not have a share in it, was standard Jewish and Christian teachings. Both Jewish and non-Jewish listing often labeled the "unrighteous."

The First Appearance of the Word Homosexual

The first known appearance of *homosexual* in print is found in an 1869 German pamphlet by the Austrian-born novelist Karl-Maria Kertbeny, published anonymously. Scholars have disputed the meaning of the term translated "homosexuals," but it seems to mean those who engage in homosexual acts, which was a common feature of Greek male life in ancient times.

For most Greek men under the age of 30, heterosexual sex was most available with slaves or with prostitutes. Roman law permitted prostitution, and it forbid fornication only if both parties were of aristocratic birth. Paul's response shows his mastery of his reader's culture and his ability to communicate Biblical truth to practical value.

The Bible forbade sex between people who were not married; the penalty for having sex with another person and

Chapter 8   The Mis-Education About the Word Homosexuality

then marrying someone else was the same as the penalty for adultery while married which was *"death."* Although this law was no longer strictly enforced by Paul during his time, it was intended to undermine the seriousness of the offense; premarital sex was an immorality considered to be adultery; including sleeping with your future spouse before marriage *(now yawl know times done changed)*.

This law is definitely outdated. It is very common today for couples to sleep together before they get married. The days of being a virgin before you are married were noble, but not common in today's time. There were many laws written in the Old Testament, but even Paul understood the times were different.

Paul was masterful at presenting an imaginary opponent similar to that of his readers, utilizing for example: *"I can get away with anything." Maybe so, but everything is not good for you. "*

When you study Romans 6, you will learn the primary focus was on *premarital sex, adultery,* and *prostitution.*

When studying the background information provided, we learn Paul is dealing with the religious legal systems designed to address religious conflicts within the Jewish, Christian and Greek communities. Now, the Jewish religious community is larger than the Christian religious community, and each one has their own internal court system.

In the Greek community, they had a voice, but in the religious community, homosexuals had no voice *(organized system)* during this time. But if you study 1Corinthians 6:1-8, you will learn the focus is not homosexuality.

*The law cannot make a man love me but the law can
stop
a man from lynching me and think that is pretty
important.* *(Rev. MLK. Jr.)*

Out of chapter six, you have the Christian community creating a mission in life to limit, restrict and legislate against homosexuals based on words lost in Bible translations and politics.

It is unhealthy for you or a love one to allow themselves to be managed by people with an unhealthy perspective, and judge your life or theirs based on "bits and pieces," of misinformation.

Loving yourself is not complicated. Loving yourself through the opinions of others is being very "tender".

Moving Yourself To The Next Level

Chapter 8 The Mis-Education About the Word Homosexuality

Each process question or thought can be viewed from the following perspectives: Same Gender Loving (SGL), Heterosexual (H) or Both (B). It is healthy to try and view from various perspectives to get insight into how others may process an issue. All perspectives are valid and should be respected and not condemned. In all thy getting; get understanding.

(1) (B) - How would you enlighten someone who is receiving wrong biblical information?

(2) (SGL) - When friends in playful manner use the word sissy, faggot or dike. What are the dangers of this language or are they not any?

(3) (B) - Effeminate men and masculine females receive negative energy from people on a daily basis. How would you enlighten a person that others may be uncomfortable with, based on their perception the person behavior is unacceptable?

(4) (B) - What would it take for you to approach an effeminate male or masculine female and tell them "I Celebrate You"? Try it!

(5) (H) - What prevents you from writing a letter to someone you feel is preaching hatred against same gender loving people?

CHAPTER 9

The Mis-Education About Jesus & Homosexuality

What Did Jesus Say About Homosexuality?

Chapter 9   The Mis-Education About Jesus & Homosexuality

Nothing!

Jesus never addressed the issue but the church made it an issue.

Jesus mission was to spread God's unconditional love to all of Gods Children. One of my all time favorite gospel songs "Jesus Is Love" written by Lionel Richie; harmoniously drives home the purpose of Jesus Christ giving his life for all of us.

The focus of this book is not to change the minds of heterosexuals, but open the minds of our Gentile Kulture, family and friends of our community.

The religious community will use some of these words in reference to Jesus; Sodom, Lust, Hell, Immorality, Sin, and the Book of Revelations. Understand this information will not stop the Bible token, non-reading religious folks *"Saved, Sanctified, Filled With The Holy Ghost, Baptized in the Blood"* from speaking condemnation in your life with the wrong information.

Who do you believe in more the church or Jesus Christ? This is the internal question you must address even when it is not popular. Jesus love made him a very unpopular person because he knew it was the right thing to do.

Love is the foundation of our faith.

> *If a person says, I love God, and hateth his brother, they are a liar: for they that Loveth not sisters and brothers whom they hath seen, how ca he love God whom he hath not seen? And the commandment have we from Jesus, That we who Loveth God love their sister and brother also. (1John 4:20)*

Love Is The Key

In the books of Matthew 22:34-40 and Mark 12:28-34 are two specific biblical accounts of Jesus referencing the two

Chapter 9   *The Mis-Education About Jesus & Homosexuality*

greatest commandments as Love being the key to a full relationship with God.

Jesus is having a conversation with the scribes/lawyer (people who were learned in the scriptures) are trying to find fault in his teachings. ***"What is the greatest commandment?"*** is a setup question by the scribes. Jesus responds so eloquently and his response can be interpreted as ***"Love Is The Key."***

Love Is The Key Matthew 22:34-40 & Mark 12:28-31 *"On these two commandments hang all the laws and the prophets"* *(Matthew 22:40)*	
<u>Old Testament</u> Thou Shalt Love The Lord Thy God With All Thy Heart And All Of Thy Soul, And All Thy Mind (Deuteronomy 6:5) Deut. book of the second law.	<u>Old Testament</u> Love Thy Neighbor As Thyself (Leviticus 19:18) Leviticus book of the first law.
Matthew 22:40 On these two Commandments hang all of the law and the prophets.	Mark 12:31 There is no other Commandment greater than these.

Charts & Figures 9.1

In the illustration, Love for God and our neighbors are above all the other laws. Jesus takes from the Old Testament the most important laws.

There is a lot in this conversation many bible teachers missed. Jesus pulls out from the Old Testament scripture and says, *"On These two commandments hang all the laws and prophets":*

- *Above your Levitical self-imposed abominations*
- *Above your legal limitations*
- *Above your restrictive covenants*
- *Above the Archbishops*
- *Above the Evangelist*
- *Above the church council*
- *Above anyone who teaches there is a limitation of Gods love*

Jesus is dealing with the some of the same issues we are dealing with today.

In the book of Mark, one of the learned men of the law repeats what Jesus says but does it very skillfully. Jesus is aware the learned man is being very cautious. Jesus responds to this individual

"Thou Art Not From The Kingdom" (Mark 12:34)

In the text, it says they "durst (dared) not ask him another question."

The scribe was trained in a religious system where the law was very strict and was challenging for many. This extraction of scripture by Christ caught them off guard because he knew what they were plotting and their hearts were in the wrong place. The scribe had to address his strict training in reflection to his spiritual walk with God.

In the church, there are many of us trapped in the method of restrictive thinking and do not leave room for change or reproofing.

It is challenging for many to let go of the old ways of thinking about the love of God.

Chapter 9 The Mis-Education About Jesus & Homosexuality

> *For the law was given by Moses,*
> *but grace and truth came by Jesus Christ*
> (John 1:17)

There will be an inner resistance for many in our Gentile Kulture to let go of the self-hate, questioning their identity and rationalizing oppressive teaching from someone they love and respect.

They are not far from the kingdom. Not far from the place called unconditional love, where the doors are opened to anyone and there is room for everyone, no more worrying, no more crying, no more sickness, no more shame, no one can kick you out and the doors are always unlocked whenever you want to come in.

> *For I am persuaded, that neither death, nor life, nor angels, nor principalities, nor powers, nor things present, nor things to come, Nor height nor depth, nor any other creature, shall be able to separate us from the Love of God which is in Christ Jesus our Lord (Romans 8:38-39)*

Misuse of Jesus and the Sodom Scriptures

Remember, the destruction of Sodom was about "Can We Find Ten Righteous In the City." (Genesis 18)

Now for the atheist or non-Christians; I am not attempting to imply you are going to hell. But the traditional Christians have booked you on a first-class ticket. My role is to explain what Christ's mission was only, and not to tell someone they will not make it to heaven. Seek the enlightenment of your understanding. One group is no better or worse than thee other.

Shall Be More Tolerable Than Sodom

Matthew 10:15 *Verily I say unto you, it shall be more tolerable for the land of Sodom and Gomorrah in the Day of Judgment, than for that city.*

Mark 6:11 *And whosoever shall not receive you, nor hear you, when ye depart thence, shake off the dust under your feet for a testimony against them. Verily I say unto you, it shall be more tolerable for Sodom and Gomorrah in the Day of Judgment, than for that city.*

The text in Matthew 10:5-42 is a biblical description about the "Twelve Apostles Receiving Instructions" to go and spread the gospel. This story can also be found in Mark 6:8-13. Also Luke 9:2-6, 12:2-10 is an account of this story, but it does not mention "Sodom."

In each one of the biblical descriptions the words preceding "Sodom" is *"shall be more tolerable."* For the sake of time, review Chapter 3 on Sodom & Gomorrah. These words Jesus used are not in reference to homosexuality, but submission to the love of God. Remember, it is more "tolerable," meaning Sodom was nothing compared to not allowing God to work in their life.

Another key point to be made in the text: we see Jesus is still in the learning process himself. In Matthew 10:5-6, Jesus says

"Go not into the way of the Gentiles, and into any city of the Samaritans enter ye not: But go rather to the lost sheep of the house of Israel"(Matthew 10:5-6)

Jesus early mission goal was to save the lost sheep of Israel. It was not until he witnessed the Gentiles relentless faith as written in Matthew 8:5-13,

Chapter 9   The Mis-Education About Jesus & Homosexuality

> *"When Jesus heard it, he marveled, and said to them that followed, Verily I say unto you, I have not found so great faith, no, not in Israel"*   (Matthew 8:10)

When a teacher believes he has learned all they can learn is enough.

Abraham Lincoln ran on a political platform to maintain slavery, but while in office, he signed the "Emancipation Proclamation" abolishing slavery.

In Bible study, allow different perspectives to be introduced to you, and they could help enlighten you.

Another Scripture Misuse By The Church

> *And thou, Capernaum, which art exalted unto heaven, shalt be brought down to hell: for if the mighty works, which have been done in thee, had been done in Sodom, it would have remained until this day. But I say unto you, that it shall be more tolerable for the land of Sodom in the Day of Judgment, than for thee. (Matthew 11:23)*

Again, the key words in the text are "more tolerable." Jesus has become disappointed with the some of the cities because they continue to operate with EGO (Edging God Out).

In Matthew Chapter 11, Jesus speaks about the religious community rejecting John the Baptist and how the religious community has rejected him also. His reference comparing Tyre and Simon to Sodom was linked to the tradition of the cities. These cities were the home of the Phoenicians, a Gentile city, and many in the city worshipped the god of Molech. In their religious practices, they sacrificed a living person, often a child, to their god. Jesus deplored this religious practice.

This statement by Jesus, I believe, was to provide a vivid picture of caution to the cities letting them know they were leading the way to their own destruction. The statement was not intended to be a reference to homosexuality, but can be taken out of context.

And Another Scripture Misuse By The Church

But I say unto you that it shall be more tolerable in that day for Sodom than for that city. (Luke 10:12)

Again our key words of reference are "more tolerable," meaning it will be worse than Sodom and Gomorrah. It is helpful to better understand the text if you review Chapter 3 in this book.

In Luke 10:1-16, Jesus Christ has sent out seventy teams of two to spread the gospel of God's unconditional love. The reference to Sodom is not about the people; it is about the religious establishment. On verse 10:12-15 see the comment.

And another …..

*But the same day that Lot went out
of Sodom it rained fire and brimstone from heaven
and destroyed them all. (Luke 17:29)*

In this text, Luke 17:20-37, Jesus is speaking about the Second Coming of Christ. The Pharisees questioning Jesus in an attempt to find away to accuse him of blasphemy (read previous chapters please). Blasphemy is not solely the questioning of scripture. True blaspheme is questioning the reverence and power of God.

Chapter 9 The Mis-Education About Jesus & Homosexuality

> *"Neither shall they say, Lo here! Or, lo there! For behold, the Kingdom of God is within you." (Luke 17:21)*

The word "within" means "in your midst" in this Biblical story. So, you are not out there misquoting scripture yourself. It is relentless pursuit of peace, understanding and good will.

Jesus & Eunuchs

In some churches the story of Jesus & Eunuchs is used to justify or support anti-homosexuality beliefs.
In Matthew 19:1-12, Jesus is having a conversation with some Pharisees who are plotting to find him in contempt of the scriptures by accusing him of blasphemy. The plot of the conversation is rooted in a question about marriage.

> *In verse 12, Jesus gives a comparison to the "eunuch." "For there are some eunuchs, which were so, born from their mother's womb: and there are some eunuchs, which were made eunuchs of men: and there be eunuchs, which have made themselves eunuchs for the kingdom of heaven's sake. He that is able to receive it let him receive it." (Matthew 19:12 KJV)*

There were different types of Eunuchs—those who chose to be eunuchs and those who were made eunuchs by groups. Jesus uses the above illustration to describe a commitment to the kingdom. This issue of being single was helpful in keeping people focused on serving the Kingdom of God.

Marriage during this biblical period was as hot a religious topic as it is today. In the religious community, many saw this as a threat to procreation. The idea of eunuchs being made castrated was not popular in many of the religious circles.

The Israelite community did not condone the practice of castrating young men. The eunuchs earned the respect of the various communities, and the religious community agreed the Lord would provide for them.

People have been beat down for so long, they cannot see away out of these negative images created by religious establishments.

The relationship with Christ is a personal commitment—not the church's, not the bishop's, not the evangelist's. It is a personal relationship.

Moving Yourself To The Next Level

Chapter 9 The Mis-Education About Jesus & Homosexuality

Each process question or thought can be viewed from the following perspectives: Same Gender Loving (SGL), Heterosexual (H) or Both (B). It is healthy to try and view from various perspectives to get insight into how others may process an issue. All perspectives are valid and should be respected and not condemned. In all thy getting; get understanding.

1. (B) - Jesus Christ died for you. Why do think people give more power to the church than to Jesus Christ.?

2. (B) - If you decided you wanted to educate your Pastor about this issue.
    a. What tools do you think you would need to complete this task?
    b. What makes you hesitant?

3. (B) - If Jesus would not remove the disciple Thomas from his presence because he constantly had questions.
    a. Could you ask questions of your Pastor/Bishop without fear of being kicked out of the church?
    b. Have you in been in a relationship wither partner, job or friendship and you were afraid to ask questions? How do you manage the relationship?

4. (B) If the law is love. Have you broken it lately?
    a. If yes. When, Why and How did you do to correct it?
    b. If no. What is your definition of the law of love?

CHAPTER 10

The Mis-Education About Love In The Bible

An exercise that I found to be very helpful; is placing the word "Love" on a ruler and use the ruler as your marker during your biblical studies. If you allow this rule to guide to guide your insight you will have a revelatory experience with scripture that will supersede the most learned in biblical studies. Love is the rule, guide and marker. If you do not see Love you see the human experience, expression and interpretation.

I have found most pro-Homosexuality in the Bible writings are more like witch hunts with the view point of any time there are two Biblical characters of the same sex developing a close relationship the interpretation is viewed as "Eros" or the layperson translation: *"see, they are gay; so, we're okay."* Noble as this may seem, it is more like reaching for Popsicles on a sunny beach; eventually, it is going to melt.

In lieu of looking for Homosexuality in the Bible, facilitate your studies using Love in the Bible as your primary tool. When you see love, you see God; when you see hate, you see the human experience refusing to be obedient to the God of Love. Love in the Bible takes you down the path of not looking for bad, but redefining what is good and recognizing oppressive language & interpretation.

The Mis-Education Against
Homosexuality In The Bible

The Bible is an historical account of a series of events. In the recording of the events we have secrecy, hidden agendas, lost records, errors in translations. No one was there in the beginning to verify any information, in the middle were many translations, and in the end we continue to have translations.

I do not identify as a conservative or a progressive theologian. It is not my want or desire to seek approval of any group or a person for the right to share my point of view.

I am challenged with the progressive religious communities that have established a platform of "outing" characters in the Bible to demonstrate the existence of the LBGT/SGL community in scripture. I am confident there are many gay characters who were very active during this ancient Biblical time, and they are not mentioned in the Bible, and there are probably writings stored away not available to the general public.

Love in the Bible gives you the green light to read for yourself. Do not let anyone tell you just because they have studied some religious books they are not the authority over your ideas and thoughts. If you really love someone, you will value or respect their point of view. Jesus was about sharing God's love:

- ☐ ·Love Your Enemies Matthew 5:43-48
- ☐ ·Love Ye One Another John 5:39-47
- ☐ ·Witness of the Scriptures John 15:12-17

Love is the Key whether you are a believer in Jesus Christ, Buddha, Allah, God of Abraham, Isaac and Jacob, The God of Your Understanding or Atheist.

Chapter 10 *The Mis-Education About Love In The Bible*

In this chapter I would like to shed some light on two old testament stories found in the old testaments (1) Ruth and Naomi (2) Jonathan and David translated by many in the gay community as a homosexual relationships in the Bible.

The primary focus of Jesus Christ teachings was the love for God and your neighbors. There will be many in the religious community who will debate this point of view. The New Testament writers attempted to put into words what was meant by God's love for us, as displayed by Jesus.

Greek Words For Love

They are four commonly used translations of the Greek word for "love" associated with the Bible: (1) Agape, (2) Philia (3) Storge (4) Eros. This word "Agape" is transformed in the New Testament as the most powerful reference for love.

As interpreted by Augustine (d. 430) a Christian theologian, love is directed first toward God. And human being is so structured as to find lasting happiness only in God, the highest good. Human pursuit of happiness by loving what is less than God is futile; the chief purpose of love is to bring one's neighbor into communion with God. True self-love and love for God are synchronized or coextensive. Augustine held that the solid rock for Christian love is the spirit, rather than the body, the urges of which lead thy self from God. Harper Collins The Bible of Religion "Christian Love" First Edition

1. Agapē is a word that hardly occurs in classical Greek, but it is the one which the writers of the New Testament used as God's special self-giving love as it was displayed in Jesus. Agapē-love, God-like love, is distinguished from the other three words of love.

2. Storgē is the natural affection between a child and a mother. The instinctive love an animal has for its offspring. But this was not the kind of love the writers of the New Testament meant by God's great love for us, so they did not use word.

3. Philia/os is the affection between friends; a compound word constructed from its roots, like "Philadelphia" (city of brotherly love & sisterly affection), is used in the New Testament and describes warm caring relationships between people.

4. Eros in classical Greek stood for sexual love; this is where the word "erotic" is derived from—*Eros;* but in the world of the Greeks and Romans, it had become so badly dishonored that it stood for lust, and the New Testament avoids it altogether.

The most important relationship is with the God of Your Understanding who provides you with the balance of mind, body and soul. The development of a healthy relationship with your family and/or partner is enhanced via a healthy relationship with the God of Your Understanding. In addition to assisting you with facilitating healthy relationships with your BriSta-z (SGL sisters and brothers) in the process.

Decide For Yourself

This is not about deciding about what is right or wrong but you should have the opportunity to make decisions for yourself and don't let anyone guilt trip about it your pursuit for knowledge.

Chapter 10 *The Mis-Education About*
Love In The Bible

In the following topics below there will be debates about the point of view. Well, I hope so.

I am not a proponent of telling someone what they are to suppose to think. This is a toxic means of education and communication. In my pursuit for truth over the years, I have listened to various perspectives, some healthy and unhealthy. In my critical thinking, I understand we all have a comfort zone and we address the issues that dramatically affect us emotionally or physically. Truth to one is not truth to another.

The Love of Ruth & Naomi
Ruth 1:16-17 and 2:10-11

Ruth 1:16-17, which is often read by couples during Heterosexual Marriage Ceremonies and Lesbian Holy Union Services:

> *Where you go I will go, and where you stay I will stay.*
> *Your people will be my people and your God my God.*
> *Where you die I will die, and there I will be buried.*
> *May the Lord deal with me, be it ever so severely,*
> *if anything but death separates you and me.(Ruth 1:16-17)*

Although this friendship appears to be very close, there is no proof that it was a sexually active relationship. There are some very theological opinions from some very well respected progressive theologians of this theory.

Ruth takes care of her mother-in-law, who, in return, helps her daughter-in-law find a good husband. Naomi was a Moabite who married a man named Elimelech. She had two sons. Both of the sons married Moabite women, Orpah and Ruth. Naomi's sons died after two years, leaving Orpah and Ruth widowed.

We know nothing of Ruth's background, origin, or family, except that she is a Moabite, meaning she's from the country of Moab (Ruth 1:3-5).

Despite the fact that she was looked down on by some Hebrews at the time as a foreigner, the Bible describes her as loyal, with personal inner strength and self-resolved. Ruth stands out as the epitome of a good daughter-in-law to Naomi. She is completely devoted and loyal to her husband's family, which she makes her own. Naomi attempts to convince Ruth her daughter in-law to return back her own (biological) family upon the death recent death of Ruth's husband, but Ruth refuses, choosing instead to follow the widow mother-in-law to her native land. After returning to Judah with Ruth, Naomi did her best to "fix her up" with Boaz, a relative on her husband's side *"So Boaz took Ruth and she became his wife and the Lord enabled her to conceive and she gave birth to a son."* (Ruth 2:1-3:18 NIV).

This point of view should generate some interesting debates in the community.

The Robert Wood Theory

This is an historical account and there is no evidence or proof if this was or was not a same-sex relationship. If you are a new student of the Bible, do not let this diminish the uniqueness of the story. It is healthy before you discuss scripture with someone that you listen to various perspectives.

Robert Wood in 1960, wrote the book, *"Christ and the Homosexual"*. He is known in the gay press as a "Pioneer For Gay Rights In America."

> Robert Wood first suggested that Ruth and Naomi were involved in a lesbian relationship with one another, in

Chapter 10   *The Mis-Education About Love In The Bible*

"Homosexual Behavior in the Bible." Few would press the text to yield evidence of physical sexual intercourse between the two women. Nevertheless, lesbians treasure this story and sometimes use these words of Ruth in a ritual in which two lesbians promise life-long love and devotion to one another.

The Loose Explanation

We have a *mother* and *daughter-in-law* developing a bond based on a life situation. In the feminist movement, women kindled, supported and nurtured each other because of societal limitations and the traditional male perceptions of a women's role.

When I was growing up, it was very normal for Sista-z to engage in an intimate relationship in which you would not generally see men engage. Sista-z are very expressive, more so than men.

My mother's name is Fannie, and her best friend in the world was also named Fannie. They have been friends since I was 5 years old. They were called "The Fannies 1 and 2." They partied on the weekends with their male friends and would get mad with each other and leave each other mad. By morning, The Fannies would be calling each other crying,

"You know you my best friend, girl; I did not mean to hurt your feelings," and this went on for years.

The Fannies could be arguing with each other, but if you got in the argument and said something that hurt the other Fannies feelings, then all hell was about to break loose.

"Don't you be talking to my friend like that!
Who do you think you are?"
"That's my sister"

And the Fannies would be ready to gang up on them. I share this story with you because I witnessed many women interact from a sisterly love perspective. Now I know the cynical one in our Kulture will say, "Maybe your mother and her best friend were lovers." That is precisely my point—every time we see women be affectionate with one another, our conclusions are that they must be gay or they are f_ _ _ _ _ g. There are many of you who have women friends at work and extended family members (same-sex attracted) and you have no desire to sleep with them, but you would give everything you had to ensure their safety and well-being. That is "philia," sisterly affection, as they would say in Philadelphia, the "City of Brotherly Love and Sisterly Affection."

In our Kulture with same-sex attracted men this is very challenging because we oftentimes encounter heterosexual men who have no desire to have relations with us but really embrace (note: be careful of the word "except) us just the way we are. I know there are some in our Kulture who is in the closet and live their life out thru others who are out. The danger is everywhere you go as soon as a man is nice to you we began to assume *"Oh they want to have me"*. This has cause problems many on their jobs and in various social circles heterosexual and homosexual.

While reviewing the story of Ruth and Naomi, it is not definitive to me if this is or is not a lesbian relationship.
It is healthy for us to look at all the Biblical text and interpretation with a critical eye regardless of whether it is a heterosexual or gay theologian.

Chapter 10　　　　　*The Mis-Education About*
　　　　　　　Love In The Bible

We have many Sista-z who will read this story and not get a Same Gender Loving relationship. It is okay if the sista-z translates and/or develop a different point of view. Keep in mind some heterosexual couples also use the language of Ruth and Naomi in their wedding vows.

In the sororities and fraternities, this love between Sista-z and Brista-z is very normal and common. The loose interpretation deserves careful consideration and can generate more confusion, but it is a very enriching dialogue.

The Beauty That Comes Out Of The Story

The beauty of the story is the "Sista-z" looked at the text and found the most valuable component and linked it to higher level of understanding:

> *16 And Ruth said, Intreat me not to leave thee, or to return from following after thee: for whither thou goest, I will go; and where thou lodgest, I will lodge: thy people shall be my people, and thy God my God: 17 Where thou diest, will I die, and there will I be buried: the LORD do so to me, and more also, if ought but death part thee and me. 18 When she saw that she was steadfastly minded to go with her, then she left speaking unto her. (Ruth 1:16-18)*

My God, our beautiful Sista-z abstracted the "philia" and attached the "Eros" aspect of love; this is beautiful. I love this. The Sista-z say whether it is or not a same-sex attracted relationship, we are using this language because it speaks to the love we have for one another "New Generation of Jumping The Broom" It is our role to establish how our Marriage Ceremonies and Services (or Holy Union Ceremonies) will be facilitated. **This is awesome.**

The universe has called upon us to modify the heterosexual model for our Kulture (LBGT/SGL). There is not always a "feminine and masculine" character; this is a gay stereotype.

Be ye not transformed by the things of this world but be ye transformed by the renewing of your mind. (Romans 12:2)

Note: In the Book of Romans 12 you find powerful language about the commitment towards God and Society. Our desire to love someone of the same sex should not distract us from the purpose to serve God of Your Understanding with your whole heart mind and soul/spirit in concert with loving your neighbors as yourself. Yes, this means the folks in our Kulture who say they do not like "transgenders" this is your neighbor and has an intrinsic value in our Kulture.

We should answer the questions for ourselves:

- *Who will give who away?*
- *Is this required today?*
- *What if both women are feminine and/or masculine?*
- *Who takes on whose name and why or why not?*
- *What does walking down the isle look like?*

Redefining the heterosexual privilege model and developing a new understanding of Jumping The Broom or Commitment for Life Ceremonies. It is your wedding; make it special for everyone, including yourself. We are the solutions to our challenges.

Our community has no idea of what organizations like the Human Rights Campaign, National LBGT Task Force, and a host of Marriage Equality organizations have done for us.

Chapter 10   *The Mis-Education About*
Love In The Bible

We owe them so much. I realized this during my sabbatical years. The tireless work of these organizations is "priceless."

The Love of Jonathan and David

The Bible story of Jonathan and David in our Kulture is a debated topic with many viewpoints even amongst the trained religious community.

Now the conservatives are going to love this point view, only because it is coming from a *"proud black gay man" (I hope yawl caught that,)* but please, do not think for one moment I am shying away from addressing the "moral midgets"; we will get to them later in this chapter.

In First Samuel and Second Samuel, among other events, is the story of a relationship of brotherly love between David and Jonathan. Jonathan is the son of King Saul, and next in line for the throne until Samuel anoints David to be the next king. This created resentment from Saul toward David.

After David's defeat of the Philistine giant, Goliath, in 1Samuel Chapter 17, David meets Jonathan for the first time.

> *1 And it came to pass, when he had made an end of speaking unto Saul that the soul of Jonathan was knit with the soul of David, and Jonathan loved him as his own soul. 2 And Saul took him that day, and would let him go no more home to his father's house. 3 Then Jonathan and David made a covenant, because he loved him as his own soul. 4 And Jonathan stripped himself of the robe that was upon him, and gave it to David, and his garments, even to his sword, and to his bow, and to his girdle.*

(1Samuel 18:1-4)

David comes in from battle after defeating Goliath, when he returns; he is met by Saul and his son, Jonathan. Jonathan instantly has a profound respect for the young warrior. The story tells us Jonathan stripped himself of his garments and his bow and his girdle.

During this ancient time, climate and social status, there were factors in determining a person's style of dress. The Israelites were scarcely influenced by the dress of surrounding countries, since their travel was limited. The fashions of Israelite men remained much the same, generation after generation. The Israelite men's "inner garments" resembled a close fitting shirt. The earliest of these garments were made without sleeves and reached only to the knees. Later, the inner garment extended to the wrists and ankles.

A man wearing an inner garment was said to be naked (1Sam 19:24, Isa. 20:24). The man's girdle was a belt or bank of cloth, cord, or leather 10 cm. or more wide. The "girdle" was utilized in two ways: as a tie around the waist of the inner garment or around the outer garment. The Israelite men wore an "outer garment" called the coat, robe, or mantle.

The clothes worn would probably not have resulted in Jonathan being totally nude. During this ancient time, clothing had a major link to the worshipping of God; when certain garments were taken off, a person was considered naked.

In the text from First Samuel 18:5-30:31, David's popularity and military achievements are advanced, and King Saul starts to become very jealous of all the attention given to

Chapter 10   *The Mis-Education About*
Love In The Bible

David. In addition, he recognizes very quickly that his son Jonathan has bonded with David.

Saul's anger was deeply rooted in jealousy, but Samuel anointed David as the future king. Saul was so angry that he used his daughter in-law, his son, manipulated his staff, sat with other religious leaders and confessed before God, never forgiving but always plotting minutes, hours, days, and weeks in advance on ways to kill David. You and I know some Saul's.

Jonathan is aware of his father's hardened heart; Saul's intentions are not loving and he knows David is innocent of any wrong doing. David is dedicated to the work of serving God and has done everything asked of him by King Saul.

Jonathan advocates on behalf of David and his father; King Saul tries to kill Jonathan, his own son.

Dr. Daniel A. Helminiak writes in his book *What the Bible Really Says About Homosexuality* the possibility David was in love with Jonathan; he also illustrates some word interpretations if applied could mean various parties had an erection in the presence of each other and there was some anal penetration. This point of view is quite impressive and educational. Dr. Helminiak in his writing often uses the word "could"; for me, this is allowing you to draw your conclusion. If it works for you; great; if it does not, fine too.

The relationship with David and Jonathan from my perspective was similar to homeboys in the hood, frat brothers; gay house brothers who have each other's back even when it is not popular, and true friendship. Solomon, the son of David, writes:

"A man that hath friends must show himself friendly: and there is a friend that sticketh closer than a brother"

(Proverbs 18:24)

In this Kulture, gay houses (i.e. House of Ferragamo, House of Estrada) are connected like Jonathan and David. In the transgender community, Jonathan and David relationships are the foundation of survival. Protecting one another at all cost, even from biological family members and modern-day oppressive homosexuals.

Cultural Perceptions vs. Reality

After the boy had gone, David got up from the south side of the stone and bowed down before Jonathan three times, with is face to the ground. Then they kissed each other and wept together but David wept the most.

(1Samuel 20:41 NIV)

Now the scripture above is pretty clear, David and Jonathan kissed and cried together.

This text is a great example of why we must be critical of all bible teachings. If you read this verse as it is presented you could say that it is pretty cut and dry. Here is how the full text reads:

And as soon as the lad was gone, David arouse out of a place toward the south, and fell on his face to the ground, and bowed himself three times: and they kissed one another, and wept one with another, until David exceeded. *(1Samuel 20:41KJV)*

Chapter 10   *The Mis-Education About*
Love In The Bible

This is why it is important to read the entire stories because David was hiding from Saul under the orchestrated by David and Saul. If you did not read the preceding scriptures this could be misinterpreted.

In many cultures kissing is a very normal greeting ritual. This would be a very normal custom in various cultures *(i.e. African, Middle Eastern, European)*. This is helpful to know if you are in a diverse religious culture and this subject were to come up. An attempt to rationalize this point of view being a homosexual act would probably offend many in the room. Many traditions practiced today originated from these ancient periods.

When I learned the translators of the *"The Living Bible"* did not like the word "kissing" found in the other translations they change the word to "shaking hands" I was very annoyed. Moral midgets, what other words have they change?

The church has manipulated us to a level we are scared to ask any questions about the bible. We have openly "gay theologians" who operate with some of the same religious egotism. (Yes, gay theologians). A person does not come out of an oppressive system and not bring some of that oppressive behavior with you.

I am distressed for thee my brother Jonathan: very pleasant hast thou
been unto me: thy love to me was wonderful passing the love of women. (2Samuel 1:26)

It appears there is a level of closeness with David and Jonathan if we read the text on a literal level. The same sex attraction is a widely used interpretation by the LBGT/SGL community.

Remember it is healthy to read or listen from different points of view. The previous scripture "could" be viewed from various points of view as illustrated:

PERCEPTIONS Vs. REALTIES		
Heterosexual	Black on Black	LBGT/SGL
Based on commitment to God **** Let nothing come between them **** Friendship grew after being tested **** Friendship never died	Homeboy is the only one that stuck with me **** When I did not have the money my friend help me	Secret love affair, Down low couple **** Best friend stuck with me when my family did not. **** Heterosexual friend has always been understanding

Charts & Figures 10.1

During ancient times and currently today in the Middle Eastern countries two men kissing is a very common greeting. The traditional greeting I believe is three kisses to the cheek. Western culture prefers a hand shake with an occasional hug and kiss on the cheek. In our Kulture we hug and kiss almost every time we see each other.

The "Eros" conclusion is open to interpretation in the progressive theology community speaking to bisexuality. In our Kulture (LBGT/SGL) we really do not understand true bi-sexuality and the community often times despises persons who

Chapter 10 **The Mis-Education About Love In The Bible**

self identify as bi-sexual. This sector of the community is viewed as confused.

They are judged without an understanding and/or knowledge what level they are at in their same sex attraction.

Biblical studies for me are a personal mission and I have seen many discuss this text and not one appeared to be very confident with their explanation. I remember talking to this guy who was trying to explain this scripture to me and I was very quiet. The guy started telling me of all the books he has read about Homosexuality and the Bible and how the books wrote about it so it must be true. I never responded to my brotha because I could hear the conviction in his heart.

It was not relevant to attempt to change his opinion because he felt comfortable with it and had supporting information. If we do not write anything different than what others are writing this is the result. If you believe pork is the other white. The pork is the other white meat. *(I have no problem with that pig).*

Just because a person has a certificate in religion does not make them a messenger for God. The slaves had to question master; they also had to question the house Negro's living up in master's quarters. It is healthy to question the church but also we should not refrain from questioning gay bible scholars.

If we do not understand any teachings and it does link together for us. Then the question should be asked.

Remember they use to tell us in school *"There is no such thing as a dumb question."* If you are clergy and get annoyed because your members (students of word) ask questions then you should seek insight within yourself as to why being questioned annoys you.

Chapter 10   *The Mis-Education About Love In The Bible*

Moving Yourself To The Next Level

Chapter 10 The Mis-Education About Love In The Bible

Each process question or thought can be viewed from the following perspectives: Same Gender Loving (SGL), Heterosexual (H) or Both (B). It is healthy to try and view from various perspectives to get insight into how others may process an issue. All perspectives are valid and should be respected and not condemned. In all thy getting; get understanding.

1. (B) What is God' unconditional love to you?

2. (SGL) Why do you think:
   a. Gay men have challenges with lesbians or transgenders?
   b. Lesbians have challenges with gay men?
   c. Transgenders have challenges with gay men?
   d. Gay men, lesbians and transgenders have challenges with Bisexuality?

3. (SGL) - Have you ever loved another person who was same gender loving but was ashamed to be seen with them in public? Why?

4. (SGL) Same-sex interracial couples often feel alienated by their own race. Why do you feel this happens?

5. (B) Do you love God?
   a. What would you do for God that would shock even you?
   b. Who would you reach out to with unconditional love on God's behalf?
   c. Do you love yourself enough to forgive someone who has hurt? How?

The Mis-Education Against Homosexuality In The Bible

CHAPTER 11

The Mis-Education About Ten Words Used Against Homosexuality

In this chapter which is *a book within itself,* you will learn about often misquoted biblical words by the religious community in reference to homosexuality. You will get a good idea of where the Christian religious community may be coming from about some of their biblical beliefs.

These words have an impact on people's lives differently, so we should be sensitive to the various reactions. If you are reading various words and they make you uncomfortable, it is all right to come back to the words. Most of these words are loading with pain and negative life experiences.

The religious system has created various economics and cultural laws for a multitude of reasons that may or may not have anything to do with homosexuality. In the book of Leviticus, you are not reading the words of God in most writings, but the ideas and thoughts of the high priest speaking on behalf of God. We are not clear in many of these writings if it was divinely inspired and politically inspired (i.e. tribal issues, upper and lower class).

Just because someone is an authority in the church does not mean they have all the answers and they are working in the best interest of God *(i.e. E.G.O. Edging God Out).*

*Chapter 11   The Mis-Education About Ten Words
Used Against Homosexuality*

1. ABOMINATION

Quotes of Judgment
'That lifestyle is an abomination unto God"

Abominations were directed toward a culture that many in society did not understand. This is one of the challenges black folks were forced to deal with because many in the European-American community were taught as children a negative image of black people.

This was birthing of negative social perceptions resulting in unhealthy programming transferred to from generation to generation. The Christian community has a history of comparing our same gender loving culture to thieves, murderers or rapists.

In comparison to today all black folks play basketball, sing, and have bad credit, like fried chicken and collard greens.

Just because someone has a Ph.D., Master's of Divinity, MSW, or LCSW does not mean they have your best interest at heart. There were people with Ph.D.s rationalizing slavery. We now have black church leaders stepping in as the new whipping masters (pharaoh).

Abomination is an English term used to translate the Biblical term to'ba (noun) or **ta'ab** (verb). The term in English signifies that which is exceptionally loathsome, hateful, wicked, or vile. In Biblical terms *to'ba* does not

carry the same sense of the exceptionable as the English term.
   a) Abhorrence; disgust.
   b) A cause of abhorrence or disgust

It simply signifies that which is forbidden or unclean according to the religion. Linguistically, it is therefore close in meaning to the Polynesian term taboo or tapu, signifying that which is forbidden, should be left alone and not touched, or (for some items) brings death by the act of touching.

Elisabeth Anne Kellogg comments on the Hebrew meaning of the term:

> *While some will point out that homosexuality and cross-dressing are in the same category as incest and bestiality, it should be noted that so are divorced people who remarry, those who have sex during menstruation and children who fight with their parents. In fact it seems that any uncleanness, any violation of Jewish Law, can be considered to'ba...*

"Abomination" Copyright compliance: "(c) Copyright 2004 Elisabeth Anne Kellogg, all rights reserved. You are expressly granted permission to copy this article provided you do not modify any portion of the text, including this copyright notice."

John 8:7, Christ himself says, **"Let anyone among you who is without sin be the first to throw a stone."** Before we start throwing stones, have we committed one or more of the various abominations?

Abomination in the Biblical sense of the word refers to:

1) No scales or fins –*i.e. Lobster and crab* (Lev. 11:10-12)
2) Pork *i.e. ribs, chitterlings, bacon* (Lev. 11:7)
3) No Blood – *i.e. Medium rare food* (Lev. 17:10 &19:26)
4) Adultery (Lev. 18:20)
5) Thou shalt not hate thy brother and bear evil against him (Lev. 19:17)
6) Do not mix fabrics- *i.e linen, silk* (Lev. 19:19, Deut. 22:11)
7) No tattoos (Lev. 19:28)
8) Christian and Jewish Old Testament scriptures refer to homosexuality (Lev. 18:22, 20:13)
9) Wages shall not be kept overnight (Lev. 19:13)
10) No Haircut - *i.e. trims, shaving* (Lev. 19:27)
11) Cross-dressing or women wearing pants (Deut. 22:5)

*Chapter 11   The Mis-Education About Ten Words
Used Against Homosexuality*

12) Cheating weights and measures - i.e. *Wall Street Greed Dishonesty in business*. (Deut. 25:13-16, Prov. 11:1, 20:10, 20:23)

13) Charging *or paying* interest (Psalm 15:5)

The law is no longer written on stone but on our hearts.

If men say, I love God, and hateth his brother, he is a liar: for he that loveth not his brother whom he hath seen, how can he love God whom he hath not seen? And these commandments have we from him, That he who loveth God love his brother.
(1John 4:20-21)

The word abomination can be linked to homosexuality but an in-depth look into the text is required to understand the cultural motives.

*Chapter 11   The Mis-Education About Ten Words
Used Against Homosexuality*

2. ANTI-CHRIST

Quotes of Judgment
*"How dare you play with the word of God like that!
You ain't nothing but the Anti-Christ!"*

The common biblical meaning of the word Anti-Christ is one who teaches a life against a commitment to Jesus Christ. The religious communities have used this word as a negative suggestion towards the Christian gay community and gay affirming pastors and churches. The Christian gay community has been an advocate for Christ and is committed to being who they are in Christ.

The Christian church propaganda uses current events as examples that these are the end times and the Lord is going to return, so you need to come to Jesus. I agree a life with Jesus is great, but not because it is the end times *(there shall be wars and rumors of wars)*. These are fear tactics used by aggressive advocates for Christ conveying to a person it's time for them to make a personal choice to follow Christ or go to hell in nonsense.

The religious community's fear teachings continue this by comparing bad weather events (i.e. hurricanes, tsunamis, floods, tornados) as a sign of the return of the Anti-Christ. These fear tactics have terrified many to coming to Christ or re-establishing a life with Jesus Christ. In truth, the weather is no different than any other time in history (outside of global warming). The weather, crime, and troubled relationships receive more airtime now thanks to 24-hour news networks (i.e. CNN, Fox) entertaining us with continuous coverage. The next time you listen to the bad weather report, you will hear the word "since." Yes, "since" is used as comparison to past events

"We have not had this kind of weather since..." Nothing new has been going on for centuries.

An enemy of Christ. Anti-Christ is the nickname of the great rival to Jesus Christ who was expected by the early Church to set himself up against Christ in the last days before the Second Coming (aka a false Christ).

The anti-Christ mentioned in the New Testament as an enemy of Jesus, who will appear before the Second Coming and win over many of Jesus' followers. The Antichrist is often identified with a beast described in the Book of Revelation, whom God destroys just before the final defeat of Satan.

Since the New Testament was written, the Christian church has frequently tried to prove an individual human being was the Antichrist. The Antichrist candidates have been Roman emperors Nero and Caligula and modern day dictators Adolph Hitler and Joseph Stalin *(both of them were probably the closest thing to evil; their crimes against humanity brings water to my eyes).*

Christian denominations disagree on the expected role of the Antichrist and what will happen in the end times, and the role the Antichrist will play. Those who believe in the Anti-Christ, of who John the Divine was writing about in the Book of Revelation, expect the Anti-Christ to arise in the future. There is a belief that sometime prior to the expected return of Jesus, there will be a period of "trials and tribulations" during which the Antichrist, inspired by Satan, will attempt to win supporters with great works, and will silence anyone or make enemies of any country that refuses their allegiance (by refusing to *"receive his mark 666"* on their foreheads or right hands). The Anti-Christ is also believed to be a group of individuals as well as organizations that, throughout history, have been trying to deceive and stifle the Christian faithful. They are finally destroyed by God on the day of Armageddon. For the sake of having some fun, let's call the 24-hour news station the Anti-Christ for always bringing bad news. Remember Ms. Evillene in *The Wiz*, *"Don't nobody bring me no bad news."*

Jesus will not come with signs and symbols

43 Now after two days he departed thence, and went into Galilee. 44 For Jesus himself testified that a prophet hath no honour in his own country. 45 Then when he was come into Galilee, the Galileans received him, having seen all the things that he did at Jerusalem at the feast: for they also went unto the feast. 46 So Jesus came again into Cana of Galilee, where he made the water wine. And there was a certain nobleman, whose son was sick at Capernaum. 47 When he heard that Jesus was come out of Judaea into Galilee, he went unto him, and besought him that he would come down, and heal his son: for he was at the point of death. 48 Then said Jesus unto him, Except ye see signs and wonders, ye will not believe.(John 4:43-54)

The term Anti-Christ has nothing to do with homosexuality.

*Chapter 11   The Mis-Education About Ten Words
Used Against Homosexuality*

3. CURSE

Quotes of Judgment
"The reason you got the AIDS is because of God cursing you for living that sinful life."

In our Kulture, many have been programmed we are a living curse. We have many in our own Kulture who will read this book and not believe even the words of Jesus Christ. It is healthy for us to love and support each other regardless of what level we are on or where we think others should be.

> *And such were some of you: but ye are washed, but ye are sanctified, but ye are, justified in the name of the Lord Jesus, and by the Sprit of God.   (1 Corinthians 6:10*
>
> *)*

The referencing of "curse" is another poor attempt by the religious community to condemn people in our Kulture. In the Bible, when Jesus is teaching, his reference to the word is never towards the condemnation of a person or group of people. In his teaching he was often trying to convey to those who have been accused of it; their accusers had no right to label them with negative images.

Judgment of the Gentiles Matthew 25:31-46

This is a good example of how the Gentiles were being warned not to repeat the behaviors of those who cursed them in the past. This is a healthy comparison for our Kulture today especially for those in openly affirming ministries. You have no right to look down on them because they chose not to follow your path.*(Matthew 25:41)*

> *"Bless them that curse you, and pray for them which despitefully use you"   (Luke 6:28)*

In Galatians 3:10-14, the main topic is about *"Christ redeems us from the Curse of the Law."* But many in the religious community love to quote verse 10:

> *For as many as are of the works of the law are under the curse: for it is written, Cursed Is Everyone That Continueth Not In All Things Which Are Written In The Book Of The Law To Do Them. (Galatians 3:10)*

Apostle Paul is writing to the churches in Galatia and it is an aggressive wording against putting works before faith. The law declares people are guilty and imprisons them; faith sets people free to enjoy the liberties of Christ.

The words above in capital letters are a Bible verse out of the Old Testament Deuteronomy 27:26. In Deuteronomy 27:11- 26 it is about the Proclamation of the Curses. They are giving instruction before they enter into *"the land that floweth with milk and honey"* (Deut 27:3) also known as The Promised Land. This has nothing to do with the cursing of homosexuals.

In Romans 12:3-21, the main focus is "Responsibilities Toward Society" and the key verse in reference to the curse is Romans 12:10,

"Bless them which persecute you: bless, and curse not"

Apostle Paul during his ministry in Rome was addressing some of the same issues we are dealing with today. People have a tendency to judge by measuring their relationships with God and the tendency to create societal systems of one group is better than another.

The word "cursing" has nothing to do with homosexuality.

Chapter 11   The Mis-Education About Ten Words
Used Against Homosexuality

4. DEVIL/SATAN

Quotes of Judgment
*"Look at that! Two women together—
that ain't nothing but the devil."*

When making statements like *"the Devil has no power,"* for many in the Christian community, it is a frightening statement within itself. Even as I was writing this section, I was a little nervous because of the old teachings of fear that remain leftover and rooted in my consciousness.

The word "devil" when reversed means "lived." Have you lived in fear of something based on good public relations, promoters and Bible totters?

Questioning the bible is not blasphemy; this is what the church wants us to believe. Blasphemy is when the power and authority of God is called into questioned (i.e. reverence, authority).

It is your responsibility to seek understanding of how various groups can perceive you and from where their perceptions could be generated.

> *Often the devil in many religions, the major personified spirit of evil, ruler of Hell, and foe of God. Used with the. A subordinate evil spirit; a demon.*

Satan [Heb., =adversary], traditional opponent of God and humankind in Judaism and Christianity. But in the New Testament it is Satan, with its Greek equal *diabolos* (the Devil), which came to dominate, displacing or demoting other names and figures.

*The Mis-Education Against
Homosexuality In The Bible*

Spirit (see the notes below) or Power of Evil. Although from time to time used to refer to demons, the term more often assigned the Prince of Evil Spirits. In the Bible, the Devil is also known as Satan, Beelzebub, and Lucifer. In post-Biblical traditions, he emerges as the tempter of humankind and is responsible for all the sins in the Bible. Christian studies describe his main task to convince humans to rejecting a Life with Christ and his unconditional love in favor of sin and death. I think I got that right. (Deep)

- **In Judaism,** Satan become known as submissive to God and as an adversary and accuser of Job and other humans

- **In the Qur'an**, the Devil is frequently associated with Iblis; he tempts the unfaithful, but not the true believer.

- **In Hinduism,** there is no main devil, although there is an assortment of demons or devilish beings.

- **In Buddhism** the reality of numerous demons, and Mara known as the Buddha's opponent and tempter, is sometimes known as a specific evil spirit.

- **In the Christian** Bible, he is well-known with the serpent in the Garden of Eden, the Jobs tempter (Job 1:6-2:13), the tempter of the Good News (Matthew 4:1-11), and the evil dragon in the Book of Revelation (20:1-9). Devil/Satan is described as hating all humanity, or more accurately creation, spreading lies, deceit among the world.

The English word "Satan" is from a Hebrew word meaning "to oppose" or "adversary." The name "Lucifer" appears in Isaiah 14 in the King James Version of the Bible.

The growing theory of Satan was a course of actions of demonizing one's opponents and attributing evil motives them. There was one religious group in the late centuries **B**.efore

*Chapter 11   The Mis-Education About Ten Words
Used Against Homosexuality*

C.hrist (or **B**.efore **C**.ommon **E**.ra) that portrayed other Jewish groups who disagreed with them as allied with the forces of darkness and themselves as "sons of light."

Early Christians adopted this approach and demonized Jews who did not acknowledge Jesus as the Messiah. In later centuries, pagans and fellow Christians who had opposing beliefs were characterized by Christians as evil and to be opposed or eradicated. Bibliography: See W. Woods, *A History of the Devil* (1974); J. B. Russell, *Satan* (1981); N. Forsyth, *The Old Enemy* (1987); E. Pagels, *The Origin of Satan* (1995)

Reprogramming those negative tapes from childhood will take some time, but the Bible says

"I can do all things through Christ that strengthens me"

This concept of the Satan/Devil has nothing to with homosexuality.

*Chapter 11   The Mis-Education About Ten Words
Used Against Homosexuality*

5. EVIL

Quotes of Judgment
"It says it in the bible, that lifestyle is evil."

The scriptures above are great examples of how Bible text can be taken out of context. I am not by any means trying to communicate that evil does not exist. That is another book within itself. My focus is helping you understand how and maybe why some groups label our Kulture(LBGT/SGL) as evil.

Evil can be overcome with love and this should to be translated into loving yourself and community.

> *Live life seeing opportunities where others see evil.*
> *Live not paranoid of evil doing or doers of evil.*
> *Live sharing kind acts of love towards all people others think are evil.*
> *Live life performing random acts of kindness overcoming evil.*
> *To live is Christ but to die is gain. (Philippians 1:20-21)*

This does not necessarily mean in a physical way but in a spiritual and emotional approach. Paul came to know the Lord through his afflictions (inner struggles). He knew how it felt to experience people considering one as evil, using unloving expressions, physical injury, questioning your past actions and decisions. To live is Christ but to die is gain.

This is not about your Christian walk but your Christian thought. When walking with Christ there may be negative thoughts you may have of yourself that continues to replay itself over and over again. To live with Christ is to recognize he will never hurt you and will be with you even unto the death. It is unhealthy when you let negative ideas, thoughts, and experiences live in your head rent-free. It is time to serve some eviction notices, foreclose on broken images of yourself.

To live with Christ is walking with an understanding, God was there with you when it first began and God is with you now.

> a) Morally bad or wrong; wicked: *an evil tyrant.*
> Characterized by or indicating future misfortune; ominous: *evil omens.*
> b) Bad or blameworthy by report; infamous: *an evil reputation.*
> c) Characterized by anger or spite; malicious: *an evil temper.*

IN BRIEF: n. - *The class of being morally wrong in principle or practice; that which causes harm or destruction or misfortune.*

In Judaism and Christianity, Evil comes as a result of being disobedient to God's will. Judaism stresses obedience to God's laws as written in the Torah and the laws. In Christianity, some religious groups stress obedience to God's law. Other religious groups emphasize Christ's statement for the love of God and love of your fellow man is the whole of the law. Still others emphasize the idea that man is inherently Evil, and in need of forgiveness.

Some forms of Christianity, as well as Judaism, do not personify Evil in Satan; these Christian groups instead consider the human heart to be naturally bent toward trickery, although human beings are responsible for their choices, whereas in Judaism, there is no prejudice in one's becoming good or evil at time of birth. In Judaism, Satan is viewed as one who tests us for God rather than one who works against God; and Evil, as in the Christian denominations above, is a matter of choice.

*Chapter 11   The Mis-Education About Ten Words
Used Against Homosexuality*

Some cultures or philosophies believe that Evil can arise without meaning or reason. Christianity in general does not adhere to this belief, but the prophet Isaiah implied that God is ultimately responsible for everything including Evil.

> *"I form the light, and create darkness:*
> *I make peace, and create Evil:*
> *I the LORD do all these things."*
> *(Isaiah 45:7)*

The word evil does not have a direct link to homosexuality.

*The Mis-Education Against
Homosexuality In The Bible*

*Chapter 11 The Mis-Education About Ten Words
Used Against Homosexuality*

6. HELL & DAMNATION

Quotes of Judgment
*"You know you going to hell
if you keep living that life contrary to the word of God."*

In some forms of Western Christian belief, damnation to hell is the punishment of God for persons with unredeemed transgressions. Damnation is often the motivator for conversions to Christianity. This concept of eternal suffering and denial of entrance to Heaven often symbolized in the Bible as burning and fire.

"Living Trying Not To Go Hell But Dying To Go Heaven"

a) The act of damning or the condition of being damned, b) Condemnation to everlasting punishment, c) Everlasting punishment, d) Failure or ruination incurred by adverse criticism

The concept of hell also known as the Valley of Gehenna (Hebrew "sheol", Greek "hades") in many traditional Christian cultures is the punishment of God's people with unredeemed transgressions and are destined to eternal damnation. The Damnation is often the motivator for people to convert to Christianity. This concept of eternal suffering and denial of a place in Heaven often symbolized in the bible with the lake of fire or burning fierce..

Most religions included the concept of a place that divided good from evil or the living from the dead. Developing an illustration or belief that hell is the final dwelling place of the damned after the last judgment is held takes place.

In Judaism, the concept of Gehenna (hell) as an infernal region of punishment for the wicked.

In Christianity, the vision of hell as the fiery domain of Satan and his evil angels and a place of punishment for those who die without repenting of their sins.

In Hinduism, hell is only one stage in the career of the soul as it passes through the phases of reincarnation.

In Buddhism, schools teach their varying conceptions of hell, usually entailing some kind of punishment or purgatory.

These words references to hell in the church have become some of the main fear tactics used by the Christian Church to bring people to Christ. The concept of hell is derived from the physical place during a biblical period of a continuous burning furnace (or trash dumps) *"where the worm dieth not and the fire is not quenched."* (Isaiah 66:24, Jeremiah 7:20).

These burning infernos were outside many of the cities and people would throw opponents, crooks, and religious leaders into the furnace as a form of punishment. Some even facilitated religious sacrifices at the burning furnace sites. Over period of time folk stories were developed and eventually ended up in the biblical written word of God.

You will discover in Mark 9:43-50, Jesus speaks to the "Warning about Hell". In the verses a keyword is to "offend" which is translated to mean *"something that makes you sin."*

In the illustration Jesus gives three qualities that should be found in our lives.
    (1) We should remember God's faithfulness, just as salt when used with a sacrifice recalled God's

Chapter 11   The Mis-Education About Ten Words Used Against Homosexuality

covenant with his people. This is a merging of salt and meat during the process and regardless of what you do to the meat once it has been salted no one can remove the salt. When you season yourself with the presence of God, no one can remove God from you. (Numbers 18:19)

(2) We should make a difference in the "flavor" of the world we live in, just as salt changes meat's flavor. *Jesus says "Ye are the salt of the earth: but if the salt has lost his savour, wherewith shall it be salted? It is thenforth good for nothing, but to be cast out, and to be trodden under foot of men (Matthew 5:13).* Where are you pouring the flavor of God in you? Who are you helping? Who are you making a difference in their lives? Your earthly encounters give you a heavenly place.

(3) We should offset the dishonest decay in humanity, just as salt preserves food from decay. When we lose this desire to "salt" the earth with love and message of God, we become useless to God. God is apart of you and will not cast thyself into a place of damnation. No one can remove God from but people distract you from believing God is in you.

God has no desire to torture you, but the Church— well that is another issue. Nice people, just a little misguided.

The words of hell and damnation are not linked to homosexuality.

The Mis-Education Against Homosexuality In The Bible

*Chapter 11   The Mis-Education About Ten Words
Used Against Homosexuality*

7. IMMORAL

Quotes of Judgment
"You know you living an immoral lifestyle!"

The words "immoral and moral" you will not find in the King James Version of the Bible. These words reflect more of a modern-day terminology.

For example it was immoral per the Bible:
- ✓ Persons with disabilities to come before the altar of God with their sickness.
- ✓ Divorce your wife
- ✓ Interracial marriage

Morality (from the Latin ***moralitaser*** "manner, character, proper behavior") has three principal meanings. In its **first** descriptive usage, morality means a code of conduct held to be authoritative in matters of right and wrong, whether by society, philosophy, religion, or individual conscience.

In its **second**, normative and universal, sense, morality refers to an ideal code of conduct, one which would be adopted in preference to alternatives by all rational people, under specified conditions. To deny 'morality' in this sense is a position known as moral skepticism.

In its third usage 'morality' is synonymous with ethics, the systematic philosophical study of the moral domain.

> The word is also commonly used interchangeably with 'morality' to mean the subject matter of this study; and sometimes it is used more narrowly to mean the moral principles of a particular tradition, group, or individual. Christian ethics and Albert Schweitzer's ethics are

examples." John Deigh in Robert Audi (ed), *The Cambridge Dictionary of Philosophy*, 1995

Webster's definition:
   a. "Moral" Violating moral principles.
   b. Licentious (wicked, shameless), lascivious (i.e. inclined to lustfulness, wanton). [1650-60]
   c. "Immorality" Immoral quality, character, or conduct: wickedness 2. Sexual misconduct
   d. An immoral act [1560-70]

Although some people might think that a moral code is simple, rarely is there anything simple about one's values, ethics, etc. or, for that matter, the judgment of those of others.

The difficulty lies in the fact that morals are often part of a religion and more often than not about culture codes.

Sometimes, moral codes give way to legal codes, which couple penalties or corrective actions with particular practices. Note that while many legal codes are merely built on a foundation of religious and/or cultural moral codes, oftentimes they are one and the same.

Sexual immorality closet reference in the bible could be found in First Corinthians 6:12-20. The key word addressing the reference is *"fornication."* During this period there were many cultural clashes between Greek mythology, Judaism, Jewish (Judeo) Christians and Gentiles.

In most Bible dictionaries, they translate the word fornication as synonymous with homosexuality and this is due in part to what is defined by the religious community as sex outside of marriage and sexual misconduct as written in the Old Testaments.

The association is heavily linked by the religious community to First Corinthians 6:1-11 concerning litigation

*Chapter 11   The Mis-Education About Ten Words
Used Against Homosexuality*

between believers and this is where the word "effeminate" is located, but learned in previous chapters the word effeminate is not about effeminate men but about wealth and living a lavish life leaving God out.

The notion to judge someone is very contradictory to the teachings of Jesus Christ. In Matthew 7:1-6 Jesus speaks to the notion of judging others:

> *Judge not so that ye be not judged. For with what judgment ye judge, ye shall be judged: and with what measure ye mete, it shall be measured to you again.*
> (Matthew 7:1-2)

When the religious community attempts to institute their moral codes in reference to immorality, they often link the immorality penalty to the "judgment seat of Jesus Christ." The "judgment seat" is the point of life when all of our actions will come before Christ. In the Bible, the judgment seat is a judicial bench in the City of Rome also known as the throne or tribunal. The trial of Jesus before Pontius Pilate was at the judgment seat (Matthew 27:19).

In the eyes of Jesus, to judge someone is not justice. Below is two illustrations how Jesus and Paul were addressing the dangers of judging others with self-imposed morality codes.

(1) Matthew 7:1-6, Christ is teaching about not judging others but evaluating yourself and holding yourself accountable for you. In Romans 14:3 there is a connection with wording in Matthew 7:1 *"that ye be not judged"* where Paul is speaking to the Principles of Christian Liberty. This is significant when you read the text; there is a morality issue about what people eat. Doesn't that sound like a current "judgment" challenge of

today: "meat eaters vs. vegans?" Knowledge about a life with Christ has a tendency to create a right and wrong with how you worship, when you worship and whom you worship with.

(2) Second Corinthians 5:9-10 is an area where the religious community oftentimes links immorality to the Judgment Seat of Christ. If a person is not learned in Biblical studies, it could be easily understood to mean you will be judged by Christ. In Romans 2:11-16 *"For there is no respect of persons with God."* For the law is written in the hearts of all.

To judge someone is not justice and we as believers are overstepping our boundaries. I know there will be people saying "what about the child molesters, rapist and killers?" This book is not about neither of them. This book is about homosexuality. If we compare our Kulture to these issues we allow them to create negative images in our mind about who we are as a community.

This is a modern day attempt to link homosexuality.

*Chapter 11   The Mis-Education About Ten Words
Used Against Homosexuality*

8. PERVERT/PERVERSION

Quotes of Judgment
"That perverted lifestyle!"

This word pervert or perversion has a very interesting history as elated to the Bible and today's modern English translation.

In the Bible, the word refers to someone who was turning people away from a committed relationship with their God *(i.e. Jesus Christ, The God of Abraham, Isaac and Jacob)*. This is a simple definition, but I am sure there are others that can be a lot more detailed.

You will discover in the five succeeding scriptures from the Old and New Testament, how the word pervert/perversion is applied with an English translation.

Webster's give us the following definitions:

(1) To lead astray morally
(2) To turn away from the right course
(3) To lead into mental error or false judgment
(4) To turn to an improper use; misapply
(5) To misconstrue or misinterpret
(6) To bring to a less excellent state
(7) A person who practices a sexual perversion (modern day definition as early 1900's)

Pervert

(1) Law of the Administration of the Judges
Thou shalt not wrest (pervert) judgment; thou shalt not respect (show partiality of anyone), neither take a gift: for a gift doth blind the eyes of the wise, and pervert the words of the righteous.

The pervert in this text is the same Webster's definition of (#4) & (#5).
> *(4) To turn to an improper use; misapply*
> *(5) To misconstrue or misinterpret*

(2) Judah is called from backsliding
> *A cry is heard on the barren heights, the weeping and pleading of the people of Israel, because they have perverted their ways and have forgotten the Lord their God. (Jeremiah 3:21)*

The word backsliding is used by many Pentecostal churchgoers as means of referring to someone who slide back into life non deemed Christian worthy. In reference to "pervert" the word in verse 21 is similar to the Webster's definition (#3).
> *(3) To lead into mental error or false judgment*

(3) Controversy with Bar-Jesus
> *You are a child of the devil and an enemy of everything that is right! You are full of all kind of deceit and trickery. Will never stop perverting the right ways of the Lord? (Acts 13:10)*

This verse is a good example of Webster's definition (#4). *(4) To turn to an improper use; misapply*

(4) Situation: The Departure From Grace
> *Which is not another; but there be some that trouble you, and would pervert the gospel of Christ. (Galatians 1:7)*

Those who troubled the Galatian believers and perverted the Gospel were zealous Jewish Christians who believed that the Old Testament practices such as circumcision and dietary restrictions were required of all believers. Because there teachers wanted to turn the Gentile Christians into Jews, they were called Judaizers.

The Galatian Christians were mainly Greek, unfamiliar with Jew laws and customs. The Judaizers were an extreme faction of Jewish Christians (sound familiar). Both groups believed in Christ, but their lifestyles differed considerably.

This verse is a good example of Webster's definition (#5) *To misconstrue or misinterpret.*

Perversion

(5)Christ's like Humility
> *That ye may be blameless and harmless, the sons of God, without rebuke, in the midst of a crooked and perverse nation, among whom ye shine as lights in the world.*
> *(Philippians 2:15)*

In many religious communities they will hang on to this verse and will not let go. It is healthy for us to read all the scriptures (Philippians 2:5-16) that pertain to this message and not just one verse.

In Paul's letter of gratitude to the church in Philippi. He is aggressive in illustrating the importance of Christ like humility. Jesus was accused of *"perversion"* because he saw himself as an image of God. Paul is emphasizing about being careful of those who try to turn you away from Christ.

Paul stresses you do not have to argue with people about your knowledge of Christ or prove to them the level of your relationship with Christ; it is more important for you to know Jesus Christ for yourself.

(3) To lead into mental error or false judgment
(6) To bring to a less excellent state

You discover from the preceding scriptures none of them have anything to do with homosexuality as defined in Webster's definition number seven. *(7) A person who practices a sexual perversion (modern day definition as early 1900's) but appropriate three and six (3) To lead into mental error or false judgment, (6) To bring to a less excellent state.*

The word pervert/perversion has nothing to do directly with homosexuality but it has become common religious rhetoric linking one to the other against homosexuality.

*Chapter 11   The Mis-Education About Ten Words
Used Against Homosexuality*

9. REPENTANCE

Quotes of Judgment
"I love you but you need to repent from that lifestyle."

Repentance is personally realizing your want or need to make a change in your life. Repentance can be an application system of right or wrong or viewed as "healthy or unhealthy" decisions. Repentance is an inner discovery of when you realize a change, series of changes or adjustments are necessary to move you from one state of mind to another.

Repentance can be healthy if you can view it as purpose driven journey. The journey creates an opportunity for you to visit *(don't build a house there; you are just visiting)* into some uncomfortable *places (i.e. abusive addictions, jealousy, low self-esteem, life set-up backs, expectations)* some journeys will require you to get off your road earlier because it causes such a mental fatigue. The journey is yours, but even loving and noble *(i.e. church leaders, best friends, co-workers, and bosses)* people can throw you off course.

In the New Testament, the word 'repentance' is a Greek word meaning *(metanoia)*. **Me-ta-noia** is therefore primarily an afterthought, different from the former thought; "change of mind and heart." A great story of self repentance found in the New Testament parable (or folk story) of the Prodigal Son found Luke 15:11-31 *"For Once I Lost But Now I Am Found."*

The true nature of repentance by some is a three-fold idea:

(1) As moving the intellect
The word here used for "repent" means to change one's mind, purpose, thought, views regarding a particular issue; it is to have another mind about a thought. This change is well

illustrated in the action of the Prodigal Son, and of the Publican in the well-known story of the Pharisee and the Publican (Luke 15, Luke 18).

(2) As moving the emotions
This meaning is exemplified by the repentant *(remorseful)* person who not only has profound regret for his past, but also the fulfilled hope in the potential of God's grace to continually bear the fruit of healing and true resolution in a person, with others, and most especially with God (Review Luke 10:13).

(3) As moving the will and disposition
One of the Hebrew words for repent means "to turn." *Then Judas, which had betrayed him, when he saw that he was condemned, repented himself (Matthew 27:3).*

In the book Genesis 32, is the story of Jacob fighting with an Angel. Jacob (Hebrew translation "trickery) received the blessing of the father Isaac via his mother's desire to have him blessed of Isaac instead of his brother Esau.

The story tells us Jacob wrestled with an angel all night long and spoke to the angel *"I will not let you go, except thou bless me."(Gen 32:26)*

Jacob's form of repentance was seeking a blessing from God for all the things he had done in the past. He wrestled with himself, wrestled with what was sent to help, wrestled with what he had achieved and wrestled with his future experiences.
Repentance "Change of heart and mind"

The desire for a change of heart. In the book of Psalms 51:10, David writes *"create in me a clean heart, O God; and renew the right spirit within me."* Our inner challenges are what haunt us. David's forgiveness was about the how he manipulated family and friends for the love of a woman and the murder of her husband because of his sexual desire for her. **Repentance "Change of heart and mind"**

Thorn In The Flesh. In Second Corinthians 12:7-10, Apostle Paul speaks about the "Thorn In The Flesh." Now, before you get deep, the Satan in the story is not about a devil with a pitchfork; it's about a physical adversary. It is a metaphor written to create a visual picture of the inner struggle same as in Hebrew poetry illustrated in Job 2:4-7. Paul illustrates he takes pleasures in his personal challenges (2Corinthians 12:10). It is in those challenges that we become strong. **Repentance "Change of heart and mind"**

A change of heart and mind is looking at the experiences not as evil or bad, but as opportunities to learn more about ourselves and become better, not bitter. Transitioning our Christian thought to guide us in our Christian walk.

This has no direct link to approval or disapproval of homosexuality.

*Chapter 11   The Mis-Education About Ten Words
Used Against Homosexuality*

10. SINNER

Quotes of Judgment
*"Living like that is a sin unto God.
You ought to be ashamed of yourself."*

The most dangerous and abusive people with the word sin are those who forget their own sins "Refusing to Love Unconditionally." They have created more havoc in people's lives than anyone in the church. They often began a conversation with

The Lord told me!
The Lord spoke to me!
The Lord gave me a word for you!

These moral midgets and bible scripture quoting fanatics, have no compassion for anyone who does not believe what they believe. They have no right to ever accuse you of living a sinful life.

"Love the sinner, hate the sin" is not a bible scripture, but just a cute little church saying that lets Christians get themselves off the hook by "choosing" not to Love. The Bible tells to "love thy neighbor as thyself (Leviticus 19:18, Matthew 22:39, Mark 12:31)." The word sin can be translated "a disobedience to God's will" and God's will is **"love"**.

Christian point of view on sin

The Greek word "sin" in the New Testament translated from Hebrew writing means *hamartia*, which literally means ***"missing the target."*** This word can be linked to the story Noah when Ham, the son of Noah, was cursed by his father. Noah did not have the spiritual authority but the patriarchal position to do what he deemed appropriate.

Both Eastern and Western Christians agree that sin obstructs one from having a relationship with God.

Many Christian groups believe due to the original sin, man has lost any and all capacity to move towards reconciliation with God (Romans 3:23; 6:23; Ephesians 2:1-3); in fact, this inborn sin turns humans away from God and towards themselves and their own desires (Isaiah 53:6).

There is difference of opinion about the origins of sin; several references are taken from Ezekiel 28:1-19 "Fall of the Prince of Tyrus," sin originated with Satan when he desired the position belonging to God (Ezekiel 28:6-9). These are debatable points but known have been proven.

The religious community has different ideas of sin

✓ **Forgivable sin** is a smaller sin and ("temporary loss of grace") will not result in a total disconnection from God and everlasting life in Hell.

✓ **Human sin** – in some religious groups a human sin is a sin that, unless you come clean and are forgiven, condemns a person's soul to Hell after death.

✓ **Original sin** – A majority of the Christianity groups understand the Garden of Eden story in The Book of Genesis (2:4-3:24) as language about the fall of man. Adam and Eve's breaking of the rules was the original sin man committed, and their *original sin* was passed on to their descendants

✓ **Lustful sin** - A strong desire many religious groups linked to sexual desire

Chapter 11   The Mis-Education About Ten Words Used Against Homosexuality

✓ **Unforgivable sin** is perhaps the most divisive sin, when someone has become a renegade (i.e. questioning the bible, biblical scholars, and God's instinct); the exact temperament of this sin is frequently unclear. (Matthew 12:31-37)

When you review the definitions of this word, you will see people measure sins from least to the greatest. The Bible says that no sin is least or greater than thee. In the John 8:1-11, (get your Bible out) Jesus shares with us the story of the woman who was about to be stoned by the townspeople.

"He that is without sin amongst you, let him first cast the stone at her" (John 8:7)

When Jesus lifted his head he saw none but the woman. (John 8:11)

There are people, not just religious folk, who have accused you of something, but they forget their own stuff.

Many of you have had the unfortunate experience of your parent's choosing to use this negative verbiage because of your Same Gender Loving relationships. It is not normal to have your parents accuse you of not being in line with God's Love.

I encourage you to love them back and keeping love them as Christ also loves you. If you are still holding on to the negative images that you are a sin…Let these scriptures **meditate on your heart.**

For when we were yet without strength, in due time Christ died for the ungodly. For scarcely for a righteous man will one die; yet peradventure for a good man some would even dare to die. But God

commanded his love toward us, in that, while we were yet sinners, Christ died for us.
(Romans 5:6-8)

For the wages of sin is death; but the gift of God is eternal life through Jesus Christ our Lord (Romans 6:23)

I truly hope this reading was helpful for you as it was for me. My goal was to provide you some of the information. The chapter is a book within itself.

CHAPTER 12
The Mis-Education of Bible Topics About Homosexuality

12.1   The Mis-Education About Cross Dressing

12.2   The Mis-Education About AIDS

12.3   The Mis-Education About Temple Homosexuality

12.4   The Mis-Education About Temple Prostitutes

12.5   The Mis-Education About Satan

12.6   The Mis-Education About Job & Satan

12.7   The Mis-Education About Punishment

12.8   The Mis-Education About Gay Clergy

12.9   The Mis-Education About Women Silent

12.10 The Mis-Education About Lust

12.11 The Mis-Education From A TV Evangelist

12.12 The Mis-Education About Sodom & Gomorrah

12.13 The Mis-Education About Destruction

12.14 The Mis-Education About Eunuchs

12.15 The Mis-Education of Homosexuality & Rape

12.16 The Mis-Education of Going After Strange Flesh

12.1
The Mis-Education About Cross Dressing

Topic: Cross Dressers
Text: Deuteronomy 22:5
Subject: *The woman shall not wear that which pertaineth unto a man, neither shall a man put on a woman's garment: for all that do so are abomination unto the LORD thy God.*

Cross Dressing has existed during the biblical period and thru out history. Thou many were not empowered to write about their life experiences and written records have been destroyed or take possession of entities who have decided this knowledge should not be shared with the general public..

The beauty of this text is behind the pages, when utilizing your bible almanacs. The book of Deuteronomy emphasis is on the common person instead of the priests as in the book of Leviticus. In many religious circles the book of Deuteronomy is a variation and development of much of the new laws from the book of Leviticus given to Moses at Mount Sinai. The book of Deuteronomy is the book of the second law and Leviticus the book of the first law.

In Deuteronomy 22:5 is our first glimpse at what could be considered cross dressing or transvestites. It would not be very helpful for you, if I attempt to explain this point of view under the assumption you understand the differences in Trans-terminologies. So here is a real crash course.

Transvestism (also called **transvestitism**) is the practice of **cross-dressing,** which is wearing the clothing of the opposite sex. **Transvestite** refers to a person who cross-dresses; however, the word often has additional connotations.

*Chapter 12   The Mis-Education of Bible Topics
Used Against Homosexuality*

Transgender is the state of one's "gender identity" (self-identification as woman, man, or neither) not matching one's "assigned sex" (identification by others as male or female based on physical/genetic sex). "Transgender" does not imply any specific form of sexual orientation; transgender people may identify as heterosexual, homosexual, bisexual, pansexual, polysexual, or asexual.

Transsexual people identify as, or desire to live and be accepted as, a member of the sex opposite to that assigned at birth. The term *transman* refers to female to- male (FtM or F2M) transgender people, and *transwoman* refers to male-to-female (MtF or M2F) transgender people, although some transgender people identify only slightly with the gender not assigned at birth.

Transvestitism existed during this biblical period and thru out history. Thou many were not empowered to write about their life experiences and written records have been destroyed or take possession of entities who have decided this knowledge should not be shared with the general public.

The beauty of this text is behind the pages when utilizing our bible almanacs. The book of Deuteronomy emphasis is on the common person instead of the priests as in the book of Leviticus. In many religious circles the book of Deuteronomy is a variation and development of much of the new laws from the book of Leviticus given to Moses at Mount Sinai. The book of Deuteronomy is the book of the second law and Leviticus the book of the first law.

We discover in our research there was not much spoken about the apparel worn by women, mainly because there appears to be only minimal differences between what men and women wore during this biblical period. Veils were a major difference and some of the clothes may have been more colorful, and some pictures indicate finer sandals on the feet of some ladies. Women wore the five basic garments as men. But if the distinctions between male and female apparel were subtle, they were nonetheless real.

The materials used to make clothing can be divided into two groups: animal and vegetable. The animal materials were mostly wool taken from sheep and goats. Hides and some camel hair also were used. Silk was also used, but because it was brought form the Far East, it was usually too expensive for all but the wealthy. Colorful clothing was possible because of the many dyes ancient people developed. Crimson came from insects, pink from pomegranate, yellow from the saffron crocus, to name a few.

This verse is a reminder of how much transvestite history as been lost and/or not recorded or destroyed. We must document the history of our Kulture past, present and future.

12.2
The Mis-Education About AIDS

Topic: Law of acceptance into the congregation
Text: Deuteronomy 23:4-6, 17-23
Subject: Religious groups used this text to rationalize why AIDS was punishment for the sin against God.

Our Christian sisters and brothers have used this text rationalizing the reason why we have AIDS today. In many Christian Churches the translation of homosexual is evil and God created AIDS as a curse and it is a blessing from God. This position has allowed them to ostracize gay men with AIDS but comfortably embrace women with AIDS because it was not the woman's fault. AIDS kills more heterosexuals than homosexuals. This disease has caused more than over four million children to be displaced to orphanages and homeless shelters.

We know today AIDS was a man made disease and was around before the public announcement in 1981. Diseases like AIDS are rooted in someone's hatred for a group of people and as shown above many have been by this disease.

The person living with AIDS did not commit an unloving act but society has created unhealthy environments, negative stigmas, lack of resources and political separation. We cannot repeat these atrocities against our own community.

Where would people get such much guided information about a disease? Who would teach unloving thoughts to parents about their children?

In the book of Job *(pronounced, Joab)* (review F) many in the religious community during the early years of AIDS used this Hebrew poetical writing as an example of why we have this disease. In other words Job is not a true story it is only poetry but many died hating themselves because biblical teachers and church goers taught and thought it of it as being real.

Job takes ill, loses his credibility and wealth because of a conversation between God and Satan *(remember this is poetry, not a true story)*. Know Job was a good and righteous man. The Hebrew poet illustrates for us Satan approached God and stress he could make Job curse him, if God would let him get a hold of Job's life.

Job is visited by four friends who are learned men of God. They all accused him of committing a great sin because they were taught you do not go through a series of challenges unless God is not pleased with you. Job allows their point of view to wear him down and eventually he succumbs to the notion that he must have committed a sin and was worthy of God's punishment. *(Sounds familiar)*

In the Book of Job 38-41, the Hebrew poet gives a strong and lengthy illustration of God getting angry with Job about questioning the power of God. In Job 42:1-6, he repents *(change of heart and mind)* and God redeems all that Job has lost.

The story of Job reflects how there are life experiences that will occur and you will not have any control them; you may experience the ripple effects linked to someone else problems, desires, unloving ways, wounded heart, manipulating spirit.

Evaluate within yourself how, when and where you have let others come between you and the relationship with the God of Your Understanding.

*Chapter 12 The Mis-Education of Bible Topics
Used Against Homosexuality*

The power of inner healing is not just about taking away the medical challenges. The power of inner healing is embracing the unconditional presence of God in your life. This can be achieved by renewing and reaffirming the purpose for you as an individual and what you have been called to do for God. This does not necessarily mean you must become an AIDS activist. Your renewed or reaffirmed spirit might conclude its time to complete:

1. Your education
2. Starting a new career,
3. Establish a business enterprise,
4. Start giving back to the AIDS Organizations that help you or one of your friends.
5. Educating others about AIDS or being a buddy to those recently diagnosed HIV/AIDS.

God loves you just the way you are. You are not a mistake or error and never have you been a mistake or error in the eyes of God. The mis-education about who you are comes from misguided teachings not God.

This scripture has nothing to do with homosexuality.

12.3
The Mis-Education About Temple Homosexuality

Topic: Sin of King Rehoboam
Text: 1Kings 14:21-24
Subject: Sodomites were known as people who practiced sex in the temples male and female and they were also pagan worshippers (idols and images)

During these biblical periods same sex attraction was common in many cultures. We discover in the story our primary character King Jeroboam's goal was to find fault and an excuse to question the character of King Rehoboam in an attempt to gain more respect and power.

Now "homosexuality" is not the issue it is someone trying to find a platform to get there name out in public view. Because King Rehoboam did not stop the homosexual activity King Jeroboam used it as a political issue (Sounds familiar). Homosexuality thru out time has always been a hot button issue and people keep pushing it.

The historical account in Deuteronomy found it necessary to warn Jewish males and females to avoid participation, but shrines which used by males prostitutes became part of Jewish life during the time of Rehoboam (1Kings 14:24) and had begun to be eradicated by King Asa (1King 15:12).

These homosexual males were not finally removed until King Jehoshaphat (1Kings 22:46).

However the corruption reappeared during the time of Josiah. King Rehoboam was the son of Solomon and successor to the throne. He was considered to be hard, brittle and not competent enough to take good advice. His reign was constantly threatened by civil war, and the internal confusion created by his own poor management of the nation.

In Rehoboam's time cult male prostitution was tolerated as well the cultural "abominations" brought into the country by Solomon's 300 wives and 800 concubines (mistresses). King Rehoboam failure to address the issue and complaints of these various cultures into a traditional system by Jeroboam ended up dividing the kingdom.

What is important to note Jeroboam was angry with Rehoboam over not just the male prostitute issue but a host of other issues primarily more so about power. Jeroboam decided he wanted complete separation from Israel. He made calves of gold at the places of Bethel and Dan as a means of breaking the custom of the people going to Jerusalem for worship.

Desodomizing the mind is an imperative step to developing healthy decision making of yourself and how you are perceive others in this Kulture (LBGT/SGL community).

Desodomization is the deconstruction of the negative images about your sexuality and reconstruction of your thoughts about your sexuality with positive and affirming images.

What makes your sexuality dirty is because you have put in the gutter. Coming out to be sexually free is not coming out. Coming out and being mentally free is truly being out.

Desodomization begins with a question for the individual or groups with the purpose of seeking enlightenment that empowers and natures their consciousness.

The pursuit for enlightenment is not about right or wrong. It is about addressing issues from a healthy or unhealthy perspective of oneself, partners, neighbors, authority, institutions and various social networks (i.e. houses, chat rooms).

Deconstructing the traditional teachings and establishing a more critical way of reviewing and managing our religious challenges; in concert with implementing healthy models to empower the mind, body, and soul.

This is a poor attempt to link an ancient custom directly to traditional homosexuality. Homosexuality is not about prostitution. Prostitution is a survival skill.

12.4.
The Mis-Education About Temple Prostitutes

Topic: Temple Prostitutes
Text: 1Kings 15:9-15
Subject: Temple prostitutes (male and female) who worshipped idol Gods. This was in conflict Christians and Jewish beliefs.

As you will learn in many of the traditions "Eros" *(see Chapter 10 Love In The Bible)* was associated with many religious practices. In modern day society the religious communities have created the image of male prostitutes having sex in the temple to bear a likeness to the LBGT/SGL persons who love the Lord.

In the biblical account the King of Judah. He was known as one of the few Kings considered to be "right in the eyes of the Lord." This recognition was given to him by his "peers" not God. He was credited with having removed all idols and male prostitution from the Kingdom of Judah. In the biblical story *(1Kings 15:16-24)* he was in constant battle with other Kings. In the second year of his death, Nadab, son of Jehoshaphat, began to reign and the biblical historians tell us he repeated the behaviors of his father by serving idol images.

If you are having sex inside of the church at the altar, get some help, Boo.

This is about pagan worship rituals, not about homosexuality.

12.5
The Mis-Education About Satan

Topic: Temptation of David by Satan
Text: 1Chronicles 21:1-4
Subject: The first time the word Satan is used in the King James Version of the Bible.

In the King James Version of the bible this is the first time you will find the word "Satan" mentioned in the bible. Historically the Christian church teaches this scripture as a concept of how Satan plots against you and tempts you.

The word "Satan" means "adversary" but not always in the context of "evil spirit" but in more of a context of human weakness or challenges with people or situations. In some religious circles "Satan" is associated with "serpent" in the story of Adam & Eve in the Garden of Eden.

When reading and understanding this scripture how can someone get homosexuality out it? You go figure! In many Christian churches almost every time the word evil or Sodom is mentioned it as an automatic association with homosexuality.

It is healthy for us in our Kulture to study the origins of their points of view and it is unhealthy for us to assume they will probably do any homework/research. ***Change Is Mandatory, Growth Is Optional.***

In some of the previous chapters I talk about the walk with Jesus. Even Christ had to change his perception of various cultures. Jesus' original mission was to save the lost sheep of Israel, but he, too, realized and learned he was here to save any who thought they were lost. (Read John 3:16-17 & Luke 15)

This has nothing to do with homosexuality.

12.6.
The Mis-Education About Job & Satan

Topic: The Life of Job (Joab)
Text: Job 1-2
Subject: A Hebrew poet illustrates a story about a conversation between God & Satan. Many new believers start their bibles studies by reading this book first. New believers should start in the New Testament reading the Gospels (Matthew, Mark, Luke & John).

In the book of Job the Hebrew poet writes a powerful image of a conversation between God and Satan. In many religious communities this is taught as a true story but it is an imaginary characterization. In the conversation, Satan approaches God and inquires about Job and seeks God permission to have access to Job. Satan in this illustration suggests to God he can convince Job to "curse him" *(question God's commitment to you)*. The story of Job tells the story of a Child of God who loses every thing—his family, his health, his wealth and struggles with the question, Why me?

The key points the Hebrew poet illustrates:
- ✓ *You belong to God*
- ✓ *God will take care of you.*
- ✓ *God is larger than the problem.*
- ✓ *God wants the best for you.*
- ✓ *God's forgiveness is free for asking.*
- ✓ *Seek God for yourself not the approval of others.*

The book is from a group of biblical poetical writings (Psalms, Proverbs, Ecclesiastes, and Song of Solomon) they characterizes the human imagination, real life experience, peoples struggles with real and profound problems. The single most important fact necessary to understanding Biblical poetry is the idea of parallelism. Biblical poetry has neither sound parallelism (rhyme) nor strict time parallelism (rhythm). Biblical poetry uses parallelism of ideas or thoughts.

In the poetical writing Job is visited by three religious friends Eliphaz, Bildad, Zophar, and Elihu seeking to be sympathetic but was very critical.

✓ Eliphaz represented the man of science. He argued from experience and from facts. He satisfied himself that Job was a "secret sinner".

✓ Bildad's arguments were based on tradition. His address was shorter and his language was rougher.

✓ Zophar was a moralist. He believed in salvation by self-merit and endeavored to prove Job's calamities were the result of his sins of omission (i.e. error, faults, mistake, and miscalculations).

✓ Elihu presented the wisdom and the power of God. He was young and inexperienced but his youth did not permit him to join in the debate but learned that wisdom is not necessarily the possession of seniors and scholars. Elihu argued that affliction could have educative value, and that God had ultimate good in store for the sufferer. He pointed out that there was no moral difference between Job and his three accusers – that all were sinners and alike needed a Savior. He thus disclosed the foundation teachings of the New Testament.

As the poet illustrates in Chapter one, neither of the educated men was present when God and Satan were having this conversation about Job. The poet also demonstrates neither of the men received a revelation from God to be shared with Job. These religious men were instructing and judging him with the trained knowledge if you are having bad times, you must not be living right. The poet clearly illustrates they were all wrong about their sin judgment.

Job over a period of time during the trials begins to believe he must to have committed a sin for all this to be happening to him. Job curses *(questions God commitment to you)* God by questioning the committed relationship between him and God. In the chapters 38-41 the poet illustrates, God gets angry with Job and bring under control him with a series of questions. Job has fallen victim to placing his faith in man, in life circumstances, in people's perceptions of him and his wealth and not in God.

In the church today many in our Kulture (LBGT/SGL) believe God does not love them and their life is sin.

This biblical poetry has nothing to do with homosexuality.

12.7.
The Mis-Education About Punishment

Topic: Gods Punishment
Text: Ezekiel 16:49-50
Subject: This is not about homosexuality but a visual illustration of God's anger with Israel by Ezekiel

> *49Behold, this was the iniquity of thy sister Sodom, pride, fullness of bread, and abundance of idleness was in her and in her daughters, neither did she strengthen the hand of the poor and needy. 50And they were haughty, and committed abomination before me: therefore I took them away as I saw good.(Ezekiel 16:49-50)*

Remember Chapter 3 of Sodom & Gomorrah we talked about the trigger words. Every time someone sees homosexuality in the bible they automatically assume it is about homosexuality. This bible scripture is not directly related to homosexuality.

Ezekiel is giving an illustration of God's point of view. The writers refer to the nation in a feminine outline. The writer tells us God first came across Israel as an abandoned baby, unwashed and unloved (Ezekiel 16:4-6). He blessed her with life and, when she came of age and beauty, made a marriage covenant with her (Ezekiel 16:7-8), see the visual image he is creating. He continues to talk about the covenant at Mount Sinai when God gave Israel his law. God was adoring, considerate and a generous husband who shared his splendor with her (Ezekiel 16:9-14).

Ezekiel, a priest and a prophet, ministers during the darkest days of Judah's history. He utilizes prophesies, parables, signs, and symbols to dramatize God's message to His exiled people.

But Israel devoted her beauty and blessings to other lovers – the neighboring nations and their pagan idols (Ezekiel 16:15-19). She sacrificed her own children to these gods, and forgot all that the true God had done for her (Ezekiel 16:20-22). She gave herself over to sacrificing her children over the fires—political alliances and mingling of fights – with Egypt, Philistia, Assyria and Babylon. And yet Israel wasn't a whore, because she paid her lovers for the privilege of their alliances.

Now God is going to expose Israel's shame and turn her lovers into enemies (Ezekiel 16:35-39). She will be destroyed by them as God's judgment on her unfaithfulness (Ezekiel 16:40-43). There is strand of paganism and immorality in Israel which comes from her Hittite origins (Ezekiel 16:44-46). Her sisters are Samaria and Sodom, who are proud and pagan enough—but Israel is worse than either of them (Ezekiel 16:44-52).

God promises to restore Sodom and Samaria – and Israel along with them (Ezekiel 16:53-58). God will punish Israel by breaking his covenant with her and allowing her to be defeated and exiled; but afterwards he will renew his commitment to her and forgive all she has done (Ezekiel 16:59-63)

Not everyone participated in the pagan worship, but everyone would have been aware of its presence.

Repeatedly, Godly kings would call for reform and purge out most of the fertility cults (1Kings 15:12, 22:46; 2Kings 23:7), but without any permanent effect.

Ezekiel has created a visual picture in this story referencing Sodom but it is not a commandment of God but a frustration he has with the direction Israel is taking.

There must have been an awful lot of homosexuals in the kingdoms for the need to eliminate them. Imagine during biblical period how many "down low /in the closet"(street synonyms) folks were around and the homosexual community always ended up resurfacing.

In verses 53-58, Ezekiel makes reference to the Samaritans being the same as the Sodomites. In the parable told by Jesus of the Good Samaritan (Luke 10:30-37), he gives a visual illustration utilizing a despised culture, in which we could conclude Jesus may have been aware of homosexuality in the City of Samaria. Jesus uses this culture of people who is not respected by some religious groups but the culture of people continued to do acts of kindness, when others refused to show their culture unconditional love.

If we are going to walk with Christ it is important we demonstrate God's love to one another even when it is not popular. That what Jesus would do.

This has nothing directly to do with homosexuality.

12.8
The Mis-Education About Gay Clergy

Topic: Gay Clergy (False Teachers)
Text: 1Timothy 1:7-10
Subject: The issue is false teachers with goal is to turn people away from a life with Christ

In this Kulture (LBGT/SGL) our new progressive thinkers will come out of the seminaries as openly and affirming same gender loving, out the bars, the hood, jail houses. These teachers will reveal what many bible scholars, prominent pastors and TV Evangelist will not comprehend.

It is important we respect the opinions of our own within our communities. This is when we as a people will see a real inclusive progress that is reflective of all of our life experiences and worship cultures.

In Second Timothy, he has been was assigned to deal with hard line religious thinkers; who saw from their point of view only and were not open to any new perspectives. Paul writes in the Second Timothy 3:16-17

> *All scripture is given by inspiration of God, and profitable for doctrine, for reproof, for correction, for instruction in righteousness: That the Child of God may be perfect, thoroughly furnished unto all good works.*

Apostle Paul, the elderly and knowledgeable messenger, writes to the youthful minister Timothy who is up against an intense responsibility within the church at Ephesus. Timothy is the son of a converted Jew (Eunice) and has a Greek father and this presents many problems with the religious community.

This was considered an "inter-racial relationship" which was not supported in many of the religious circles during this ancient time. In our communities today people still frown upon it. Paul was a strategist to his heart so to counteract if they were to find out Timothy's father was Greek; Paul had him submit to circumcision.

In the book of First Timothy, Paul reminds his readers that Timothy is authorized to act on his behalf. In addition, Paul is instructing the church about being careful of continuous bible babbling.

In the text First Timothy 1:10, there is much conflict with the wording of homosexuality. In various bibles, the verses take different translations (i.e. fornicator, homosexual). The reference to homosexuality is greatly debated in many religious circles but our challenge has been mostly Christian Fundamentalists have been the primary bible publishers. See the illustration below how different groups translate the reference scripture.

10 For whoremongers, for them that defile themselves with mankind, for men stealers, for liars, for perjured persons, and if there be any other thing that is contrary to sound doctrine
(1Tim 1:7-10)

See illustration

*Chapter 12   The Mis-Education of Bible Topics
Used Against Homosexuality*

1Timothy 1:10 Bible Comparison	
✓ For them that defile themselves with mankind (King James Version)	✓ These laws are for people who are sexually immoral, for homosexuals (New Living Translation)
✓ For adulterers and perverts (New International Version)	✓ Immoral men and homosexuals (New American Standard Bible)
✓ And immoral men and homosexuals and kidnappers and liars and perjurers, and whatever else is contrary to sound teaching, (New American Standard Bible)	✓ [For] impure and immoral persons, those who abuse themselves with men (Amplified Bible)

Charts & Figures 12.1

What the text will not tell you if read without any supporting information. During this period slave trade was growing, women and children (boys & girls) were often kidnapped and made to be prostitutes. There is deeper underlying message in the scripture about the importance of freedom and people who are victims of greed.

Paul and his scribes were attempting to address many devout religious believers. It would be safe to say this was typical political environment. *(biblical politics aka "ecumenical politics" are similar to traditional politics probably more vicious.* This was list of issues addressed to inform people of their ecumenical and social political positions.

In was customary for the letters addressed to the leadership to be read out loud and shared with the community. Paul letters always had an ecumenical agenda (church politics) with a spiritual covering.

Most dominant religions and the philosophers condemned empty, worthless talk, including arguments about words and the verbal skills of wordy rhetoricians unconcerned with the pursuit of truth. The Gospels reveal to us Jesus challenged with those who were publicly recognized as teachers of the law.

The writings leave much for interpretation but you determine what it means to you. Read the scriptures through the eyes of love and the revelations will jump out and grab you.

Our Kultural clergy (i.e. LBGT/SGL) have a daunting task to study and teach about an open relationship with Jesus Christ. They are called to the lost sheep of our community. This group has received criticism from all sides.

- ✓ LBGT/SGL has questioned them
- ✓ Christian church has rejected them
- ✓ Family has denied them
- ✓ Friends will not support them

You have to really love the Lord when so many forces are trying to distract you from sharing the Teachings of Jesus Christ. This is a special breed of individuals.

*Chapter 12   The Mis-Education of Bible Topics
Used Against Homosexuality*

Their major challenges will be embracing a diverse culture of worship styles and refraining from rebuilding or mimicking the oppressive systems they were trained in.

The church historically has become one of the most racist, sexist, homophobic institutions in the world. We are called to interweave various racial, gender and socio economic groups into a worship life enhancing experience. It is okay to have a faith center and different services to accommodate the worship styles. If you have a congregation that is 75% Caucasian and 25% Latino; it is healthy for church to offer alternatives to the minority groups if they feel the need.

It is dangerous to compare yourself to another church. Just because something works across the street does not mean it will work at your church.

We must refrain from repeating the limited perception of Jesus Christ the same way the traditional Christian church does with their perception of our lifestyle. No worship style is the "Holy Grail." It is important for you seek out a worship center that embraces all of you Mind, Body, Spirit and yes that includes your sexuality. Our community has a need for a new breed of teachers, preachers and administrators.

This scripture has nothing to do with homosexuality.

12.9
The Mis-Education About Women Being Silent

Topic: Women to be silent
Text: 1Cor 14:34-35, 1Timothy 2:11-12, 1Peter 2:15
Subject: The issue is false teachers with a goal to turn people away from a life with Christ

> *Let your women keep silence in the churches;*
> *for it is not permitted unto them to speak;*
> *but they are commanded to be under obedience,*
> *as also saith the law.*
> *And if they will learn any thing,*
> *let them ask their husbands at home:*
> *for it is a shame for women to speak in the church*
> *(1Corinthians 14:34-35)*

Why is this important to Lesbians? The same sista-z that have been oppressed in the traditional church themselves will attempt to oppress you. Learn your bible and help others see the aweness in God. Oh yes, many sista-z in the Christian Church are struggling with their sexuality and you might be the one to help guide them towards a healthier understanding of God's unconditional love.

I love the work of the sista-z in the Unity Fellowship of Christ and Metropolitan Community Church movement. They are smart, strong, beautiful and in control of their destiny. Same Gender Loving women must cross the lines of gay ministries by building a sisterhood that insures the wellbeing of other sista-z.

I question biblical authority figures who rationalize that certain people should or should not teach the gospel. Women

*Chapter 12   The Mis-Education of Bible Topics
Used Against Homosexuality*

are wonderful teachers on any subject they put their minds to. In the Progressive National Baptist Movement a majority of the churches will not let a woman sit in the pulpits. The Roman Catholic Church has yet to ordain women Cardinals and it continues to be a male dominated society.

Women during this biblical period became a political issue. Women played a significant role as the infant churches struggled to stand. It was not a man's church, though most of the official leadership was male. Ladies such as Lydia accepted the Good News eagerly (Acts 16:14-40). Priscilla played an important part of teaching such Apostles as Apollo's (Acts 18:24).

Many women aided in the ministry of Jesus Christ as evidenced by the fact that Paul paid homage to eight women in the closing chapter of Romans. Women worked as deaconesses and the four daughters of Philip acted as prophetesses (Acts 21:9). We do not know the context of their prophecies, but they certainly were messages from God.

There are, of course, some unresolved difficulties in the New Testament concerning the role of women. In his letter to the Corinthian, Paul tells women to keep silence in the church (1Cor. 14:33-36). They are also prohibited from taking positions of authority over men or teaching them.

*Let the woman learn in silence with all subjection.
But I suffer not a woman to teach,
nor to usurp authority over the man,
but to be in silence.*
(1Timothy 2:11-12)

Paul is a strategist whose ecumenical political skills were superior to many of his colleagues and he understood the political climate during this time. Women were becoming very vocal in the church but the learned men continued to see women as subservient. Although they were supposed to be learned men of God, they were really *"sexist learned men of God."*

Our lesbian's sista-z must be mindful of men trained in historical sexist environments and call the questions when they are in doubt. Just because he is out and gay does not remove him from being a sexist.

I know of this gay male clergy who is challenged with having a lesbian Bishop as his overseer but no one calls the question. When he needs advice he calls his male Bishops and tolerates the opinions of the female Bishops and challenges her every move.

The more church antics we bring from these oppressive hierarchical systems the more of this behavioral stuff will come with it. The brotha-z need the sista-z and the sista-z need the brotha-z.

This scripture has nothing to do with homosexuality.

12.10
The Mis-Education About Lust

Topic: The Source of Temptations: Lust
Text: James 1:14-15, James 4:2-6
Subject: *You Be The Judge*: Lust for Sex vs. Lust for Money

But every man is tempted,
when is drawn away of his own lust, and enticed.
Then when lust hath conceived it bringeth forth
sin; and sin, when it is finished, bringeth forth
death

(James 1:14-15)

The word lust has several translations; the most often known meaning is associated with sexual thoughts and actions.

In these scriptures the translations are known in Greek as "epithemuo"

to turn upon a thing; to have a desire for,
long for, to desire; to lust after, covet

The reading is associated with the long desires for financial riches and power at any cost

If someone is reading the scripture without understanding the information behind the pages, it could be used in error. This is not saying a person should not aspire for financial riches.

It is illustrating if your desires take your attention away from your God, then you are lusting after something ahead your God.

Theologian John Calvin once said;

"Make all you can, Save all you can, Give away all you can."

> Jesus says, *"No man can serve two masters: for either he will hate the one, and love the other; or else he will hold (be loyal) to the one, and despise the other. Ye cannot serve God and mammon (riches)"*
>
> *(Matthew 6:24)*

> *But seek ye first the kingdom of God, and his righteousness; and all these things shall be added unto you.*
> *(Matthew 6:33)*

Unquestionably James is one of the most down-to-earth books in the New Testament. The writer's main focus is faith and dealing with everyday affairs, covering such matters as a persons dialogue, business ventures, the respect of persons, disagreements between Christian brethren, relations between employers and employees, and a number of other things.

The word temptation in the writings is a reference to the outward pressures which bear hard upon the Christian community. It illustrates that temptations are there by God's permission, designed to test our faith and have a promise of reward. There's also sexual temptation that arises from within; James interprets it is the result of man's own nature but it does not come from God (James 1:13).

> *Let no man say when he is tempted, I am tempted of God: for God cannot be tempted with evil, neither tempted he any man* *(James 1:13)*

James' focus is (lust) materialism because many people are challenged with lustful desires and this leads to the pursuit of erotic love (Eros). They pursue the flesh more than developing a relationship with God. The Christian Church will redirect this biblical account with homosexuality.

Jesus is not talking about sexual desires but seeking a relationship with him. Your sexual desires are not God but things you have acquired. Understand sexual desires for the same sex and sex escapades are two different issues.

Sexual Escapades are venturing to express your sexual desires (i.e. online sites, bars, clubs, parks, parties)

The truth seeking journey for you is learning to understand
1. Who do you need to disempower in your thoughts to have an open and honest relationship with God?
2. Why do you love they way you do?
3. If you are uncomfortable with your sexual desires for the same sex. Seek out someone who can assist you in understanding and addressing your challenges.
4. Does your sexual escapades leave you feeling with shame, guilt or somewhat embarrassed? Why and what do you do with those feelings?

This scripture has nothing to do with homosexuality.

12.11
The Mis-Education From A TV Evangelist

Topic: Unfeigned Love
Text: 1Peter 1:22-25
Subject: Love One Another

This is funny. I was watching one TV Evangelists on the Trinity Broadcast Network (yes, I do watch it) and he said *"the book of 1Peter talks about homosexuals and their unfeigned love of the brethren"* and I almost fell out my chair. This is always a problem; people just talk to us any kind of way. They took the verse out its entire context and shared it with millions of viewers to be repeated over and over again.

In 1 Peter 1:22-25 the scripture is Loving One Another and word "unfeigned' means" "sincere".

King James Version
Seeing ye have purified your souls in obeying the truth through the Spirit unto unfeigned love of the brethren, see that ye love one another with a pure heart fervently:

New International Version
Now that you have purified yourselves by obeying the truth so that you have sincere love for your brothers, love one another deeply, from the heart.

Webster's Dictionary
unfeigned - not pretended; sincerely felt or expressed; "genuine emotion"; "her interest in people was unfeigned"; "true grief"
Feigned - insincere – lacking sincerity

We are challenged with Christian bible teachers and readers who misinterpret words and then just run with it. The

*Chapter 12   The Mis-Education of Bible Topics
Used Against Homosexuality*

end result is they end up wounding people with scriptures. Read the text and it will bless you.

You must be careful of using mainstream media as your source of information. Just because someone is on the radio broadcast, television show or a flashy web presence does not make them an authority on a subject matter.

This has nothing to do with homosexuality.

12.12
The Mis-Education of Sodom & Gomorrah

Topic: And turning the cities of Sodom & Gomorrah into ashes
Text: 2Peter 2:6
Subject: The scriptures focus is about false teachers.

> *And turning the cities of Sodom and Gomorrah into ashes condemned them with an overthrow, making them an ensample unto those that after should live ungodly*
>
> *(2Peter 2:6)*

In the bible many writers would use Sodom as an example of destruction on the basis of God's disapproval of people's action. This has resulted in many linking the word Sodom to homosexuality.

Jewish teachers during this time often coupled Sodom with the flood generation as summary to the written works of wickedness; the Old Testament prophets also use Sodom repeatedly as an image of an alternative scene.

It is very important to note, Jesus never killed anyone, but people continue to preach a character of Jesus as one who punishes his believers:

> *For God so love the world, that he gave his only begotten Son, that whosoever believes in him should not perish, but have everlasting life. For God sent not his Son into the world to condemn the world; but that the world through him might be saved (John 3:16-17).*

In the religious community today these types of scriptures are used against our LBGT/SGL ministries who chose to teach the love of Jesus Christ. These ministries are not encouraging us to separate from Christ. Their mission is to guide you to a life with Jesus Christ.

In Second Peter 2:6, the writer illustrates about the concern with false teachers in the church. These teachers were claiming new insights and experiences which, they say, put them on a higher spiritual level than other people and the teachings of Jesus Christ was not necessary to reach a heavenly place or space in their life.

There were groups known as "Gnostics" who claimed to have secret information on the ways to heaven. The Greek word gnosis which means *"knowledge"* is often used in Greek philosophy in a manner more consistent with the English word of *"enlightenment"*.

Gnostic philosophy and religious movements began in pre-Christian times. During this time, ideas from Greek Gnosticism intermingled with Early Christianity. The name "Christian Gnostics" came to represent a segment of the Early Christian community who believed that salvation was not in merely worshipping Christ, but in psychic or pneumatic souls learning to free themselves from the material world via the revelation.

I have seen our LBGT/SGL ministries deeply divided over the various belief systems we come to accept and incorporate in our worship services. We must always keep in mind we are all teachers of Gods unconditional love.

You will repeat master's *"my-way-or-the-highway"* mentality if you are committed to just your way of worship, teaching, and outreaching. Our community has a very rich and diverse make up with many traditions and worship attitudes.

No worship style is the law it is only what you have been taught.

This has nothing to do with homosexuality.

12.13
The Mis-Education About Destruction

Topic: Sodom in written words of destruction
Text: Revelations 11:8
Subject: *And their dead bodies shall lie in the street of the great city, which spiritually is called Sodom and Egypt, where also our Lord was crucified.*

In the Christian church, whenever they see the word Sodom, they automatically link it to homosexuality. Many of the biblical writers used Sodom as a visual illustration of destruction not as a focus on homosexuality.

The devil after all these years has been driving you crazy but Revelations 20:10 says, he was thrown in the pit he designed for everyone else.

> *And the devil that deceived them was cast into the lake of fire and brimstone, where the beast and the false prophet are, and shall be tormented day and night for ever and ever. (Rev. 20:10)*

People will slander your name, curse your efforts and cause you mental frustration, but in reality they never get away with it, because they create their own internal hell within their heart. Jesus says pray for those who persecute you and falsely accuse you (Matthew 5:44).

*Chapter 12   The Mis-Education of Bible Topics
Used Against Homosexuality*

As much as I would love to expound on the book of Revelations, I would recommend you be very careful reading this book. Historically, many Christian

Denominations use this book to bring people to Christ with the fear Christ will not receive them and they are out of the will of God.

In many academic circles there is much debate about who was the writer of this book but it was definitely not Jesus, even though in the King James Version, it uses the red writing as recognizing when Jesus is speaking.

The title means "unveiling" or "disclosure." It is the story John, The Divine, during his exile on the island of Patmos. He was sentenced to the island by Nero Caesar because he would not stop spreading the gospel of Jesus Christ.

Revelations centers on visions and symbols of the resurrected Christ, who alone has authority to judge the earth, to remake it, and to rule it in righteousness. There are many well-known symbols generated from the book, the most notable are:

1. There were seven letters sent to designated city churches.
(Rev. 2-3)

2. The one white horse carried a bow and wore a crown was to conquer, one red horse carried a sword and was to take peace from the earth, one black horse carried a balance and was to produce famine conditions and one pale horse followed death by hell and was to kill by sword, famine, death and wild beasts.   (Rev. 6:1-8)

3. Only 144,000 believers per the bible shall be caught up in the rapture when Jesus returns. (Rev.7:1-8, 14:1-13)

4. The mark of beast "666" in which during this time numbers were used as a coding system and the numbers "666' was a translations meaning "Nero Caesar". In a majority of Christian churches it is believed the mark of the beast will be left on the foreheads of non- Christians after the Second Coming of Christ.   (Rev 13:18)

In Revelations 11: 8, the reference is made about Sodom from the images of a dream. It would be vain of me to attempt to interpret someone else's dream when I can't interpret most of my own dreams.

Many of the writers used Sodom as a visual illustration of destruction not as a focus on homosexuality.

This reference to Sodom has nothing to do with homosexuality.

*Chapter 12   The Mis-Education of Bible Topics
Used Against Homosexuality*

12.14 The Mis-Education of Eunuchs

Topic: Some are chosen as Eunuchs, born Eunuchs, die as Eunuchs
Text: Daniel 1:9, Acts 8:26-38
Scripture Reference: *Now God had brought Daniel into favour and tender love with the prince of the eunuchs.*

A eunuch received the right to worship but could not change who they were. There were eunuchs who were born that way and there were eunuchs who became that way; but the religious community believed they could have a limited relationship with God.

During this biblical period eunuchs, served various roles. Many were assigned to oversee the ruler's court, and were often given positions as trusted officials. A eunuch has come to be known by many as a man who was not very masculine in the courts of the ancient rulers.

In the Bible, you will find three common types of Eunuchs: (1) House Servant (2) High Ranking Official (3) Guard

Eunuchs were assigned domestic chores such as making the beds of their ruler, hygiene services *(bathing him, haircuts)*, transporting him in his royal chair. Eunuchs were known to relay private messages and many earned *"their superiors ear"* and were considered to be a trusted confidante of the imperial courts or the primary ruler. The eunuchs were also servants of commanders, and other ranking eunuchs.

The logic in various cultures during this biblical time was, they could not procreate nor had no interest in accumulating wealth because they had no family to inherit their wealth. They would appoint their best candidates to oversee the treasuries, harems and children of the royal families.

The Jewish tradition did not condone making people eunuchs; this was more of an eastern custom. In the Jewish tradition, the idea of causing young males the inability to procreate was a threat to the growth of Israel.

There were eunuchs who earned a high level of respect but they were perceived usually as second-rate citizen. Eunuchs could be replaced or killed with no consequences.

Dr. Daniel A. Helminiak illustrates a healthy critical thought from the book of Daniel and the Eunuch's as follows:

> The book of Daniel offers still another case,
>
> *"Now God allowed Daniel to receive favor and compassion from the palace master." (Daniel 1:9)*
>
> Another translation reads,
>
> *"By the grace of God Daniel met goodwill and sympathy on the part of the chief eunuch."*
>
> This text <u>could</u> also be translated to read that Daniel received "devoted love." Moreover, there is some serious speculation that the servants at court or the "eunuchs" in ancient mid-East were not necessarily castrated men but rather men whose sexual interest was only for other men. For this reason they could be trusted around the harem. So some people <u>suggest</u> that Daniel's role

Chapter 12   The Mis-Education of Bible Topics
Used Against Homosexuality

> in Nebuchadnezzar's court included a homosexual liaison with the palace master. The romantic connection would explain in part why Daniel's career at court advanced so favorably. And, of course, the Bible sees Daniel's success as a blessing of Divine Providence.
>
> "What the Bible Really Says About Homosexuality" by Dr. Daniel A. Helminiak, the Millennium Edition Pg 127

Dr. Helminiak has been thorough in his research. He provides us with key phrasing that even many LGBT/SGL theologians over look the words "could & suggest". This leaves open the discussion of others interpretation. If you are having a conversation and using this as your supposition, then it is healthy for you to have clarity on the writings. Dr. Helminiak's writings have spiritually freed so many and mentally feeds many more.

Phillip & The Eunuch

In Acts 8:26-38, is the story of Phillip and The Eunuch. Phillip heard the a royal eunuch reading outloud and the spirit of the Lord moved upon Phillip to speak with eunuch. During this biblical period, reading out loud was customary practice. When Phillip inquired with the eunuch, the eunuch asked him to explain a passage out of the text.

> and like a lamb dumb (silent) before his shearer, so opened he not his mouth **8:33** in his humiliation his judgment was taken away: and who shall declare his generation? For his life is taken from the earth.

The eunuch had great authority over treasures and people, but he still felt empty inside. The eunuch was taught since childhood he is not worthy of place in the Kingdom of God. The eunuch desired a relationship with Jesus Christ and a deeper understanding the writings. While reading the scriptures, he was able to connect with redemptive nature and love of Jesus Christ.

Phillip guided him with an understanding that coming to Christ just as you are is not complicated. The story tells us the eunuch wanted to be baptized. Phillip came upon a creek filled with water.

> Phillip said,
> *If thou believe with all thy heart, thou mayest And the eunuch answered I believe that Jesus Christ is the Son of God And Phillip took the eunuch down to the creek baptized him in the water. When the Eunuch came out of the water, Phillip was gone.*

The Lord never established an eternal law to put away the eunuchs from His house. Any eunuch, who is willing to obey the Lord's commandments and follow the Lord, will be accepted in the Temple of the Lord; and the Lord says the believing eunuchs can have a special place in the Temple. The Lord promises they will not be forgotten.

This has nothing to do with homosexuality.

12.15
There Is Nothing Spiritual About Being Raped.

Topic: Tribal Immorality
Text: Judges 19:11-30
Subject: *But the men would not hearken to him: so the man took his concubine, and brought her forth unto them; and they knew her, and abused her all the night until the morning: and when the day began to spring, they let her go.*

While in bible study one Wednesday night, I listen to a theologian linking this text to Sodom and Gomorrah. This is so far from the truth. While writing this book in all of my research it appears this is a consensus thought by many scholars but I beg to defer. The only relation between these two stories is that they are both found in Chapter 19.

In the book of Genesis 19 was a potential rape but in Judges 19 it was an actual rape. The angels did not let Lot's daughter be raped but the Levite let his concubine be raped. There are some valuable lessons and social conscious insights we can exegete from the despicable incident.

When you read from Genesis 19 the story of Sodom and Gomorrah, it was about two angels coming into the city looking for ten righteous people that loved the Lord and the citizens wanted to get *"to know them"(have sexual relations).* In Judges 19 the story illustrated was about a Levite man traveling with his concubine looking for a place to rest for the evening and found shelter in the city of Gibeah (Judges 19:15) What is implied here is that no one met the Levite's party along with his concubine as they entered the village, unlike in Genesis 19:1, and they were forced to seek shelter in the city square ("rehob"). The fact that the Levite in Judges 19 is forced to go to the city square demonstrates a basic failure on the part of the citizens of Gibeah to offer him hospitality. This is where the phasing of "hospitality not homosexuality "is appropriate.

The concubine is a secondary wife and was often a foreign prisoner of war but they could also be Israelites, as was probably the case in this story. However, in most cases in which a marriage contract is made with the father of a woman who will be considered a concubine, there is an assumption of a lesser status than a regular wife. Thus the Levite may have simply contracted for a sexual partner, since his social status would ordinarily have required a wife of certain attributes (Leviticus 21:7). This may explain why he was in no hurry to bring his concubine home (Judges 19:2).

A Levite and his party, on their way home from a trip to the concubine's father, are offered lodging by an old man in the town of Gibeah. The house is surrounded by some townsmen who demand that the Levite be brought out to them (Judges 19:22). As he recounts the events later, the Levite understood that they intended to kill him (Judges 20:5). The Levite instead pushes out his concubine, who is gang raped throughout the night (Judges 19:25). She dies on the doorstep in the morning. On returning home, the Levite dismembers her body in order to send its pieces to the tribes of Israel as a bloody call for revenge. The Israelites assemble an army that finally succeeds in killing the inhabitants of Gibeah.

This was nothing spiritual about this experience. The Levite could have saved the concubine if he would have acknowledged her as one of his wives. The tribal violation was these men raped one of their own women. We should never condone rape regardless of what a person social status may be or their rational.

One the most respected Theologians St. Augustine is quite clear that the citizens of Sodom wanted to rape the male angels, In his narrative of the Old Testament history within the City of God, Augustine gives as reason for the destruction of Sodom that it was a place where "debaucheries in men" (stupra in masculos) flourished by custom. That is why Lot tried to offer his daughters instead. Better for men to violate women that to violate other men. *(Augustine De ciuitate Dei 16.30/ Dombart-Kalb 48:535.3-5)*

It is our responsibility to protect every child of God from being raped regardless of our race, gender, social status or religion. There is never any thing spiritual or logical about condoning anyone being raped.

This text has nothing to do with homosexuality.

12.16
The Mis-Education of "Going After Strange Flesh"

Topic: False Teachers
Text: Jude 7
Subject: *Even as Sodom and Gomorrah, and the cities about them in like manner, giving themselves over to fornication (sexual immorality), and going after strange flesh, are set forth for an example, suffering the vengeance (punishment) of eternal fire.*

The scripture provides us with some valuable lessons within the same gender loving community. The primary focus has been in reference to (1) Even as Sodom and Gomorrah, (2) After strange flesh.

The letter of Jude focuses on apostasy—when people turn away from God's truth and embrace false teachings. Jude was a brother of James, who was one of the leaders in the early church. Both of these men were Jesus half-brothers (Mark 6:3). Mary was their mother. Joseph was the father of James and Jude.

In the Old Testament and even more so in later Jewish tradition: Sodom came to be viewed as the epitome of wickedness. This was very common when referred to through out the scriptures in the New Testament as well in Jude 7 "Even as Sodom and Gomorrah." In the scripture Jude is Sodom as an example of what he perceives as wickedness.

"Strange flesh" is these scriptures has been viewed as sex with angels, which is hardly unlikely since Jewish traditions would not call angels "flesh" and the Sodomites in Genesis 19:5 did not realize the visitors were angels. Strange flesh is literally "other" flesh, but this could also mean "other than natural," rather than "other than their own kind." Then again, "in the same way" as those of verse 6 might imply angels and people having intercourse with each other. Apart from Philo, few ancient Jewish writers stressed the Sodomites homosexual behavior; most instead stressed the Sodomites lack of hospitality, arrogant sin or sexual immorality in general, which in the Jewish perspective included but was not limited to homosexual acts. In many cultures homosexuality was very common but in the Jewish culture it was an abomination. This belief continued even when Jews became Christians.

Jude is challenged with the false teachings of many of those who he feels have watered down the teachings of Christ. They have come to be known to us as Gnostics. Gnostics opposed two of the basic foundations of Christianity (1) The incarnation of Jesus Christ *"the word was made flesh and dwelt amongst us "John 1:14)* and (2) Christian ethics (religious dogma). Some scholars interpret strange flesh as people who are non-Jewish and practice another religion. In addition the false teachers (Gnostics) claimed that they possessed secret knowledge which gave them authority. Jude letter was about aggressively addressing these false teachers and to encourage true Christine doctrine and right conduct by the Christian standard.

Surprisingly many scholars attempt to connect the angel's theory of having sex to the story of the giants illustrated in Genesis 6:1-4. In reality the correlation of the word "flesh" gives us logical assumption that the flesh issue is reference to racial or tribal difference.

The scripture does open up insight into our own racial and sexual bias about who should be doing what, who they should be doing it with and how they should do it. In laymen's term your hidden issues with inter-racial couples, your hidden issues with masculine women or effeminate men, your hidden morality issues of people having multiple partners.

In Same Gender Loving community we are challenged with our own he feel because we remain Christian we are not following the spiritual path that God has revealed to them. We are not a religious or spiritually monolithic people as Jude so desired of all those who are Christians.

Same Gender Loving Christians have many moral complexities rooted in years of religious rhetoric that has inspired generations to operate on self and disconnect from their spiritual journey.

If you wanted to make a case that this was about homosexuality you could but your case would weak and very questionable, especially if you factor in Jewish, Christian and Gentile traditions. Jesus questioned all traditions *"why do you question the tradition of the elders"* (Matthew 15:2).

CHAPTER 13

The Mis-Education About Same Gender Loving Sexuality

The number thirteen is perfect for this subject. It time to file chapter 13 bankruptcy on the negative images about your sexuality.

Science has long debated the question of whether homosexuality is a natural a natural condition or psychological disorder. For many years it was considered a disorder. But in 1973, the American Psychiatric Association reversed its long-held position on homosexuality. It declared that homosexuality is biologically predetermined and is not a disorder that can be cured. The decision has been the foundation linked to why society should now accept homosexuality and forbid discrimination against the same gender loving community.

Contemporary research is today uncovering new facts that are producing a rising conviction that homosexuality, far from being a sickness, sin, perversion, or unnatural act, is a healthy, natural, and affirming form of human sexuality for some people. Although the research is still in its infancy, relatively speaking, but it has demonstrated a capacity to confront and challenge sexual fear and prejudice that has become entrenched by centuries of repetition.

Despite centuries of belief to the contrary, it is slowly dawning on us that the seat of sexual arousal is the brain, not the genitalia. To put it bluntly, this means that the brain is the primary sex organ of the body. A person's sexual orientation and what he or she finds sexually exciting are functions of that person's brain. An understanding of these new findings in the field of human sexuality must therefore begin with a look at modern discoveries about neurophysiology and its role in human learning.

Since the evidence points to the conclusion that homosexual persons do not choose their sexual orientation, cannot change it, and constitute a quite normal but minority expression of human sexuality, it is clear that heterosexual prejudice against homosexuality must take its place alongside slavery, women rights, inter-racial marriages, and other ignorant beliefs and oppressive institutions that we have abandoned.

Sexual Orientation is sexual attractions to males or females. Attractions to individuals of the opposite sex are called heterosexual. Attractions to individuals of the same sex are called homosexual. Attractions to both sexes are called bisexual.

Discovering who you are attracted to and having words to describe those attractions are important challenges for all is same sex attracted individuals.

Human sexuality makes us feel alive. It helps us to fall in love and express ourselves as sexual beings. Understanding and valuing your sexuality is an important part of your journey.

Your attitudes and feelings are an important part of your sexuality. Think consist of what you think is right and wrong about sexuality. It includes knowing yourself and your sexual attractions. In also comprises being comfortable with your sexual orientation.

Chapter 13   The Mis-Education About SGL Sexuality

Having sex with the same gender during your adolescents ---male or female—doesn't make you homosexual (key word "adolescent"). Likewise, having sex with the opposite gender doesn't make you heterosexual. During the adolescent years it is common for youth to experiment with sex. This experimentation allows teens to work out what is healthy for them or feels normal to them. It is not about who you experimented with but how you felt about the experience. You decision to love another human being should be decided by what makes you the most comfortable and being honest with yourself.

Some people confuse sexual orientation with gender. Most people in the same gender loving community embrace their gender as it is. The same gender loving stereotypes can be linked to some of these challenges (1) All same gender loving men are effeminate (2) All same gender loving women are masculine (3) Internalized oppression by other SGL's if you are a male that is not effeminate you are uncomfortable with you sexuality or women who is not masculine is the viewed the same.

However, some of our Sista-z and Brotha-z identify as the opposite sex and come to be known as "Transgender, Transvestite and Transsexuals."

Experts have yet to determine a person's sexual orientation. However, they do know it is not a choice. Sexual orientation appears to be set early in life, probably by age eight. The events that can bring one into their sexual orientation can be linked to the following

(1) Born Gay
(2) Opportunities to have sexual experiences

(3) Negative events (i.e. molestation, rape, emotional or physical abuse)

Early in life, we learn from our parents what it means to be male or female. Puberty usually begins around ages 9 to 11. During puberty, the adolescent body begins to produce hormones. These hormones prepare the body for adulthood, sexual activity, and reproduction, or having a child. Girls typically begin puberty earlier than boys do.

Sexual desire increases during your puberty stage. The production of hormones fuels this sexual attraction to others. It is common again for teenagers to experience a variety of sexual attractions during puberty with healthy or unhealthy (I will explain more about healthy and unhealthy decisions). It is very common to have same-sex as well as opposite-sex attractions way into your late adulthood.

We are all different when it comes to learning about sexual attractions. Some people know who they are attracted to and accept it. For others, learning about sexual attractions can be a confusing experience, especially when it conflicts with their religious teachings. The beauty for many is they become accepting of their sexuality when they fell in love.

Cultural and religious beliefs can affect how we think and feel about our sexuality. Your sexuality is dirty if you put in the gutter. If you see it as dirty then it is dirty. If you see it as normal for you then it is normal.

It is your moral responsibility to yourself to find others who you can trust and talk about your challenges.

Chapter 13   The Mis-Education About SGL Sexuality

Developing A Healthy Sexuality

When you are developing your sexuality it is helpful in understanding your attractions and being comfortable with who you are. The same gender loving community has taught researchers some important things. They have taught that pride in a person's identity is an important part of sexual health.

There are healthy behaviors and unhealthy behaviors?

We learn these behaviors by experiences and experimenting. They are learned and acquired by viewing pictures or dreams about what they look, feel, and taste like. Our community cultures popular opinion sources teaches us attitudes, behaviors, visual tools, toys and diverse social networks.

Whatever your sexuality may be, learning who you are sexually is a gradual process. Learning to appreciate your sexual identify is part of the process. The process can happens over weeks, months or even years.

Our images of our bodies often develop challenges with our self-esteem. This is no different than opposite sex attractions of portraying thin women and muscular built men as the social standard of acceptability.

Developing your sexual behavior can be challenging but is important to your overall whelm being. When we possess negative images of ourselves we often compromise our sexual partner selection.

How you begin your sexual experience may vary from one person to the next regardless if you are male or female. Sex does not have to involve intercourse but if it does, then it does. It is only right if you do not feel right about what you are doing. In the beginning stages we were all nervous and somewhat insecure. That too will pass.

In the same gender loving community sexual intercourse is not a "do this or do that" rule.

> 1. All same gender loving men do not engage in anal sex
> 2. All same gender loving women do not have a desire to penetrated by their partners (i.e. toys, fingers)
> 3. All same gender loving women or men do not indulge in oral sex
> 4. Some same gender loving individuals prefer using sex toys to satisfy each other

There is no rule but there are healthy and unhealthy behaviors.

In the early stages of male sexuality many feel pressured or it is their role to be penetrated but to find out years later they enjoy penetrating. In the early stages of women challenged with their sexuality they feel pressured to be penetrated because they think it will change their desire for another women but only to find out later the feelings are not going away.

When you fall in love for the first time is normally when most same gender loving folks come to grip with their sexuality. Love is a powerful and wonderful feeling to give and receive. Love will have you telling anyone who questions your sexuality "Go to hell."

However finding that special someone can present challenges.

1. Where do you meet the "Partner" versus "Piece?"
2. You were taught how love someone of the opposite sex. How do you love the same sex when there are so many moral complexities?
3. Why are you uncomfortable with effeminate man trying to love,
4. Why are you uncomfortable with masculine female trying to love you?
5. Doing you really want a lover or do you just want to have sex? Either one is okay, but be truthful to you.
6. What is a lover to me and what is a friend?
7. Are you comfortable being in love all by yourself? What does that mean to you?

Coming Out

Coming out is the process of naming, valuing, and celebrating your sexual identity.

The phrase "coming out" is used in reference to being "in the closet" or "on the down low" about your sexual attraction to the same sexes.

Coming out has many cultural challenges regardless of race, gender, religion or geographic (i.e. south vs. north). The decision to come out and celebrate who you are can be a traumatic decision.

Coming out to experience sexual expressions is not truly coming out. True coming out is about being mentally free of the negative images about your sexuality.

For many same gender loving persons this process since their childhood has not been dealt with. If you are not comfortable coming out that is your decision and should be respected by all those who are aware of your same sex attraction. If you are verbally bashing people who are out then you loss the right to have your same sex attraction on the down low.

There is no right or wrong way coming out to be mentally free. In your coming out process, you should address some questions within yourself.

1. Why do you want to come out?
2. How will this affect you job/career? If it will have a negative affect.
3. What is the affect and will it threaten your income or destiny?
4. When should you have this discussion with your parents? Role the conversation in a mirror.
5. If you have children under 18 yrs old. How will this affect them? Who can you talk to about this process?
6. If you are married to the opposite sex? How should you tell your spouse? Do you feel any potential physical harm?
7. If you are being pressured or encouraged by someone else. How does your coming out impact their life?
8. What community leader or popular opinion leader can you talk about your coming out decision?
9. Who you should or should not tell?
10. If you are less than 18 yrs of age seek a same gender loving affirming counselor. (Search the internet for local Youth Pride organization or national registry). There are a lot of loving and caring people ready to assist you. I do not recommend you go at this alone.

Chapter 13   The Mis-Education About SGL Sexuality

Coming can be easy if you begin to disempower how others see you in a negative light. It can be challenging but if you are reading this book; then you are well on your way to coming out and being mentally free. Remember anything you give more power and authority than you God has too much power.

Empowerment Networks

Developing you a network of friends and family members you trust and can talk openly with should have a cross section of the following:

✓ Male and Female partners you are not in a sexual relationship with who are accepting and will challenge you about your sexuality.

✓ If you are Christian, a person with some spiritual and/or biblical knowledge.

✓ Social network groups promoting moving you to the next level in your life.

✓ People who can be instrumental in your life not judgmental.

Your empowerment network will serve you on multiple levels. You are more than your sexual orientation. This is only a part of who you are.

1. Parents are an important part of your empowerment network.

✓ Supportive parents allow a person to grow into their sexuality without the internal family baggage.

✓ Non-Supportive parents provide internal personal challenges for both genders oftentimes the male seeking the validation of mother and the female seeking validation of the father. This is not always the case but seems to be a behavioral pattern.

2. Siblings/Aunts/Uncles/Cousins are on a need to know bases. You should share your sexuality with who you are comfortable with but not as a moral obligation. If the issue comes or fear that it will come up then begin to discover ways to address it. If you decide to address it all. It's your peace of mind that is most important.

3. You're Children – Seek guidance from others who are openly LGBT/SGL with children in addition to books about this family topic. Be careful speaking to people with no children about this issue. Their perspectives maybe very limited and often un-insightful. Your children deserve the utmost care and sensitivity. Your decisions will affect their lives.

4. Clergy/Spiritual Counselors – If you spiritual teacher/pastor/bishop is not supportive of your lifestyle choices then it is not healthy for you to inform them. If you decide to discuss the issue with them. Ask yourself the following questions first:

- ✓ What do you want them to do?
- ✓ What if they do not agree with you?
- ✓ What are your options if they request for you to denounce your sexuality?

✓ What if they take it as an opportunity to make a pass at you? What will you say?
✓ Can I allow someone to be my spiritual covering if they do not respect the whole person in me?

5. Friends should be told on a need to know basis. This is not an option for effeminate men or masculine female. Your decision are about affirming who you are as an individual and celebrating who you are.

Dealing With Emotions

Society has programmed itself as heterosexuality as social norm. As a result, many heterosexuals and homosexuals do not accept homosexuality as being normal. When in fact "there is nothing strange in the universe."

The result of this programming instituting emotional abusive and feeling of inferiority, building the foundation for "internalized homophobia."

Homophobia is an irrational fear of persons who are same sex attracted or being same sex attracted. Internalized homophobia is when people are scared of their own homosexual feelings. These emotions keep cause a person to be on a continual emotional rollercoaster with feelings of doubt, shame, guilt, loneliness, separation.

Homophobia is based on myths and stereotypes, or overly simple opinions, For example, one myth is that gay and lesbian people molest or mistreat children. This is untrue fact. The fact is heterosexual males commit 95 percent of sexual abuse of children.

Managing Emotions

Dealing with emotions surrounding homosexuality can be painful. Feelings of fear or rejection from peers (i.e. friends, colleagues) can be very stressful. This can lead for some to thoughts of suicide, compulsive behaviors (i.e. alcohol, drugs, and sex or internet sex websites).

Although these may appear to be some of the same problems that heterosexuals may deal with but the root of the problem is different.

The root of most the negative images and language of the problems generate from our religious community. Some religious institutions are very hard-line against homosexuality. While some others just never address the issue "silence = death." There are many groups now offering workshops to change a person from homosexual to heterosexual. Research shows that these groups do not work and can increase the negative images a person may have of themselves. The American Medical Association and the American Psychiatric Association both warn that trying to change sexual orientation can harm your self-esteem.

In the LBGT/SGL community spirituality and religious practices are very important in our lives. It is healthy for you to find a balance of where you receive your spiritual feedings and religious training. If you're spiritual covering or religious trainer does not have any working knowledge of homosexuality in the bible then you should be seeking it out for yourself. This is about you.

Your sexual identity develops over time and takes effort. Accepting and understanding one's sexual orientation is just one part of sexuality, and it is an important part.

Chapter 13   The Mis-Education About SGL Sexuality

Developing ways to do this in a positive and healthy manner is a sign of maturity about your sexuality.

You can be your own biggest support by learning to accept who you are as a person and building your self-worth. Do not discount who you are, see yourself at full value. Try writing positive messages about yourself and reading about others sought out to discover themselves.

Your sexuality is much about integrity, or completeness, as it is about sex. Knowing yourself, being honest about who you are and knowing your sexual preference are important parts of your sexual health.

You may experience multiple partners before you find the committed partner or relationship. You should always have a conversation with your partner about the type of relationship you both want. Being in a committed relationship is not the moral standard in the same gender loving community. It you decide to be single this is okay.

Each person needs to determine his or her personal readiness for a sexual relationship. To be ready for an emotional and sexual relationship, you should understand the risks and responsibilities involved. You need to be able to communicate open and honestly with your partner about each other's feelings. You should be prepared to accept if the person does not want the same thing you want. Keep your heart open to honesty. It is a horrible feeling being in a relationship and you do not realize to latter on that you are the only one in love in the relationship.

They are not rejecting you. They are expressing what they want at this time during their life. You should detach from the outcome and not create fall expectations.

Stay Away From Morality Declarations

There are many people that fear accepting homosexuality will mean that critical judgment must be suspended from all forms of homosexuality behavior. That, too, is an irrational manifestation of prejudice. All forms of heterosexual behavior do not receive approval just because we affirm the goodness of heterosexuality. Any sexual behavior can be destructive, exploitative, predatory, or promiscuous, and therefore evil, regardless of the sexes of the parties involved. Whenever any of those conditions exist, a word of moral judgment needs to or will be spoken. The difficulty comes when a society evaluates heterosexuality per se as good and homosexuality per se as evil. Such moral absolutes eventuate in preferential ethical treatment of heterosexuals.

Distinctions will be for heterosexual people between life-giving and life-destroying behavior, while any and all patterns of sexual behavior arising form a homosexual orientation are condemned as sinful. Such a moral position leaves same gender loving persons with no options except denial and suppression. Indeed, many an ecclesiastical body has suggested that these are in fact the only moral choices open to homosexuals. We should be mindful that large numbers of heterosexual people engage in promiscuity, prostitution, rape, child molestation, incest, and every conceivable form of sadomasochism. Further, by refusing to accept any homosexual behavior as normal, this homophobic society drives many, same gender loving people into the very behavioral patterns that heterosexual fear and condemn.

The next stage is being entered when we begin to regard both the homosexual orientation and the heterosexual orientation in and of themselves as neither good nor evil, but

Chapter 13   The Mis-Education About SGL Sexuality

only as real and true. Both aspects of human sexuality will ultimately be seen as natural. The recognition is growing that there is a majority orientation and minority orientation and that both have roles in the enrichment of human life. This change will take time, for ignorance and fear are both tenacious, and prejudice covers human irrationality, making it difficult and frightening to relinquish.

Supplementary Support

There are various LGBT/SGL support hotlines and online networks. In many of the networks you do not have to give your name. Contact the National LBGT/SGL Hotline 1 (888)843-4564 or do web engine search (i.e. Google, yahoo) LBGT/SGL networks or gay and lesbian centers in your city or state.

Moving Yourself To The Next Level

*Chapter 13 The Mis-Education About
Same Gender Loving Sexuality*

Each process question or thought can be viewed from the following perspectives: Same Gender Loving (SGL), Heterosexual (H) or Both (B). It is healthy to try and view from various perspectives to get insight into how others may process an issue. All perspectives are valid and should be respected and not condemned. In all thy getting; get understanding.

1. (SGL) - It is healthy to build your self-esteem and assertiveness about your sexuality?

2. (SGL) - If your parents do not know about you.
    a. Why are you uncomfortable with them knowing about your same sex attraction?

3. (SGL) - If you want to be in a relationship with someone of the same sex. What are you looking for?

4. (SGL) - What do you need to work on within you, before you bring someone into this part of your life?

5. (E) - It is healthy to build yourself an empowerment network.

6. (E) - If your people you respected found out someone know if same gender loving.
    a. How would you talk to them about it?
    b. Who someone who you really did not have that much respect and you found out they were same gender loving. What would you do?

Chapter 13   The Mis-Education About SGL Sexuality

7. (E) - How would I talk to someone about them talking to their parents about their sexuality?

8. (H) - When you were growing up. How did you learn about your sexuality?

9. (H) - How did you learn to have a conversation with your partner about sex?

10. (H) - If you were to talk to someone about sexual relationships. What would you tell them to be careful of?

CHAPTER 14

The Re-dedication of Christians Who Happen To Be LBGT/SGL

When you begin to re-educate or enhance your spiritual growth using the teachings of Jesus Christ. The emphasis should be on your *"Christian Thought not Christian Walk."* What you think determines where you walk in your career, education, friendships, intimate relationships, spiritual growth, ministry commitments and acts of kindness.

You are called to look at the scriptures differently but this time with you in the scriptures. Let the scriptures open up your mind, body and spirit. Meditate on them and listen to what God will reveal specifically to you; not to parents but to you, not to your pastor but to you, not to your partner but to you, not to your problem but to you. God will reveal what God has for you when you see yourself in the word of God.

God is not asking who you are sleeping with, for God already knows and why you are sleeping with them. Let yourself be cradled in the arms of God and feel the love and comfort of God that will never run out.

The following scriptures are from the King James Version of the Bible for quick reference, as a guide to help LBGT/SGL folks begin or enhance their life utilizing the teachings of Jesus Christ. In addition to encouraging healthy and challenging social and organized group discussions within the community.

Nothing shall separate us from the Love of God, which is in Christ Jesus our Lord. (Romans 8:39)

If you are more comfortable using inclusive language, please feel free to change the scriptural language. Be mindful, it is healthy for us to respect all Christians; even the ones who may not have been exposed to the logic and application of inclusive language ideology. We should refrain from proselytizing (preaching) to them; about what is the politically appropriate way to re-write any of these historical writings. We are commissioned to teach one and reach one. Let the wonderful Love of God cover everything in your life. Let the Word of God, the Logos meet you at the point of your needs. The teachings of Jesus Christ can take you to the next level in your life along with many other wonderful spiritual teachings.

Chapter 14   The Re-dedication of Christians Who Happen To Be LBGT/SGL

Abandonment

Even if my father and mother abandon me, The Lord will hold me close.
(Psalm 27:10)

We are hunted down, but God never abandons us. We get knocked down, but we get up again and keep going.
(2Corinthians 4:9)

[12] Not as though I had already attained, either were already perfect: but I follow after, if that I may apprehend that for which also I am apprehended of Christ Jesus. [13] Brethren, I count not myself to have apprehended: but this one thing I do, forgetting those things which are behind, and reaching forth unto those things which are before, [14] I press toward the mark for the prize of the high calling of God in Christ Jesus.   (Philippians 3:12-14)

Even if your family rejects or neglects you, God will never abandon you. This is a promise God has made to every man, woman and child, regardless of their sexual orientation.

God promises to be present with you, in you and beside you in all circumstances. Never give any situation (i.e. individual or groups) more power than the God of your understanding. If God created the universe, God can create a healthier situation for you even when the abandonment experience does not look to be in your favor *"Faith is the substance of things hoped for, the evidence of things not yet seen" (Hebrews 11:1).*

In the LBGT/SGL community, it is important that we know God has control of everything. Any life experience you've had, God was always there and will continue to always be there. Looking back on your abandonment experiences should not be seen within yourself you should have forgotten them now. Don't let the abandonment experiences keep you from moving forward. Don't let any life experience take your eyes off of your spiritual journey. The more you keep looking back at the abandonment experience, keeps you from looking forward toward your God experiences. Let go and let God guide your path.

Acceptance
> *Knowing that a man (person) is not justified by the works of the law, but by the faith of Jesus Christ, even we have believed in Jesus Christ, that we might be justified by the faith of Christ, and not by the works of the law: for by the works of the law shall no flesh be justified.*
> *(Galatians 2:16)*

We live in a society that circulates myths, fears, and irrational beliefs about homosexuality. It is no small wonder then, that among persons with a gay or lesbian sexual orientation, a common concern is a sense of rejection and isolation-- from friends, family, and society-at-large. Prejudicial and misinformed social attitudes often lead gays and lesbians to feel anxious, depressed, and guilty. Such feelings are often significant hurdles in the process of developing a positive sense of self-identity and esteem.

While these feelings are real and may feel overwhelming at times, they seem to be a response to myths and negative, self-defeating stereotypes.

*Chapter 14   The Re-dedication of Christians Who
Happen To Be LBGT/SGL*

The Judaizers (Jewish Christians) accused Paul of watering down the Gospel to make it easier for Gentiles to accept, while Paul accused the Judaizers of nullifying the truth of the Gospel by adding conditions to it. Paul was not saying the Law was bad, but instead has an important role to play in the life of a Christian. The Law cannot possibly save us, but Law can be a valuable guide for living as God commands.

In the LBGT/SGL community, if you do not accept who you are then you give others more power over your life than God. The true law of God is love. We over step our authority when representing God; when we do not accept people just the way they are. We are all made in the likeness and image of God whether other people believe it or not.

Addiction(s)

And be not conformed to this world: but be ye transformed by the renewing of your mind, that ye may prove what is that good, and acceptable, and perfect, will of God.   *(Romans 12:2)*

All addictions have a source of origin. The addiction *(i.e. drugs, sex, alcohol, shopping, abusive behaviors, and dysfunctional personalities)* is not the problem; it is the series of events that leads you to the problem. Freedom from your addictive behaviors come as you change your focus and change your mind. This is about seeking the truth about your behaviors and seeking out compassionate people or groups that will not let you address the addiction in a denial mode. You can do this by trusting the God of Your Understanding and connecting with others who want a positive change in their life.

In the LBGT/SGL community it is important not to assume that homosexuality causes drug or alcohol abuse. When gays, lesbians and bisexuals internalize society's homophobic attitudes and beliefs, the results can be devastating. Society's hatred becomes self-hatred. *As a minority group; same gender loving folks are victims of systemic and ongoing oppression. It can lead to feelings of alienation, despair, low self-esteem, self-destructive behaviors, and substance abuse (Nicoloff & Stiglitz, 1987).*

The first step toward getting help is recognizing that your alcohol, substance abuse or sexual addiction is a problem, search within yourself and ask some of these questions.

- Do you feel irritated when other people comment on how much you drink/use drugs?
- Do you ever drink or use drugs when you are alone?
- Have you had periods of time while you were drinking or using drugs that you could not remember later?
- Have you ever had problems with friends, school, or work, or arrested as a result of drinking or using drugs?
- Have you ever wondered whether you have a drinking or drug problem?
- Can you go without having sex daily?
- Can you go a day without signing unto a sexual website (i.e. hook up, videos, and photographs)?
- Do you find yourself signing onto sites as soon as you log your computer on?
- Do you watch porn more than you watch television?
- Does it irritate you when people talk negatively about others having multiple sex partners?

Chapter 14   The Re-dedication of Christians Who Happen To Be LBGT/SGL

The process of recovery allows you to heal by working through those feelings you have pushed down with alcohol, drugs or sex. It is often said that when you have a substance abuse problem, your emotional development stops when you start abusing the drug. When you medicate your feelings, you numb yourself from conflicts and reality. Once you decide to no longer abuse, those feelings and emotions will surface and may be overwhelming. Sexual addiction is still a very taboo subject in the same gender loving community. Self-help groups offer a safe and supportive environment where people share common experiences, strength and hope.

Adversity
My sisters and brothers, count it all joy when ye fall into divers temptation; Knowing this, that the trying of your faith worketh patience. But let patience have her perfect work, that ye may be perfect and entire, wanting nothing.   (James 1:11)

Adversities that threaten and try us are the very tools that God uses to strengthen and mature us. We learn how venerable we are to circumstances and how certain people can make us forget our faith. As we endure, we gain greater wisdom, integrity, and courage to face whatever comes our way.

In the LBGT/SGL community, to assist you in dealing with the reactions and opinions of certain people in 'main-stream' society, it may be beneficial for you to become involved in the local gay, lesbian, bisexual and transsexual community (clubs, organizations or local business attractions). You are also surrounding yourself with more positive people who are ready and willing to face the social pressures of society head-on.

Aging

They shall bring forth in old age; they shall remain vital and green.
(Psalms 92:14)

Trusting in the Lord involves knowing and believing in the Lord. This can lead to a satisfying life and often a long life as well. Regardless of our age, we can be productive and vital while telling others about God's unconditional love.

In Genesis 18, Sarah & Abraham were old in age but forgot God promise them a child. The angel asked Sarah *"Is there anything to hard for God" (Genesis 18:14)*. You are never too old to receive a blessing from God. It is not about your sexuality; it's about your trust in a God who never forgets a promise.

- If you think you are too old to love, start a new career, develop or enhance your relationships then you have put your trust in what you think you know.

- If you think you are too young to pursue dreams, receive your promise then you have put your trust in what you think you know.

In the LBGT/SGL community, while there are times when a life is cut short by circumstances, we may or may not understand, we should continue to have our trust in the Lord.

Chapter 14   The Re-dedication of Christians Who Happen To Be LBGT/SGL

Regardless of your age when you begin to define or redefine your purpose in life put God first in your plan. As many of us age financial concerns and periods of loneliness are a daily challenge. It is a social reality that many in the LBGT/SGL community may be their only source of income for greater period of their lives. This should not be an excuse to limit yourself from moving to the next level in your life regardless of what the world may think of you. We are what we think.

Anger

[15] Moreover if thy brother shall trespass against thee, go and tell him his fault between thee and him alone: if he shall hear thee, thou hast gained thy brother. [16] But if he will not hear thee, then take with thee one or two more, that in the mouth of two or three witnesses every word may be established. [17] And if he shall neglect to hear them, tell it unto the church: but if he neglect to hear the church, let him be unto thee as an heathen man and a publican. [18] Verily I say unto you, Whatsoever ye shall bind on earth shall be bound in heaven: and whatsoever ye shall loose on earth shall be loosed in heaven. [19] Again I say unto you, That if two of you shall agree on earth as touching any thing that they shall ask, it shall be done for them of my Father which is in heaven. [20] For where two or three are gathered together in my name, there am I in the midst of them. (Matthew 18:15-20)

The teaching of Jesus Christ discourages us from giving into anger. Do not retaliate against people who have hurt you. God wants you to reach out to your sister or brother in the name of Love and try to resolve the matter. Giving into anger invites the other person to strike back even harder. Seek the enlightenment of God (i.e. understanding, wisdom, right speak) to address the challenge with gentleness and resist the urge to respond back in anger.

In the LBGT/SGL community many of us have been hurt by others. This leads us to make decisions about our experiences while we are still hurting. Don't let someone guilt trip you for being angry with someone but seek a way via the enlightenment of God to turn the negative experience into a positive learning experience. The scripture says *"thy enemy is thy footstool" (Psalms 110:1, Hebrews 10:13).*

Your challenging situation is designed to take you to the next level; it's your footstool. What is the next level about you? What does the situation teach you about yourself? The bible tells us the enemy is our footstool (Psalms 110:1). Your footstool can be viewed as your life challenges but the challenges require you to move yourself to another level. What level does your footstool thinking move you towards? Yes, the negative life experiences did happened; now what level are you going to transform towards? *"Be ye not conformed to this world but transformed by the renewing of your mind that you may prove what is that good, and acceptable, and perfect, will of God" (Romans 12:2)* It's not the challenge that is the challenge; it's how you address the challenge that is the challenge.

Assurance
My sheep hear my voice, and I know them, and they follow me: And I give unto them eternal

Chapter 14   The Re-dedication of Christians Who Happen To Be LBGT/SGL

> *life; and they shall never perish, neither shall any man pluck them out of my hand. My Father, which gave them me, is greater than all; and no man is able to pluck them out of my Father's hand. I and My Father are one.*
> *(John 10:27-30)*

The assurance of God's love gives us courage to bring any challenge, struggle or concern to God. Our prayers are never received as an interruption to God. When we seek God, know that God is always reachable. Our confidence should be rooted in God's Power; not on how powerful we think we are, for it is the power of God that resides in us. God's love is eternal.

The insurance of God is the protection; a policy was paid by the blood of Jesus shed on Calvary. The assurance is God's promise that whosoever wants a relationship with God in no way will God cast them out or deny them.

In the LBGT/SGL community there is a point in your life when you must let go the power you have given to the church/temple and give it back to God. Jesus says, *"Destroy this temple, and in three days I will raise it up" (John 2:19).*

There are people coming to this new temple that will be seeking the promise and will know when they hear God's voice via the Word taught and the actions of those in this new temple. The protection of God we have already received at the cross. The assurance of God is what we seek. The assurance is rooted in our faith in God. When we let go of what others may think of us we disempower them and empower our God; operating in the protection and promise of God.

Beginnings

> *Therefore if any man be in Christ, he is a new creature: old things are passed away; behold, all things are become new.*
> *(2Corinthians 5:17)*

Those who apply the teachings of Jesus Christ are not simply turning over a new leaf; they are changing their inner spiritual being to become more Christ like. God has already begun the work of transforming every aspect of our lives. We invite God to work in our relationships, our jobs/careers, our recreation, our ministries, our children and, yes, our enemies.

We don't just make New Year's Resolutions but New Season Resolutions to begin anew and seed planting with the expectation your harvesting period is coming. God renews every season and an abundance of mercies to us every day. We can choose to be burdened by yesterday's temporary disappointments or missed opportunities. We can choose to change our Christian Thought as we walk into our new seasons.

In the LBGT/SGL community, your new beginnings may call you to relent everything you have been taught about a God with limitation, lack, anger and jealousy, *"the God of the will not."* How you think about God determines how you walk within the life experiences and how you decide to walk out the life experiences; *"change is mandatory; growth is optional."*

Betrayal

> *Dearly beloved, avenge not yourselves, but rather give place unto wrath: for it is written, Vengeance is mine; I will repay, saith the Lord. Therefore if thine enemy hunger, feed him; if he thirst, give him drink: for in so doing thou shalt*

*Chapter 14   The Re-dedication of Christians Who
            Happen To Be LBGT/SGL*

> *heap coals of fire on his head. Be not overcome
> of evil, but overcome evil with good.
> (Romans 12:19-21)*

Betrayal is a challenging life experience to manage. It wounds the core of your spiritual being and can hide itself in your daily living. It often disguises itself as a feeling of release, the more often you think and talk about the experience.

Your trust is damaged and you oftentimes go on a dangerous skid; it's like hitting a sheet of ice, but God can and will throw sand on the road to stop you from sliding. We anchor our faith in God, not in people's personalities or positions. The unhealthy response to betrayal is to give in to the desire for vengeance. The healthy response to betrayal is to stop the cycle of retaliation in your thoughts and begin a path of healthy thinking; taking control and putting the negative experience in its proper perspective in your life.

In the LBGT/SGL community our forgiveness must involve both attitude and actions. Forgiveness is not condoning a person's behavior, it's about taking control of the negative feelings and emotions generated by their actions. Rethinking how you manage the negative experience is what empowers you to move yourself to the next level.

If you find it hard to feel forgiving of someone who has hurt you this is normal and a valid feeling. This is not about acceptance, this is about you letting go. Send them a card, call them or take it to the cross and just commit to yourself that it is time to let this go in the name. This leads to healthy thoughts and the purging of those unhealthy thoughts.

Bible

16 All scripture is given by inspiration of God, and is profitable for doctrine, for reproof, for correction, for instruction in righteousness: 17 That the man of God may be perfect, thoroughly furnished unto all good works. (2Timothy 3:16-17)

The bible is a compilation of historical accounts, fables, human ideas and revelations about God. Through the Holy Spirit, God revealed His plan to various believers, who documented God's message for His people (2 Peter 1:20-21). This process is known as "inspiration." The writers wrote from their own personal, historical, and cultural contexts. But, even though, they used their own minds, talents, language, and style, they wrote what God wanted them to write.

In the LBGT/SGL community in our zeal for the truth within the Scriptures, we must never forget that its purpose is to equip us to do good for others (i.e. servitude). We should not study God's Word simply to increase our own knowledge. Do not serve or develop an arrogant appearance displaying we are more knowledgeable about God than others. It's about us being missionaries not dignitaries. Our mission is to spread God's unconditional love and teach the Bible from a loving perspective.

We are saved by grace, not of ourselves; it is a gift from God. We should study scripture for guidance to know how we should carry out God's Will in the uttermost parts of our community; even where the most self righteous of dignitaries will not journey *(i.e. bathhouses, book stores, clubs, bars, television, radio, spade parties, online social networks)*. Our knowledge of God's Word is not useful unless it leads us to the good works of helping others. Our work is about being missionaries not dignitaries.

*Chapter 14   The Re-dedication of Christians Who
Happen To Be LBGT/SGL*

Blessings
*He that hath pity upon the poor lendeth unto the
Lord; and that which they have given, God will
repay you.   (Proverbs 19:17)*

This proverb identifies with the poor as Jesus did in Matthew 25:31-46. When we help the poor, we show honor both to our Divine Creator and to the human creation. God accepts our help as if we had offered it directly to God.

God's blessing encompasses all the days of our lives. God promises to bless those who do more random acts of kindness. God sometimes blesses people we do not like and some of them appear to be receiving more blessings than those who are committed to loving God. Don't let that take your eyes off what God wants you to do.

In the Matthew 20:1-16 is the parables of laborers. God agreed to bless those who started work in the early morning with a full days blessing, those who started in the afternoon with a full days blessings and those who started at the later part of the day with a full days blessing. What God has for you, it is for you. When you are tempted with discouragement because you do not feel like the blessings are coming your way, just remember that God promised to bring you into your harvest season at the appointed time.

In the LBGT/SGL, God has promised in the covenant to bless us and we are called to be a blessing to others. What does the poor look like for us? The young women and men on the corner selling their bodies, the youth being kicked out of their parents' house because they are same gender loving. What does being under a bridge look like for us? There are people walking around in openly LBGT/SGL churches who are at the front door of homelessness. How do we become a blessing to our elderly LBGT/SGL family?

We are called to be a blessing as we are blessed. We cannot be choosy about who we are called to be a blessing to. God has blessed you to be that blessing in someone's life that will shock you.

Challenges
> *My sisters and brothers, count it all joy when ye fall into divers temptations; Knowing this, that trying of your faith worketh patience. But let patience have her perfect work, that ye may be perfect and entire, wanting nothing. (James 1:2-4)*

Nothing is too small for God. When you commit your plans to the Lord, God commits resources to you. At the moment of your commitment, God conspires on your behalf for your victory. The promise of victory is embedded in your commitment to trusting in God, even when you cannot see your desired outcome. Instead of being dispirited by the size, length or degree of the task, depend on and be encouraged by the inexhaustible power of God. *"For no weapon formed against you shall proper." (Isaiah 54:17)*

In the LGBT/SGL community your commit to what God has in store for you is not limited or based on your sexuality but on your faith in God. Our faith infuses our works and is made perfect in our serving of God. There is nothing that any religious institution can do to stop God from moving on our behalf and being our protection.

*Chapter 14   The Re-dedication of Christians Who
Happen To Be LBGT/SGL*

Character

But the fruit of the Spirit is love, joy, peace, longsuffering, gentleness, goodness, faith, meekness, temperance: against such there is no law.
(Galatians 5:22-23)

The "fruit of the Spirit" is the spontaneous work of the Holy Spirit in us. The Spirit harbors these character traits, which are found in everyone and is the natural ingredient of all God's children. All fruit begins as a seed that's planted in some form of dirt. Every seed has its season to reveal itself to the world. Every seed knows its destiny and waiting to be planted to become what it is predestined to become.

In the LBGT/SGL community, if you want to experience spiritual growth, you should seek a spiritual journey for your inner truths. Your spiritual journey with the teachings of Jesus Christ will challenge everything you think you know. All fruit begins as a seed that is planted in dirt within environments and geographical conditions designed specially for seed. Every seed has its harvest season to reveal itself to the world. Your present situation is not a fair indicator of your future. You are in the midst of your growth as seed that is developing and constantly changing to become what God has predestined to become. You will not look the same once you have grown out of the dirt. You do not have a character flaw; you have an opportunity to grow.

Communion

[26] And as they were eating, Jesus took bread, and blessed it, and broke it, and gave it to the disciples, and said, Take, eat; this is my body.
[27] And he took the cup, and gave thanks, and gave it to them, saying, Drink ye all of it; [28] For this is my blood of the new testament, which is

shed for many for the remission of sins. ²⁹But I say unto you, I will not drink henceforth of this fruit of the vine, until that day when I drink it new with you in my Father's kingdom. (The Lord's Supper) – *(Matthew 26:26-29, Mark 14:22-25, Luke 22:19, 20)*

²³For I have received of the Lord that which also I delivered unto you, that the Lord Jesus the same night in which he was betrayed took bread: ²⁴And when he had given thanks, he broke it, and said, Take, eat: this is my body, which is broken for you: this do in remembrance of me. ²⁵After the same manner also he took the cup, when he had supped, saying, this cup is the new testament in my blood: this do ye, as oft as ye drink it, in remembrance of me. ²⁶For as often as ye eat this bread, and drink this cup, ye do shew the Lord's death till he come.
(1Corinthians 11:23-26)

In the old covenant (agreement) the people could not approach God unless they came through the priest or a sacrificial system. In the new covenant (agreement), the death of Jesus Christ was the ultimate sacrifice. This established the way, the truth and the life of all people having the right to approach and communicate with God.

The new covenant completes, rather than replaces the old covenant, fulfilling everything the old covenant looked forward to *(Jeremiah 31:34-34)*. Eating the bread and drinking the cup shows we are remembering Christ's death for us and renewing our commitment to him. Jesus said, *"This do ye, as oft as ye drink, in remembrance of me."* It does not make a difference if communion is facilitated on the first Sunday, or

*Chapter 14   The Re-dedication of Christians Who
Happen To Be LBGT/SGL*

third Sunday of the month or every Sunday. This ceremony can be done on a daily basis over your home, family, business or whatever you want to commit unto Christ.

In the LBGT/SGL community, we should take communion on behalf of our relationships with our partner, take communion for our family configurations (include your children), and take communion before your medical reports, home and your business. Communion is a commitment unto God for everything in your life and we do this often as remembrance of Christ giving His life as a living sacrifice.

Conflict

The Lord is my light and my salvation; whom shall I fear? The Lord is the strength of my life; of whom shall I be afraid? When the wicked, even mine enemies and my foes, came upon me to eat up my flesh, they stumbled and fell. Though an host should encamp against me, my heart shall not fear: though war should arise against me, in this will I be confident.
(Psalms 27:1-3)

Conflict in life is inevitable. The worse way to manage conflict that directly affects your life is to avoid it. In your spiritual development you should be seeking guidance in how to manage the conflict in your life. You will experience many types of conflicts (i.e. life partners, job, parents, friends and co-workers). God does not keep you out of conflict but resides inside you to help you manage the conflict.

In the *"Christian principles of paradox": blessed when cursed, give when threatened, and feed those who would take our food.* This principle unleashes God's power into the conflict. When you learn how to manage conflict; you quickly learn that all conflict does not deserve your attention. The four areas of conflict that deserve your immediate attention are anything that threatens your (1) Family (2) Money (3) Destiny (4) Or The Mistreatment of Others (i.e. violence, verbal or emotional abuse, hungry). You do not have to run from conflict but seek the enlightenment of God to understand how to manage the conflict. In some cases managing conflict as a reflection of number four could be as simple as calling the police.

In the LBGT/SGL community it is important to know the peace of God is in the power of love, not the love of power. It's not about winning or losing but about seeing things from all sides and approaching the conflict from a win-win perspective and in some cases allowing the other party to win. Our inner and external conflicts have many moral complexities but they create an opportunity for all of us to grow spiritually with God.

Courage

> *I can do all things through Christ which strengthened me.*   *(Philippians 4:13)*

Courage is about trusting the presence of God. Everyone has the power within to achieve and receive their heart's desire. When we detach ourselves from the nonessential things in life and attach ourselves to the spirit within us we see no lack or limitation in our lives or the lives of others.

Our thoughts seek to transform to a more open point of view of self and others. It is not necessarily about praying the problem away or for it to end; but seeking the courage to face the problem. It's not the problem that is the problem; it's how you address the problem that is the problem. *Romans 8:37 says*

Chapter 14   The Re-dedication of Christians Who Happen To Be LBGT/SGL

"Nay, in all these things we are more than conquerors through him that loved us."

In the LBGT/SGL community we have the propensity not give ourselves credit for being courageous. Look at your past courageous actions; even though, the most prominent faith institutions have done all they could to convince you being same gender loving is wrong. You still found the courage within yourself to be same gender loving against their negative perceptions. You have reached out to other same gender loving folks to establish a relationship that works for both of you. That took courage and you conquered that fear, even though, the masses objected. You are a conqueror, you have always been a conqueror and you will always be a conqueror. You can achieve whatever you want when you disempower the things around you and empower the anointing within you.

Depression

Come unto, all ye that labour and are heavy laden, and I will give you rest.
(Matthew 11:28)

Depression is a time of soul-searching to identify the origins of the mental challenges. When you are depressed, you need time to remind yourself that God has been faithful in the past and will be faithful in the present. Stop listening to the voices of discouragement and listen instead to the soft voice of God within your heart. God wants to guide us but sometimes we are resistant to the blessings God has provided us. Never underestimate the power of God's affirmation and God's willingness to provide you with all we need in life.

In the LBGT/SGL community, if you are challenged with the symptoms of depression seek out a professional, an affirming peer or group that can help you work through the daily challenges of depression. Depression can be a biological challenge or the result of a series of negative events. In many cases the signs and symptoms have been instilled within your everyday living and you were not aware of the long term effects of the inner neglect. You are not a mistake or error. You are challenged by some life experiences. Let God lead you to a having peace of mind and guiding the right people towards you in your life to find this peace of mind.

Discernment

> *For when for the time ye ought to be teachers, ye have need that one teach you again which be the first principles of the oracles of God; and are become such as have need of milk, and not of strong meat. For every one that useth milk is the word of righteousness: for he is a babe. But strong meat belongeth to them that are of full age, even those who by reason of use have their senses exercised to discern both good and evil.*
> *(Hebrews 5:12-14)*

Discernment is the ability to interpret events and to understand the true nature of people and situations. Discernment is an aspect of wisdom. It enables you to see behind the charades that mask the truth. Discernment shows you the way through the maze of options that face you. Like the sun that burns away the fog, discernment cuts through confusion and distractions. Whereas the devil (accuser/slanderer) is the *"father of lies,"* God is the father of the truth, and He gives discernment to those who seek it.

Discernment enhances the quality of our life and our discipleship. Your spiritual journey seeking wisdom and understanding can guide you away from or assist you in

Chapter 14   The Re-dedication of Christians Who Happen To Be LBGT/SGL

managing the lies and deceptions of your accusers, slanderers or challenging people in your life.

In The LBGT/SGL community, the teachings of Jesus Christ will provide spiritual paths to a new perspective on life, *"For God hath not given us the spirit of fear but of power, and of love and of sound mind".* (2Timothy 1:7) God has given you everything you need but since you were a baby you have been taught about lack or limitation in a *"God of the cannot and will not."* You must embrace the discerning spirit God has instilled in you. You have the anointing within you, coming from the anointed one (Christ) and guided by the Word of God. If you lean and depend on the Holy Spirit it will guide your thoughts and decisions. Just because someone is older than you does not mean they are more discerning than you. Just because you are young does not mean you do not have the ability to discern for yourself. Spiritual discerning is not about age, it is about your maturity with God.

Doubt

But let him ask in faith, nothing wavering. For him that wavereth is like a wave of the sea driven with the wind and tossed.
(James 1:6)

Doubt often arises because you look at the problem instead of looking towards God. God is not limited by your circumstances, lack of resources or abilities. All things are possible with God; Moses parted the Red Sea, Daniel sat in the pit with a lion, Sarah conceived a child at an old age; many others of God's people across the centuries have learned that God can do anything God decides to do. When Peter was walking out on water to greet Jesus, he was overcome by doubt. Jesus did not punish him because of his doubt; he questioned his belief but still reached out to save him. Doubt is normal for us all. The question for the believer is how long will you doubt God. Will you get in the middle of the storm then fall apart?

In the LBGT/SGL community, we doubt many times the world will ever change its oppressive ways toward our community. We should know that when a mind "wavers" it is not completely convinced that God's way is best. It is indecisive between feelings, the world's ideas, and God's commands. To stabilize your wavering or doubtful mind, commit your thoughts, purpose and mission to God.

We seek to learn more about our Lord and about our faith. Let your doubts drive you into the word of God and draw you into healthy relationship with the Lord. When you fill your mind with the promises of God, God fills your life with the provision and blessing of the promises. Doubt eats away at your confidence, but God's promises should inspire your faith and hope *"for faith is substance of things hoped for the evidence is things not yet seen." (Hebrews 11:1)*

Endurance

And shall be hated of all men for my name's sake: but he that shall endure unto the end, the same shall be saved. (Mark 13:13)

Endurance comes from keeping your thoughts on the promise of the harvest, not the problems of the moment. You do not endure your own strength alone. God is at work in your life. God gives you the strength to keep going when you are exhausted and the vision to keep believing even when you are discouraged.

Endurance is like the fire that purifies precious metals and hardens valuable pottery. It cleanses, clarifies, and

Chapter 14   The Re-dedication of Christians Who Happen To Be LBGT/SGL

solidifies your faith. Living through the trials and tests of life is often the most significant way to discover the riches of your faith.

In the LBGT/SGL community, our endurance is what sustains us with God. God sees the injustices we suffer. Just as God was pleased with Jesus' submission on the cross, God is pleased when we are honored to serve on God's behalf *"nothing shall separate us from the love of God, which is in Christ Jesus our Lord." (Romans 8:39)* Endurance is an essential quality within the teachings of Jesus Christ. Although you have been promised eternal life, God promised that those who endure will not only survive, but have an abundant life.

Faith

[22] And Jesus answering saith unto them, Have faith in God. [23] For verily I say unto you, That whosoever shall say unto this mountain, Be thou removed, and be thou cast into the sea; and shall not doubt in his heart, but shall believe that those things which he saith shall come to pass; he shall have whatsoever he saith. [24] Therefore I say unto you, What things soever ye desire, when ye pray, believe that ye receive them, and ye shall have them.
(Mark 11:22-24, Matt 21:20-22)

Matthew 17:20   [20] And Jesus said unto them, Because of your unbelief: for verily I say unto you, If ye have faith as a grain of mustard seed, ye shall say unto this mountain, Remove hence to yonder place; and it shall remove; and nothing shall be impossible unto you.
(Matthew 17:20)

*Now faith is the substance of things hoped for,
the evidence of things not seen.* (Hebrews 11:1)

Faith is our lifeline to God. Faith in God frees us from the pressures, priorities, and perspectives of this world. It links us to God's peace and power. Our faith is divinely inspired by the Holy Spirit working through the word of God. The strongest faith is not one based on physical senses but on spiritual conviction. The mustard seed was often used to illustrate the smallest seed known to man. Jesus says that faith is not a matter of size or quantity. We do not have to have great faith in God; we have to have faith in a great God.

In the LBGT/SGL community, our faith should be solely depended unto God; not into church doctrines, bishops or evangelist. We work for God and rely on God's power not our own to do God's will. Our faith in God is about the Power and aweness of God, there is no other name above God and God is Omnipotent (All-Powerful), Omniscient (All-Knowing) and Omnipresence (Everywhere). We do not have to have great faith in God; we have to have faith in a great God. Our God is great and greatly to be praise and will shall not put anything above God. We work for God and our faith empowers our works, not our works of faith.

Failure

And Peter went out, and wept bitterly. (Luke 22:62)

Often our sense of failure is determined by the level of approval from others. God rewards our faithfulness even if we appear to fail in the eyes of the world. Our failure demonstrates how God loves us unconditionally. God's love is not different than a caring parent who may be hurt or saddened by a child's

Chapter 14 The Re-dedication of Christians Who Happen To Be LBGT/SGL

worldly failures or habits, that failure doesn't make them love the child less. In fact, failure often awakens greater tenderness and support toward the child. Just as God understands our weaknesses, our failures help us depend on God's marvelous grace.

Peter wept bitterly, not only because he realized he had denied his affiliation with Jesus the Messiah, but also because he had turned away from a very dear friend, a person who had loved and taught him. Peter said he would never deny Jesus as the Christ, despite Jesus' prediction he would deny him three times *(Luke 22:33, 34)*, but when questioned was he one of Jesus followers within just the next twelve hours he became frightened and he went against what he had boldly promised. He wept because he believed that he failed as a disciple and as a friend but Peter did not fail God; Peter failed to trust in his God.

In the LBGT/SGL community, your failures (aka temporary disappointments) do not determine your identity or your self-worth. It is temporary disappointment but a great opportunity to learn more about you. God uses our temporary disappointments as opportunities to enlighten us and prepare us for the next level. Failure is not a dead end but the doorway to possibilities. When you see local, state and federal ballot initiatives defeated and won; they are only temporary victories. God has a plan that is going to shock even you.

Family
While he yet talked to the people, behold, his mother and his brethren stood without, desiring to speak with him. Then on said unto him, Behold, thy mother and thy brethren stand

> *without desiring to speak with thee. But he answered and said unto him that told him, Who is my mother? And who are my brethren? And he stretched forth his hand toward his disciples, and said, Behold my mother and brethren! For whosoever shall do the will of my Father which is in heaven, the same is my brother, and sister, and mother.* *(Matthew 12:46-50)*

Too often we think of our relationship with God in individualistic terms. God cares about families, too. We can pray for our families and for future generations, knowing that God wants to redeem them and care for them.

Jesus was not denying his responsibility to his earthly family. On the contrary, he had earlier criticized the religious leaders for not following the Old Testament command to honor their parents. He provided for his mother's security as he hung on the cross *(John 19:25-27)*. His mother and brothers were present in the upper room at Pentecost (Acts 1:14). Instead Jesus was pointing out that spiritual relationships are as binding as physical ones, and he was paving the way for a new community of believers (the universal church), our spiritual family.

In The LBGT/SGL community, our family configurations should encourage us to seek a committed relationship with God. Your family configurations may not look like or mimic the social norms whether heterosexual or within homosexual community. We should encourage that our family configurations develop a real appreciation and hunger for God's truth and the wisdom for living a healthy lives. Honoring your family configurations is one

Chapter 14 The Re-dedication of Christians Who Happen To Be LBGT/SGL

of the key pathways on your spiritual path to receive all the promises that God has stockpiled for you.

Parents, regardless of what your family configurations may consist of you are entrusted to teach and direct your children to walk with God and to discipline with love. Children are to respond with respect and obedience. When these happen, good things follow. If people do not like your family configurations then place your family in places that respect and support your family configurations. The Grace of God promises to bless your family. You can trust your families in God's everlasting care.

Fear

And the Lord said, What is that in thine hand? And Moses said, a rod. And God said, Cast it on the ground. And he cast it on the ground, and it became a serpent; and Moses fled from before it. And the Lord said unto Moses, Put forth thine hand, and take it by the tail. And he put forth his hand, and caught it, and it became a rod in his hand.   (Exodus 46:3-4)

Instead of fearing others, we can face them with courage and confidence because we know their limitations. We also know our enemies will ultimately answer to God. God's care is the antidote to our despair and God's power helps us resolve our problems. It reminds us that while the threats in this world are seemingly endless, the promise of God's protection is infinitely greater. When we are faithful, we will sometimes find ourselves in very tough situations.

God told Jacob to leave his home and travel to a strange and far away land. But God reassured him by promising to go with him and take care of him. When new situations or surroundings frighten you, recognize that experiencing fear is normal. To be paralyzed by fear, however, is an indication that you question God's ability to take care of you.

In the LBGT/SGL community, our fear can come from human intimidation, fueled by irrational anxiety. Let God's presence calm your panic. God does not want us to focus on the life experiences, people or groups that threaten us, but the Lord God Almighty who loves us *" If God be for us, who can be against us." (Romans 8:31).*

Forgiveness

[22] Jesus saith unto him, I say not unto thee, Until seven times: but, Until seventy times seven. (Matthew 18:22)

[25] At that time Jesus answered and said, I thank thee, O Father, Lord of heaven and earth, because thou hast hid these things from the wise and prudent, and hast revealed them unto babes. [26] Even so, Father: for so it seemed good in thy sight.   (Matthew 11:25-26)

Forgiveness is not based on the magnitude of the human experiences of shame, guilt, betrayal or abandonment but the magnitude of the forgiver's love. No negative life experience is too great for God's complete and unconditional love.

God has never done anything to hurt you. Your mother/father God wants the best for your life. Your faith institution may have hurt in the name of God with their misguided teachings. God knows why you are angry and when

Chapter 14   The Re-dedication of Christians Who Happen To Be LBGT/SGL

you became angry. When you decide you do not want God's forgiveness, God knows why and still forgives you anyway. It's your issue with God not God issue with you.

Forgiveness means that God looks at us as though we never missed the mark. We are blameless before God. Just as God forgives us without limit *"how many times should thy forgive, I say not unto thee until seven times; but until seventy times seven" (Matthew 18:21-22),* we should forgive others without keeping score. Jesus forgave the two thieves nailed beside him. God wants us to respond to others' sins against us by blessing them.

In the LBGT/SGL community, we have some justifiable reasons for not forgiving some people or groups. God is asking us to forgive them anyhow. In the LGBT/SGL community, we have people in our own community that have really hurt us but God is asking us to forgive them also. You should forgive the ex-lover who hurt you and broke your ability trust and now others who are trying to love you can't get through. You should forgive the person or groups that you gave the power of your life. Forgetting about the experience is not forgiving. The experience is like a thought not forgotten but hidden in your attic (mind/thoughts). Forgiveness is the action step to cleaning things out of your attic (mind/thoughts) that is living rent free in your thoughts.

We receive God's forgiveness when you are willing to forgive others. This removes them out of a prominent place in your thoughts and places God as first and foremost in your life. Being unwilling to forgive, demonstrates that you have not surrendered it to God for forgiveness. God is always more ready to forgive than we are ready to change our heart and thoughts. A broken spirit is the quickest way to spiritual wholeness with God. Surrender unto to God and expect dramatic changes in your life.

Giving
> *6 But this I say, He which soweth sparingly shall reap also sparingly; and he which soweth bountifully shall reap also bountifully. 7 Every man according as he purposeth in his heart, so let him give; not grudgingly, or of necessity: for God loveth a cheerful giver.* (2 Corinthians 9:6-7)

Giving/Tithing is God's means for supplying a variety of needs for God's people. As you fulfill God's command to meet the needs of others, God will graciously meet—and exceed—your own needs. God promises to provide for us as we give to others. God promises to meet our needs far and above our gifts in thy honor.

We cannot outgive God. While we should not give in order to get, God has promised to bless us in response to our giving. Those who trust him find that they always have what they need when they really need it. God blesses the generous with things that money can never buy. The simplest gifts bring the most sacred rewards. No gift is too small, and no act of kindness is too insignificant to go unnoticed by the Lord.

In the LBGT/SGL community, you should be giving to faith-based institutions that empower you as a whole person of mind, body and spirit. If you are not in an openly LBGT/SGL or affirming faith church and/or you are not out of the closet, you should search your heart as to where your sowing of your tithes and offerings are most productive for doing God's work. If we give, God has promised to give to us more than we can imagine! Those who trust this promise realize they always have what they need when they need it.

Grace

In whom we have redemption through his blood, the forgiveness of sins, according to the riches in his grace; Wherein he hath abounded toward us in all wisdom and prudence. (Ephesians 1:7-8)

Grace is God's favor. What we believe about God is the most important aspect about our relationship with God. If we believe that God is always angry, we will be defensive, fearful, or antagonistic toward God. When we believe the depth of his love and grace toward us, we enter into peace, joy and happiness.

In the LBGT/SGL community, it is important to know that we do not have to earn God's love or work our way to heaven. By grace, we are forgiven and restored to full fellowship with God.

Guilt

9 What then? are we better than they? No, in no wise: for we have before proved both Jews and Gentiles, that they are all under sin; 10 As it is written, There is none righteous, no, not one:
(Romans 3:9-10)

All are guilty before God. Most of our guilt is rooted in shame and regrets over what you have done or what someone perceives you should be doing in the eyes of God. Sometimes it is hard to believe the degree of God's unconditional love towards you when others have planted a limited perception of a

God *"For there is no respect of persons with God." (Romans 2:11)*

You do not need God to save you from anything; you need God to save you from yourself. God knows why you feel guilty and where the guilt originated but God is ready to intercede on your behalf. When you trust in God, the strength and prominence of your guilty feelings will be removed.

In the LBGT community, we have a long history of being guilty of a sin, because who you choose to love. In the scripture above the Gentiles where being guilt tripped because they wanted to love God without conditions. Your guilty feeling and perception you are a sin does not originate from God. Your sexuality is only dirty because you have allowed the church to convince you that it is from the gutter. Your sexuality is beautiful for there is nothing strange to God. God did not ask the Gentiles to deny who they were and you should not deny who you are.

Heaven

[29] Jesus answered and said unto them, Ye do err, not knowing the scriptures, nor the power of God. [30] For in the resurrection they neither marry, nor are given in marriage, but are as the angels of God in heaven. [31] But as touching the resurrection of the dead, have ye not read that which was spoken unto you by God, saying, [32] I am the God of Abraham, and the God of Isaac, and the God of Jacob? God is not the God of the dead, but of the living. [33] And when the

> *multitude heard this, they were astonished at his doctrine.*
> *(Matthew 22:29-33, Luke 27, 40, Mark 12:24-25)*

Heaven is described most often in terms of being our spiritual home; where we are all one with God living in peace and harmony. Jesus' resurrection gives us the promise and assurance of our place in heaven and eternal life.

In the LBGT/SGL community, many doubt they will make it to heaven because they are same gender loving. The truth of the matter is heaven is not a place where gender is relevant. We are all spirits and there is nothing strange in a place of heavenly spirit. There is not one person or faith institution that can deny you a place in heaven. You don't even have the authority to deny yourself a place in heaven. So don't be distracted with earthly decisions but be attracted to the heavenly commission *"for we that if our earthly house of this tabernacle were dissolved, we have a building of God, an house not made with hands, eternal in the heavens."(2 Corinthians 5:1)* We cannot comprehend the full Glory of the Lord, it is too wonderful, too awesome, it is God being God all by God's self.

Hope

> *Brethren, I count not myself to have apprehended: but this one thing I do, forgetting those things which are behind, and reaching forth unto those things which are before, I press toward the mark for the prize of the high calling of God in Christ Jesus.* *(Philippians 3:13-14)*

Expectation builds endurance. You can get through a great deal when we realize the wonderful gifts God has for you in this lifetime. We oftentimes hope and expect too little from God.

Our hope is rooted in the wonderful historical acts of God and God's integrity and faithfulness. Your life challenges may cause you to question or not rely on God. Especially when it appears everything is falling apart; this is when we lean on the everlasting power of God. Jesus knew Peter was going to deny him three times but he forgave before Peter denied himself. The denial experience was for Peter but the trial experience was about Christ. Your hope is not in the denial or the trial, it is in the Christ. Your hope is not in the situation but in your exaltation of Jesus Christ above all your situations in your life.

In The LBGT/SGL community, we have endured so much from the church community. We have endured them while they were out casting us, we have endured them while they were denying us, and we have endured them while we were trying to love ourselves *"And ye shall be hated of all men for my name's sake: but he that endureth to the end shall be saved." (Matthew 10:22)* The hope we should have is not about the church or church folk. This is about your personal commitment to endure on the Lord's behalf even when others question who you are. A hope that endures; a hope that is relentless; a hope that is shared with those who feel hopeless.

Humility

1 At the same time came the disciples unto Jesus, saying, Who is the greatest in the kingdom of heaven? 2 And Jesus called a little child unto him , and set him in the midst of them, 3 And said , Verily I say unto you, Except ye be converted , and become as little children, ye shall not enter into the kingdom of heaven. 4 Whosoever therefore shall humble himself as

Chapter 14 The Re-dedication of Christians Who Happen To Be LBGT/SGL

this little child, the same is greatest in the kingdom of heaven. 5 And whoso shall receive one such little child in my name receiveth me.
(Matthew 18:1-5)

Jesus used a child to help his self-centered disciples get the point. We are not to be childish, but rather childlike, with humble and sincere hearts. The disciples had become so preoccupied with the organization of Jesus' earthly kingdom; they had lost sight of its divine purpose. Instead of seeking a place of service, they sought positions of advantage.

Humility is not about condoning embarrassing people but humbling ourselves regardless of our titles or position. Just because a minister has left the traditional church does not mean they left the oppressive ways of treating all God's children.

We are called to serve even when it is not popular *"Peter saith unto him, Thou shalt never wash my feet. Jesus answered him, If I wash thee not, thou hast no part of me."(John 13:8)* This illustration of humility is about servitude. Who's feet will you wash? The more titles you have; the more feet you should be washing. We are responsible for leading by example, as Christ did with the disciples.

In the LBGT/SGL community, we are prone to repeat the behaviors of the religious institutions we were ostracized from. If we rebuild the same hierarchical ministry structure, we set the path for our bishops, pastors, ministers, deacons, community leaders to fight amongst themselves for positions and titles. They lose sight of what God called them to do. We should be childlike not childish in our decision about serving God. Children are very forgiving; humility calls for you oftentimes to forgive people even when they may have knowingly done you wrong. Your role to serve in the church is to humble yourself but even your leaders must humble themselves. No leader has the right to abuse you verbally or emotionally. That is not God speaking through them. That is them speaking without God authority. Humiliation and discipline are two very different things. The more titles a person has attached to their name the more humble they are called to become.

Hunger for God

> *But seek ye first the Kingdom of God, and his righteousness; and all these things shall be added unto you.* *(Matthew 6:33)*

Too often we misunderstand our own desires and over time come to learn there are careers, relationships and financial successes that will never satisfy the deepest longings of our hearts. When you are seeking God's plan for your life everything else falls into proper perspective. Your faith in action assures you God will provide all your needs and abundantly more. Faith does not mean inaction. The Lord invites you to earnestly pursue your desires to serve or come closer to God. As you do, God promises to lead you into peace, joy, happiness and a sense of purpose.

In the LBGT/SGL community, the hunger for God is as natural as rain falling from the clouds and stars lighting up the sky. The challenge is when you give people more authority over your lives than God. To hunger for God is the desire to seek the fullness of God in your life *"And Jesus said unto them, I am the bread of life: he that cometh to me shall never hunger; and he that believeth on me shall never thirst."(John 6:35)* This is not about your sexuality but about yearning for that holy relationship and that abounding love of God. Let Christ be your bread, let Christ be your drink, let Christ be first and foremost in your life not your sexuality. When you fill yourself with faith, hope and charity (love) you will find greater life within your sexuality and a greater sense of purpose.

Integrity
> *Let integrity and uprightness preserve me; for I wait on thee.* *(Psalms 25:21)*

Integrity helps you from walking into the trap of dishonesty and self destruction. Your integrity can affect your ability to worship open and honestly with God. God has provided through the Holy Spirit the ability to maintain loving attitudes, positive thoughts, and healthy decision making.

Integrity (honor) is about being what we say we are and how we will walk accordingly to those ways. Uprightness (respectability) is seeking what God wants us to know and do, and then moving into action. Uprightness says this is how God wants us to move forward. Your integrity is not about your mother, father, siblings, pastor or friend's honor and respectability but about your honor and respectability on God's behalf. It is hypocrisy when you say you have faith in God and still be ashamed of someone in our community *"Yea, let none that wait on thee be ashamed". (Psalms 25:3)* Our honor and respectability calls us to serve whosoever desires a relationship with Christ regardless of their sexual orientation.

In the LBGT/SGL community, our honor and respectability can provide us with valuable ethics about how we treat one another and respect each other's mission. Our honor is linked to the principles of unconditional love without judgment. Our respectability is we embrace everyone in our community just the way they are. Everyone you meet is not going to be out of the closet; honor and respect their process. Everyone we meet is not going to be a masculine male or effeminate woman; honor and respect them. We are called to "wait"; this means serve. Serve those who others will not touch, desire to be associated with, are judged as immoral, hungry, naked and unsheltered.

Judging

1 Judge not, that ye be not judged. 2 For with what judgment ye judge, ye shall be judged: and with what measure ye mete, it shall be measured to you again. 3 And why beholdest thou the mote that is in thy brother's eye, but considerest not the beam that is in thine own eye? 4 Or how wilt thou say to thy brother, Let me pull out the mote out of thine eye; and, behold, a beam is in thine own eye? 5 Thou hypocrite, first cast out the beam out of thine own eye; and then shalt thou see clearly to cast out the mote out of thy brother's eye. 6 Give not that which is holy unto the dogs; neither cast ye your pearls before swine, lest they trample them under their feet, and turn again and rend you. (Matthew 7:1-6)

Jesus' statement "Judge not" is addressing the hypercritical, judgmental attitudes to tear others down in order to build themselves up. It is not a blanket statement against all critical thinking, but a call to be discerning rather than being negative with your thoughts and words.

The teachings of Christ illustrates to us that we should examine our own motivations to measure others instead of judging one another. The behaviors that are troubling to us in others are often the behaviors we dislike in ourselves or a reflection of a negative experience. Do you find it easy to magnify others faults while ignoring your own? When you are

Chapter 14   The Re-dedication of Christians Who Happen To Be LBGT/SGL

ready to criticize someone you should check to see if you deserve the same criticism. Judge yourself first, and then lovingly forgive and help your neighbor.

In the LBGT/SGL community, we are prone to judge masculine women or effeminate men. We are often judging on what society says is the social norm of behaviors. What is normal? Jesus is illustrating to us the dangers of measuring those who are different because we are only measuring ourselves. Who you are is not defined by how you measure up to others but how others measure in your life. How you see others determines the type of beam in your eye.

Lords Prayer

9 After this manner therefore pray ye: Our Father which art in heaven, Hallowed be thy name. 10 Thy kingdom come . Thy will be done in earth, as it is in heaven. 11 Give us this day our daily bread. 12 And forgive us our debts, as we forgive our debtors. 13 And lead us not into temptation, but deliver us from evil: For thine is the kingdom, and the power, and the glory, for ever. Amen. 14 For if ye forgive men their trespasses, your heavenly Father will also forgive you: 15 But if ye forgive not men their trespasses, neither will your Father forgive your trespasses. (Matthew 6:9-15)

The Lord's Prayer was given by Christ to the disciples. It is easy to ask God's forgiveness, but difficult to grant it to others. Whenever we ask God to forgive us, we should ask ourselves "Have I forgiven the people who have wronged me?"

The phrase *"Our Father which art in heaven"* indications that God is not only magnificent, divine and loving.

The phrase *"Thy kingdom come"* is a reference to God's divine sovereignty. The phrase *"Thy will be done,"* means we are not giving up on ourselves to disaster, but praying that God's perfect purpose will be accomplished in our lives. When we pray *"Give us this day our daily bread,"* we are acknowledging that God is our Sustainer and Provider. Jesus is not implying that God leads us into temptation. God has promised that He won't allow us to be tempted beyond our endurance.

In the LBGT/SGL community, it is imperative to seek God's help when you recognize temptations and for God to give you strength to overcome it. Jesus stresses the need to forgive ourselves and others. When we do not forgive others, we are denying our need of God's forgiveness.

Love

> *He that loveth not knoweth not God; for God is love.* (1John 4:8)
>
> *Love worketh no ill to his neighbour: therefore love is the fulfilling of the law.* (Romans 13:10)

God is the source of our love. We are all just an expression of the inner manifestation of God's love. God's love is shocking and will contradict what you may have been trained to think about the love of God. God's love surpasses religious laws.

In your daily life, love is your choice resulting in an action. We are called to treat all people as we would want to be treated. We should not ignore the rich, because then we would be withholding our love. But we must not favor them for what they can do for us, while ignoring the poor because we think

*Chapter 14   The Re-dedication of Christians Who
Happen To Be LBGT/SGL*

they can offer us little in return. When we fail to love, we are actually breaking God's law.

In the LBGT/SGL community, our love for one another must exceed any negative perception the world may attempted to convey to us as righteousness. We are called to examine our attitude and actions toward others not displacing blame on the heterosexual community. When we are ready to criticize one of our sisters or brothers we should be asking ourselves; "Is this what God is expecting of me?"

The love for God and the relationship with God is linked to how we treat all of our sisters and brothers, even when there is something about their behavior that challenges our perception of them. We are all just an expression of the inner manifestation of God's love. We are all made in the likeness and image of God because of God's love *"For God so loved the world, that he gave us his only begotten Son, that whosoever believeth in him shall not perish, but have everlasting life". (John 3:16)* God gave us the very best He had and wants us to give the best of ourselves to help others.

Our sacrifices for God are not about going without; it is about Love. Love for one another, love for all our sisters and brothers *"Greater love hath no man than this, that a man lay down his life for his friend." (John 15:13)* During the civil rights movement it was love that brought white and black folks together to fight the injustices. It was love that during the early years of AIDS when gay men were afraid to touch their own brothers many of our lesbian sisters became care givers even when they did not have a full understanding of the disease *"If a man say, I love God, and hateth his brother, he is a liar: for he that Loveth not his brother whom he hath see, how can he love God whom he hath not seen? And this commandment have we from him, That he who loved God love his brother also".* (1John 4:20-21) We are commissioned to love one another.

Ministry

6 Who also hath made us able ministers of the New Testament; not of the letter, but of the spirit: for the letter killeth, but the spirit giveth life. (2Corinithians 3:6)

8 Unto me, who am less than the least of all saints, is this grace given, that I should preach among the Gentiles the unsearchable riches of Christ; (Ephesians 3:8)

When God calls, God equips. When Apostle Paul described himself as "least of all the saints," he was saying that without God's help, he would never be able to do God's work. Yet God chose him to share the Gospel with the Gentiles and gave him the power to do it. If you feel useless, you may be right—you may have forgotten what a difference God makes. People are ready to hear and receive the Good News of God's love, but with this promise comes the responsibility of putting the promises of God to work. The Lord wants us to fully enter into thy work of reaching the world with the love of God.

Fear comes when we believe the deceptions and distortions of others. Faith and empowerment come from believing the promises of God. As we serve God, we have the promises of God's presence and power.

God gave Apostle Paul the ability to share effectively the Gospel of Christ. You may not be an apostle or even an evangelist, but God will give you opportunities to tell others about Christ's unconditional love—and will provide you with the ability, courage, and power. Whenever an opportunity presents itself, make yourself available to God. As you focus on the other person and his or her needs, God will communicate your caring attitude, and your words will be natural, loving and compelling.

In the LBGT/SGL community, our ministries will develop and take shape in many forms within our cities, denominations and community centers. You are called to go where others are uncomfortable. You are called to go deeper in the wilderness where even the noblest people of faith will not journey that far into the wilderness. It is not about them, it's about you taking the mission of spreading God's unconditional love in places where you may also be uncomfortable but your trust will be in God alone.

Our wilderness experience will require us to use new resources, develop more insightful perspectives, teach to enlighten the most unlearned, develop more simple tools for understanding, and protect those weak in spirit but strong in character, challenge our traditions and operate with integrity.

As followers of Christ, we are part of the church. God has promised that we will overcome and claim victory. We must not be on the defensive, thinking we will one day lose. We should take the offensive and overcome evil with good.

Obedience

Woe unto you, scribes and Pharisees, hypocrites! For ye pay tithe of mint and anise and cumin, and have omitted the weightier matters of the law, judgment, mercy and faith: these ought ye to have done, and not to leave the

> *other undone. Ye blind guides, which strain at a gnat, and swallow a camel.* *(Matthew 23:23-24)*

Obedience is the visible expression of our love. Obedience to God is an intrinsic element of our covenant relationship with God. Sin is not about breaking the law but breaking the covenant with God. God's call for obedience is based on His own commitment to our well-being. When we obey, we have a clear conscience and uninterrupted fellowship with the Lord. We honor other people and manage conflict not run away from it.

It's possible to obey the details of the laws but still be disobedient in our general behavior. For example, we could be very precise and faithful about giving ten percent of our money to God, but refuse to give one minute of our time in helping others. Tithing is important, but paying tithes does not exempt us from fulfilling God's other directives. Even as a river flows through an unblocked channel, so does God's grace and provision flow through us when we follow God's ways.

The Pharisees strained their water so they wouldn't accidentally swallow a gnat—an unclean insect according to the Law. Meticulous about the details of ceremonial cleanliness, they nevertheless had lost their perspective on inner purity. Ceremonially clean on the outside, they had corrupt hearts.

In the LBGT/SGL community, we should emphasize the power God gives us is through the Holy Spirit not through the church. Where God calls us, God empowers us. God guides us in the ways that are best for us, and God gives us the power to live according to those ways. Even as the breath we breathe empowers our physical bodies, so the Holy Spirit empowers our spiritual lives.

Chapter 14   The Re-dedication of Christians Who Happen To Be LBGT/SGL

Planning

Take therefore no thought for the morrow: for the morrow shall take thought for the things of itself. Sufficient unto the day is the evil thereof.
(Matthew 6:34)

As we seek God, He will guide us in making our plans. Our plans cannot mess up God's plans. A plan is only as good as the information upon which it's based. Our human intellect is limited and inadequate. Apart from the Lord, our plans are liable to fail. The Lord promises wisdom to those who rely on God's word and depend on the Spirit of God.

Planning for tomorrow is time well spent; worrying about tomorrow is time wasted. Sometimes it's difficult to tell the difference. Careful planning is thinking ahead about goals, steps, and schedules, and trusting in God's guidance. When done well, planning can help alleviate worry. The worrier, by contrast, is consumed by fear and finds it difficult to trust God. The worrier lets their plans interfere with their relationship with God. Don't let worries about tomorrow affect your relationship with God today.

In the LGBT/SGL community, we should never forget God is in control of all things and always has been. Do not doubt God's good intentions for us. The wonders of creation, the evidence of God's constant care, and the priceless gift of Jesus Christ for our salvation gives us confidence that God will establish all who trust God.

Power of God

And the Lord said unto him, What is that in thine hand? And he said, a rod. And he said, Cast it out on the ground. And he cast it on the

> *ground, and it became a serpent: and Moses fled from before it.* (Exodus 4:2-4)

God's power is greater than any of the skills or resources we have at our disposal. While we may use the means that God has provided to us, we know that victory comes from God alone. God's power does not depend on human strength and power. In fact, our resources can get in the way if we rely on them instead of on the Lord. God's power flows through our weaknesses like electric currents through a wire. The wire is simply a conductor, with no power in it. But without the wire, the current doesn't flow. God is looking for people who are wired for his service.

A shepherd's staff was commonly a three-to six-foot wooden rod with a curved hook at the top. The shepherd used it for walking, guiding his sheep, killing snakes, and many other tasks. Still, it was just a stick, but God used the simple shepherd's rod Moses carried to teach him an important lesson. God sometimes takes joy in using ordinary things for extraordinary purposes. What are the ordinary things in your life—your voice, a pen, a hammer, a broom, a musical instrument? While it is easy to assume God can use only special skills, you must not hinder God's use of the everyday contributions you can make. Little did Moses imagine the power his simple staff would wield when it became the rod of God.

In the LBGT community, it is important for us to know this power is ours also as we grow our trust in God, obey and honor God. We should not look at the size of the problem but the size of our God. When there are great things to be done, we have a great God who will do them through us. God's power comes from thy presence within us.

Chapter 14 The Re-dedication of Christians Who Happen To Be LBGT/SGL

Our spiritual growth is likely to stir spiritual opposition. Spiritual battles require spiritual power. God's armor provides power against the schemes of the world, the flesh, and the accuser and slanderers *"For we wrestle not against flesh and blood, but against powers, against the rulers of the darkness of this world, against spiritual wickedness in high places. Where fore take unto you the whole armour of God, that ye may be able to withstand in the evil day, and having done all, to stand". (Ephesians 6:12-13)* When we seek and affirm the power of God that resides inside of us; we are called to be prepared not scared of those in our community, government and faith institutions who will not approve of the unleashing of this power. It's not just our time; it's our turn.

Presence of God
For in time of trouble he shall hide me in his pavilion: in the secret of his tabernacle shall he hide me; he shall set me up upon a rock.
(Psalms 27:5)

God's presence is like the sure hand of a guide who steadies us on a steep and slippery trail. We walk confidently because we know we are not walking alone. Even when we feel distant from God, we are assured God is with us. The sooner we break with our denial of the presence of God in our lives, the sooner we will be able to deal with the things we are trying to hide that challenge us. The promise of God's presence holds the promise of our freedom.

During the Old Testament times, God's presence was expressed in limited ways. For example, the high priest could enter the Holy of Holies only once a year. In Jesus Christ, the veil between us and God is torn away, and we all enter freely into his presence.

We often run to God when we experience difficulties. But David sought God's guiding presence every day. When troubles came his way, he was already in God's presence and prepared to handle any test.

In the LBGT/SGL community, we are call to invite our sisters and brothers to experience the presence of God in their lives. God is present with us, even when it does not look favorable for us. God's presence should be in our relationship with our partner, friends, business projects and missions. We are to call upon the presence of God in all aspects of our life.

Protection
Keep me as the apple of the eye, hide me under the shadow of thy wings. *(Psalms 17:8)*

Spiritual battles require spiritual protection. Our protection is directly related to the character, competence, and capability of our protector. The Lord is unsurpassed in all areas. God's hold on us---not our hold on God—is our ultimate basis for confidence. This does not diminish our call to trust and obey God, for we are saved by God grace. God never tires of saving us. The "shadow of thy wings" is a figure of speech symbolizing God's protection. God guards us just a mother bird protects her young by covering them with her wings.

In the LBGT/SGL community, when our enemies attack us, they are really attacking the Lord. We are continually reminded that victory is assured when we let the Lord fight our battles. God can turn our enemies against each other so that they destroy themselves while we walk away unscathed.

Chapter 14   The Re-dedication of Christians Who Happen To Be LBGT/SGL

God guards us from the dangers that stalk us. God is a refuge, a shelter, and a place of safety from all threats. God's promises shield us and inspire our faith and courage. The teaching of Jesus Christ illustrates we should protect ourselves through discernment, self-discipline, and the confident exercising of our authority in Christ.

Purpose/Mission

For whom he did foreknow, he also did predestinate to be conformed to the image of his Son, that he might be the firstborn among many brethren.   (Romans 8:29)

As you pursue your purpose in Christ; the Lord promises that your life will have lasting significance and eternal results. As you pursue your God-given purpose, don't get discouraged even when it appears that nothing is happening. God wastes nothing.

Discovering God's purpose begins with a wholehearted commitment to God. We give ourselves to the Lord and God will provide for us. God promises to make thy will known to us as we make ourselves available to him.

When we commit ourselves to fulfilling God's purpose for our lives we will find meaning for ourselves and lead others to know the truth of Jesus Christ.

In the LBGT/SGL community, our purpose in life was designated yet before we were born; the call on your life whether it is working with youth, elderly, homeless, parenting ministry or starting your own business. Your mission is revealed by how open you are to accepting the responsibility and commitment. Even when the people you respect and admire do not agree with your mission *"and who Knoweth whether thou art come to the kingdom for such a time as this?" (Esther 4:14)* We all have been positioned in place to serve others and grow our financial resources to do God's work. Poverty while serving God is a position not a purpose *"seek ye first the kingdom of God and thy righteousness and these things shall be added unto to you". (Matthew 6:33)* In many cases we are called to help in ministries that have multiple service layers and in other cases we are called to become a gift in someone life. You are either in the right place to help now or your path is leading you there for such a time as this.

If you are uncomfortable and doubt your abilities then you are on your way towards your mission. Your purpose aligns you with God to become totally dependent. *This battle is not yours it is the Lords (1Samuel 17:47).*

Relationships

[31]There came then his brethren and his mother, and, standing without, sent unto him, calling him. [32]And the multitude sat about him, and they said unto him, Behold, thy mother and thy brethren without seek for thee. [33]And he answered them, saying, Who is my mother, or my brethren? [34]And he looked round about on them which sat about him, and said, Behold my mother and my brethren! [35]For whosoever shall do the will of God, the same is my brother, and my sister, and mother. (Mark 3:31-35, Matt 12:46-50, Luke 8:19-21)

Jesus was not denying his responsibility to his earthly family. Instead Jesus is pointing out that spiritual relationships are as binding as physical ones. Jesus is paving the way for a new community of believers (the universal church), our spiritual family.

Chapter 14   The Re-dedication of Christians Who Happen To Be LBGT/SGL

Jesus' mother was Mary, and his brothers were probably the other children Mary and Joseph had after Jesus. Many Christians, however, believe the ancient tradition that Jesus was Mary's only child. If this is true, the "brothers" were possibly cousins (cousins were often called brothers in those days). Some have offered yet another suggestion: when Joseph married Mary, he was a widower, and these were his children by his first marriage.

Although Jesus cared for his mother and brothers, he also cared for all those who loved Him. Jesus did not show partiality. He allowed everyone the privilege of obeying God and becoming part of His family. He shows us how to relate to other believers in this new way. God's family is open and doesn't exclude anyone. Christ offers us an intimate family relationship with Him.

In the LBGT/SGL community, our relationship with the Lord requires us to receive everyone in our family as a child of God. We are called to care for them even when they may not agree with our lifestyle chooses. Our relationship with Christ guides us to having a more loving relationship with family, partner, friends and strangers. The foundation of the family is love. Love does not care about image. Jesus illustrates that we are all God's children and our God wants us to have the best in life like any parent wants for their children. God is father and mother of us all *"for we are made in the likeness and image of God". (Genesis 2:27)*

Salvation

For by grace are ye saved through faith; and that not of yourselves: it is the gift of God:
(Ephesians 2:8)

God created us for a purpose. Salvation enables us to fulfill that purpose through the power of God at work within us. God has both the power and the desire to save whosoever. We are saved by faith, putting our confidence and trust in what God has done for us in Christ.

Being saved means accepting a relationship with Christ and applying the teachings of Christ in our daily lives (i.e. love and service to others). The salvation of God provides a new pathway to an inner peace. As Christians, even after we have been given the gift of salvation, still feel duty-bound to try to work our way to God. Our salvation is a gift that we receive with gratitude, praise, joy and serving others.

In the LBGT/SGL community our lives are salvation is tied to the gift of God given to all. It is not tied to your sexuality but your individuality. Spirituality before sexuality and no one can take away your individuality. You are unique in God's own way. There is no one like on but you. You were saved by grace by the blood of Jesus Christ shed on a hill called Calvary. Grace is the favor that was given to all of us a gift from God. Thank God on a daily for the gift of grace *"Amazing grace how sweet the sound that saved a wretch like me. I was once lost but now I am found; I blind but now I see."*

Sins

For all have sinned, and come short of the glory of God   *(Romans 3:23, Galatians 3:22)*

10:4 For it is not possible that the blood of bulls and of goats should take away sins.
                              (Hebrews 10:4, 10:15-17)

Chapter 14 The Re-dedication of Christians Who Happen To Be LBGT/SGL

Where of the Holy Ghost also is a witness to us: for after that he had said before, 16 This is the covenant that I will make with them after those days, saith the Lord, I will put my laws into their hearts, and in their minds will I write them; 17 And their sins and iniquities will I remember no more. *(Hebrews 10:15-17)*

Your sexuality is not the sin. The sin is letting others lead you into questioning your relationship with God and creating the doubt whether God loves you. Your sexuality is not a surprise to God. God knew what you were before you knew yourself *"Before I formed thee in the belly I knew thee; and before thou camest forth out of the womb I sanctified thee, and I ordained thee a prophet unto the nations". (Jeremiah 1:5)* The sin knowledge is acquired. You were born out of love, by love to love.

Some sins appear to be bigger than others because of their learned civil or moral consequences as being much more serious. Murder, for example, seems to us to be worse than hatred, and adultery seems worse than lust. All sin makes us sinners for there is no sin least or greater in the eyes of God.

In Hebrews, the writer illustrates that God will never remember your sins. Christ forgives completely, so there is no need to confess our past sins repeatedly. As believers, we can be confident that the sins we confess and renounce are forgiven and forgotten.

Animal sacrifices could not take away sin; they provided only a temporary way to deal with sin until Jesus came to deal with it permanently. In the Old Testament believers were following God's command and he graciously forgave them when, by faith, they made their sacrifices. This practice was no longer necessary when Christ made himself the ultimate sacrifice.

In the LBGT/SGL community, we must not get embarrassed, paranoid or annoyed every time we hear the word sin. The sin nature is in all of us. For sin is the disobedience to God's will and God's will is for us to love one another. We should be taking our unloving thoughts and ways to the Lord, not pouring out our hearts at a mock altar. Jesus sacrifice of his life was the ultimate altar "the cross", "the crucifixion" it is a symbol and reminder of Him giving His life for all our sins. We are called to love God with our whole heart, mind and soul. God does not keep track of your sins (non-loving actions). God forgives and forgets them, you should try taking Gods lead *"For my yoke is easy and my burden is light" (Matthew 11:30).* This invitation is not limitation or restriction but to guidance for you daily. This invitation is not about carrying the burden of sins but letting the Lord carry the burdens with you. God will take care of you *"Come unto me, all ye that labour and are heavy laden, and I will give you rest". (Matthew 11:28)*

Strength
> *He given power to the faint; and to them that have no might he increaseth strength. Even the youths shall faint and be weary, and the young men shall utterly fall: But they that wait upon the Lord shall renew their strength; they shall mount up with wings as eagles; they shall run, and not be weary; and they shall walk, and not faint.*   *(Isaiah 40:29-31)*

We all need regular times to listen to God. Waiting upon the Lord is expecting God's strength to help us rise above life's

*Chapter 14   The Re-dedication of Christians Who
Happen To Be LBGT/SGL*

distractions and difficulties. Strength starts in the heart long before it is exerted in other aspects of life. Having the strength to obey, endure, and triumph in all circumstances.

God's strength in us is a result of God's love for us. In God's strength we have the power to do things that we could never do on our own. We can withstand the toughest attacks and can take the offensive to overcome our problems. Believing in God's strength we can learn to manage our fears. Even people who appear to be consistently strong get tired at times. God's power and strength will never diminish. God is never too tired or too busy to guide and protect.

Our strength is not about walking around throwing our weight around or puffing up our chest. No, that is E.G.O. *"edging God out"*, the scriptures tell us *"But God has chosen the foolish things of the world to confound the wise; and God hath chosen the weak things of the world to confound the mighty". (1Corinthians 1:27)* Our strength is about our belief in a God with awesome power and there is nothing too hard for God to do. Our strength in God will shock not just ourselves but our adversaries to changing their ideas and agendas about who we are.

In the LBGT/SGL community, our strength in the Lord is needed to assist us in managing the many internal and external challenges we face daily. When we begin to rely on God's strength within us, it calls us to seek guidance, fairness, commonality, perseverance, courage, wisdom and peace of mind.

Never underestimate the strength and power of God. The strength of God is in the power. The strength of God brings down the walls of Jericho, the strength of God tells the sea to part, the strength of God tells your storms to be still, the strength of God can speak a word in the distance and change your life. The strength of God also resides in you.

Wealth

> *33 But seek ye first the kingdom of God, and his righteousness; and all these things shall be added unto you.* (Matthew 6:33)
>
> *³⁴For where your treasure is, there will your heart be also.* (Luke 12:34)

To seek *"first the kingdom of God, and his righteousness"* stresses that you should turn to God first for help and fill your thoughts with God's desires for your life. What is really important to you; career, relationships, finances, new job, family, education, health or ministry? Commit to making God first and foremost in your life and all those other things in life will be revealed to you.

Having a relationship with God does not mean you are required to be financially poor. This is the result of some of misguided teachings that to serve God is to have lack and surrender everything. This is so far from the truth within the teachings of Jesus Christ. Your wealth, career achievements, or educational desires should not take precedence over serving God. Let God be in all those areas of your life.

In the LBGT/SGL community, we are considered by marketers to have a lot of disposable income. Our wealth ambitions are important to establishing financial self sufficiency. If you were to get sick, who is going to take care of you? If you were to lose your job, who is going to pay your bills? The odds are you may be your only source of income for a greater part of your adulthood. Whether this is true for you or not, seeking a relationship with God to cover every project you are working on in life will bring you all of your heart's desires. John Calvin says, *"Make all you can, save all you can, give away all you can."*

God has no desire for you to live in poverty but desires for you to receive your blessings so that you may bless others in need. Serving God connects you to an infinite source of resources that money does not provide. You can have financial stability and still feel empty inside and lonely even when you are in a room full of people. God presence as the foremost thing in your life makes all things valuable but not put value in all things that would go above God. Commit to God as being first and foremost in your life and all the blessing you desire will come your way.

Witnessing

18 And Jesus came and spake unto them, saying, All power is given unto me in heaven and in earth. 19 Go ye therefore, and teach all nations, baptizing them in the name of the Father, and of the Son, and of the Holy Ghost: 20 Teaching them to observe all things whatsoever I have commanded you: and, lo , I am with you always, even unto the end of the world. Amen. *(Matthew 28:18-20)*

26 For as the body without the spirit is dead, so faith without works is dead also. *(James 2:26)*

Sharing our faith is a natural expression of our fellowship with Jesus. God promises to direct us and put us in the path of those in our community who are ready to hear the good news (Gospel) of God's love for us.

Our witnessing is not about making people become self righteous but self reliant on a God of love, compassion, grace and mercy. Our faith fuels our works to journey into places even the most self righteous openly LBGT/SGL believers will not go *"And the Pharisees and scribes murmured, saying, this man receiveth sinners, and eateth with them". (Luke 15:2)*

God is there to give us the words and the strength to proclaim our love and relationship with God. When the enemy tries to intimidate us with lies about our inadequacies, we can call upon the promise that the truth will set us free to share our faith boldly.

In the LBGT/SGL community, our witnessing to others in our community must not be rooted in shame, guilt or preconditions. Our witnessing is not an Apostolic, Baptist, Holiness, Lutheran, Methodist Presbyterian or Unitarian method. Our witnessing must be rooted in a message of unconditional love, hope, courage, prosperity and peace of mind.

God's love does not care about image. God loves says go where others will not go and spread the message of love, hope, grace, mercy forgiveness, reconciliation and redemption. We must use all the available tools we have; texting messaging, internet social networks, issue target brochures, radio, network TV, cable, bible studies, conferences and peer to peer outreach.

*Chapter 14   The Rededication of Christians Who
Happen To Be Same Gender Loving*

Appendix A
Scripture Reference

Chapter 1 The Mis-Education About The Bible, pg 1
Romans 3:18, Psalms 36:1, Proverbs 6:23, 2Timothy 3:16, John 3:16-17

Chapter 2 The Mis-Education of Adam & Eve, pg 15
Genesis 1:27, 2:21, 1:2 , 1:31-2, John 1:14, Hebrews 11:1-2, Genesis 2:7, *2:8*, 3:8 3:2, 1:3, 1:26, 2:7 , 2:22, 2:15, 2:23, 2:9, 2:17, 3:5 , 3:7, 2:17-19, 3:24, 1Corinthians 15:47, Genesis 2:25, 2:24, 3:10, 2:8-15, 3:2-5, 3:12-13, 3:14-15, Mark 10:2-12, Wisdom of Solomon 2:24, Romans 8:22,16:20, Genesis. 3:16, 1:28-29, 2:15, 3:20, 3:21, 3:18, 3:22, 3:24, 12, Deuteronomy 24:16, Genesis 4:9, 4:16-17

Chapter 3 The Mis-Education of the Rainbow, pg 39
Matthew 5:11, Matthew 7:1, Genesis 6:8 – 9, 9:19-28 (NIV), Matthew 7:1-2, Genesis 7:2, 9:18, Genesis 9:24, 9:23, 9:25, 10:6-20, 9:22, 6:5, 7:7 Jeremiah 1:5

Chapter 4 The Mis-Education About Sodom & Gomorrah, pg 50
Genesis 19, Genesis 18, Genesis 19:1-3, Genesis 19:5 (KJV), Genesis 19:5 (NIV) Genesis 19:8-10, 9:13-16, Matthew 7:7

Chapter 5 The Mis-Education About Being An Abomination, pg 71
Leviticus 18:22, 20:1-5, Matthew 15:21-29. (NRSV), Matthew 15:26, Leviticus 18:6-17, 18:19, 18:20, 18:23, 17-26, 20:13-14, 19:13, 19:17-18, 19:19 19:26, 19:27, 19:28, 19:30, Matthew 12:1-8, Matthew 6:33, Matthew 12:9-13

Chapter 6 The Mis-Education About Gay Marriage, pg 85
Matthew 22:23-33 - *22:29* , Luke 1.34-37, Deuteronomy 7:3, Deuteronomy 25:5 (KJV), Deuteronomy 25:5 (BBE) , Exodus 20:3

Chapter 7 The Mis-Education of Present Day Gentiles (same gender loving), pg 109
John 8:7, Romans 1:16-17, Luke 14:7-14, Romans 1:26-27, Leviticus 18:22 and 20:13, John 3:17, Matthew 15:1-3, Galatians 2:11-20, Galatians 2:11, Romans 2, Romans 2:11-16, Romans 2:17-29, Galatians 4:21-31, Romans 3:1-8, Romans 3:8-9, **Matthew 7:1-** Romans 3:9-31, Romans 3:9-10, Romans 3:21 John 3:16-17, Matthew 9:11

Chapter 8 The Mis-Education about the Word Homosexuality, pg 131
First Corinthians 6:9, Matthew 6:21, Matthew 6:24, Jude 1:4, Deuteronomy 28:54, 56, Isaiah 3:15-24, 2Kings 22:19, Job 23:16, Psalms 55:21, Isaiah 7:4., 1 Corinthians 6, 1Corinthians 6:1-8 , 1Corinthians 5:1-2, 1Corinthians 6:9

Chapter 9 The Mis-Education About Jesus & Homosexuality, pg 141
1John 4:20, Matthew 22:34-40, Mark 12:28-34, Deuteronomy 6:5, Leviticus 19,

*The Mis-Education Against
Homosexuality In The Bible*

John 1:17 Romans 8:38-39 **Genesis 18**, Matthew 10:15 Mark 6:11 Matthew 10:5, Mark 6:8-13, Luke 9:2-6, 12:2-10, Matthew 10:5-6, 8:5-13, 8:10, 11, 11:23, Luke 10:12 , 10:1-16, 10:12-15, 17:29, 17:20-37, 17:21 Matthew 19:1-12

Chapter 10 The Mis-Education About Love In The Bible, pg 157
Ruth 1:16-17, 2:10-11, 1:3-5, 2:1-3:18, 1:16-18, Romans 12:2, 1Samuel 18:1-4, 19:24, Isa. 20:24, 1Samuel 18:5-30:31, Proverbs 18:24, 1Samuel 20:41 (NIV), 1Samuel 20:41(KJV)

Chapter 11 The Mis-Education of Ten Words Used Against Homosexuality, pg 177
1. Abomination   John 8:7, Lev. 11:10-12 11:7, 17:10, 19:26, 18:20, 19:17, 19:19, Deut. 22:11, Lev. 19:28, 18:22, 20:13, 19:13,19:27, 22:5, Deut. 25:13-16, Prov. 11:1, 20:10, 20:23, Psalm 15:5, 1John 4:20
2. Anti-Christ   John 4:43-54 43
3. Curse   1Corinthians 6:10, Gentiles 25:31-46, Matthew 25:41, Luke 6:28, Galatians 3:10-14, Deuteronomy 27:11- 26, Deuteronomy 27:3, Romans 12:3-21 Romans 12:10
4. Devil/Satan   Job 1:6-2:13, Matthew 4:1-11, Revelation 20:1-9, Psalms 109:1-6, Psalm 109:6, Matthew 12:22-30
5. Evil   Philippians 1:20-21, Isaiah 45:7
6. Hell & Damnation   Isaiah 66:24, Jeremiah 7:20, Mark 9:43-50, Numbers 18:19, Matthew 5:13
7. Immoral   1Corinthians 6:12-20, 6:1-11, Matthew 7:1-6, 7:1-2, 27:19, Romans 14:3, 2Corinthians 5:9-10, Romans 2:11
8. Pervert/Perversion   Deuteronomy 16:19, Jeremiah 3:21, Acts 13:10 Galatians 1:7, Philippians 2:15, 2:5-16
9. Repentance   Luke 15:11-31 Luke 15, Luke 18, Luke 10:13 Matthew 27:3, Genesis 32, 32:26, Psalms 51:10, 2Corinthians 12:7-10
10. Sinner   Romans 3:23; 6:23, Ephesians 2:1-3, Isaiah 53:6, Ezekiel 28:1-19 Ezekiel 28:6-9, Genesis 2:4-3:24 Matthew 12:31-37, John 8:1-11 John 8:7, John 8:11, Romans 5:6-8, Romans 6:23

Chapter 12 The Mis-Education of Bible Topics And Homosexuality, pg 217
12.1 The Mis-Education of Cross Dressing
Deuteronomy 22:5
12.2 The Mis-Education about AIDS
Deuteronomy 23:4-6, 17-23, Job 38-41, Job 42:1-6
12.3 The Mis-Education of Temple Homosexuality
1Kings 14:21-24, 1King 15:12, 1Kings 22:46

12.4. The Mis-Education of Temple Prostitutes
1Kings 15:9-15, *1Kings 15:16-24*

12.5   The Mis-Education about Satan
1Chronicles 21:1-4, John 3:16-17, Luke 15
12.6   The Mis-Education About Job & Satan
Job 1-37
12.7   The Mis-Education About Punishment
Ezekiel 16:49-50 , Genesis 3
Ezekiel 16:4-6, 16:7-8, 16:9-14 ,16:15-19, 16:20-22, 16:35-39, 16:40-43, 16:44-46, 16:44-52, 16:53-58, 16:59-63, 1Kings 15:12, 22:46; 2Kings 23:7, Luke 10:30-37
12.8   The Mis-Education about Gay Clergy
1Timothy 1:7-10, 2Timothy 3:16-17,
12.9   The Mis-Education About Women Silent
1Cor 14:34-35, 1Timothy 2:11-12, 1Peter 2:15
12.10   The Mis-Education About Lust
James 1:13, 1:14-15, James 4:2-6, Matthew 6:24, Matthew 6:33
12.11   The Mis-Education From A TV Evangelist
1Peter 1:22-25
12.12   The Mis-Education of Sodom & Gomorrah
2Peter 2:6, John 3:16-17
12.13   The Mis-Education About Destruction
Revelations 11:8, 20:10,   Matthew 5:44, Revelations 2-3, 6:1-8, 7:1-8, 14:1-13, 13:18
12.14   The Mis-Education of Eunuchs
Daniel 1:9, Acts 8:26-38, Acts 8:32-33, Acts 8:37
12.15   The Mis-Education of Homosexuality & Rape
Judges 19:11-30, Genesis 19, 19:1, 19:15, Leviticus 21:7, Judges 19:2, 19:22, 20:5, 19:25
12.16   The Mis-Education of Going After Strange Flesh
Jude 7, Mark 6:3, Genesis 19:5, John 1:14, Genesis 6:1-4, Matthew 15:2

Chapter 13 pg 263 No Scriptures References

Chapter 14 The Rededication of Christians Who Happen To Be LBGT/SGL , pg 281

Abandonment   Psalm 27:10, 2Corinthians 4:9, Philippians 3:12-14, Hebrews 11:1
Acceptance   Galatians 2:16
Addiction(s) Romans 12:2
Adversity James 1:11
Aging   Psalms 92:14, Genesis 18:14
Anger   Matthew 18:15-20, Psalms 110:1, Hebrews 10:13, Romans 12:2
Assurance   John 10:27-30, John 2:19
Beginnings 2Corinthians 5:17
Betrayal   Romans 12:19-21
Bible 2Timothy 3:16-17
Blessings Proverbs 19:17
Challenges James 1:2-4, Isaiah 54:17

The Mis-Education Against
Homosexuality In The Bible

Character Galatians 5:22-23
Communion Matthew 26:26-29, Mark 14:22-25, Luke 22:19, 20, 1Cor. 11:23-26
Conflict Psalms 27:1-3
Courage Philippians 4:13, Romans 8:37
Depression Matthew 11:28
Discernment Hebrews 5:12-14, 2Timothy 1:7)
Doubt James 1:6, Heb. 11:1
Endurance Mark 13:13, Romans 8:39
Faith Mark 11:22-24, Matt 21:20-22, Matthew 17:20, Hebrews 11:1
Failure Luke 22:62
Family Matthew 12:46-50
Fear Exodus 46:3-4, Romans 8:31
Forgiveness Matthew 18:22, Matthew 18:21-22
Giving 2Corinthians 9:6-7
Grace Ephesians 1:7-8
Guilt Romans 3:9-10, Romans 2:11
Heaven Matthew 22:29-33, Luke 27, 40, Mark 12:24-25, 2Corinthians 5:1
Hope Philippians 3:13-14, Matthew 10:22
Humility Matthew 18:1-5, John 13:8
Hunger for God Matthew 6:33, John 6:35
Integrity Psalms 25:21, Psalms 25:3
Judging Matthew 7:1-6
Lords Prayer Matthew 6:9-15
Love 1John 4:8, Romans 13:10, John 3:16, John 15:13, 1John 4:20-21
Ministry 2Corinithians 3:6, Ephesians 3:8
Obedience Matthew 23:23-24
Planning Matthew 6:34
Power of God Exodus 4:2-4, Ephesians 6:12-13
Presence of God Psalms 27:5
Protection Psalms 17:8
Purpose/Mission Romans 8:29, Esther 4:14, 1Samuel 17:47
Relationships Mark 3:31-35, Matt 12:46-50, Luke 8:19-21, Genesis 2:27
Salvation Ephesians 2:8
Sins Romans 3:23, Galatians 3:22, Hebrews 10:4, 10:15-17, Jeremiah 1:5, Matthew 11:30, 11:28
Strength Isaiah 40:29-31, 1Corinthians 1:27
Wealth Matthew 6:33, Luke 12:34
Witnessing Matthew 28:18-20, James 2:26, Luke 15:2

Appendix

Appendix B
Charts & Figures

What Would Jesus Do? (Chapter 4, pg 64 Charts & Figures 4.1)

Should The City Be Destroyed?	
Sodom & Gomorrah (Genesis 19)	**City of Samarians** (Luke 9:51-56)
Outcast because of worship practices	Outcast because of mixed race
Visited by Angels	Visited by messengers from Jesus
Lot showed hospitality with a place to sleep	City refused to provide a place to sleep
Destroy with fire from heaven	Threaten to be destroyed by fire from heaven
Chose not to shake off the dust from their feet	Jesus chose to shake off the dust from his feet
Seeking Righteousness	Unrighteous Spirit
Destroyed life	Jesus Saved Lives

Charts &Figures 4.1

The Mis-Education Against
Homosexuality In The Bible

What Would Jesus Do? (Chapter 4, pg 65 Charts & Figures 4.2)

City Samaria Rejects Christ And He Does Not Destroy The City (Luke 9:51-56)			
New American Standard Bible (NASB)	**The Bible in Basic English**	**New International Version (NIV)**	**King James Version (KJV)**
9:54 When His disciples James and John saw this, they said, "Lord, do You want us to command fire to come down from heaven and consume them?"	**9:54** And when his disciples, James and John, saw this, they said, Lord, may we send fire from heaven and put an end to them?	**9:54** When the disciples James and John saw this, they asked, "Lord, do you want us to call fire down from heaven to destroy them?"	**9:54** And when his disciples James and John saw this, they said, Lord, wilt thou that we command fire to come down from heaven, and consume
9:55 But He turned and rebuked them, [and said, "You do not know what kind of spirit you are of;	**9:55** But turning round he said sharp words to them.	**9:55** But Jesus turned and rebuked them,	**9:55** But he turned, and rebuked them, and said, Ye know not what manner of of spirit ye are of.
9:56 for the Son of Man did not come to destroy men's lives, but to save them."] And they went on to another village.	**9:56** And they went to another small town.	**9:56** and they went to another village.	**9:56** For the Son of man is not come to destroy men's lives, but to save them. And they went to

Appendix

Fourteenth Amendment (Chapter 4, Pg 89 Charts & Figures 6.1)

> **Fourteenth Amendment (Amendment XIV)**
> *Section 1. All persons born or naturalized in the United States, and subject to the jurisdiction thereof, are citizens of the United States and of the State wherein they reside. No State shall make or enforce any law which shall abridge the privileges or immunities of citizens of the United States; nor shall any State deprive any person of life, liberty, or property, without due process of the law; nor deny to any person within its jurisdiction the equal protection of the laws.*

Charts & Figures 6.1

Deuteronomy 25:5 (Chapter 6, Pg 97 Charts & Figures 6.2)

Deuteronomy 25:5

King James Version	Bible In Basic English
If brethren dwell together, and one of them die, and have no child, the wife of the dead shall not marry without unto a stranger: her husband's brother shall go in unto her, and take her to him to wife, and perform the duty of an husband's brother unto her.	If brothers are living together and one of them, at his death, has no son, the wife of the dead man is not to be married outside the family to another man: let her husband's brother go in to her and make her his wife, doing as it is right for a brother-in-law to do.

Charts & Figures 6.3

Ballot Initiatives (Chapter 6, Pg 98 Charts & Figures 6.3)

2008 State Ballot Initiatives	
Arizona Proposition 102: Ban on Gay Marriage	Passed
Arizona Proposition 202: Hiring Illegal Immigrants	Passed
Arkansas Initiative 1: Ban on Gay Couples Adopting Children	Passed
California Proposition 8: Ban on Gay Marriage	Passed
California Proposition 4: Abortion Limits	Failed
Colorado Amendment 46: End Affirmative Action	Failed
Colorado Amendment 48: Human Life from Moment of Conception	Failed
Florida Amendment 2: Ban on Gay Marriage	Passed
Nebraska Initiative 424: End Affirmative Action	Passed
South Dakota Initiative 11: Abortion Limits	Failed

Charts & Figures 6.2

Appendix

Slavery and LBGT/SGL Comparison
(Chapter 7, Pg 127 Charts & Figures 7.1)

Slavery and LBGT/SGL Comparison	
Slave	**Our Kulture(LBGT/SGL)**
Slave Master (Oppressor)	Pastors with Anti Gay Position
Slave Master (Liberator)	Love and Accepting Ministry—teach how to read for ourselves, sacrificed family, potential financial gain and alienation from peers.
Field Negro	Out and acknowledges same gender attraction.
House Negro	"House Homo" will not talk with master, even though they have a prominent position in his house *(i.e. Church Clergy, Media Personalities, Entertainers, Executives).*
Abolitionist	Heterosexuals who speak about the inclusion of LBGT/SGL community
Freedom Fighters	LBGT/SGL Activists

Charts & Figures 7.1

The Mis-Education Against
Homosexuality In The Bible

Love Is The Key (Chapter 9, Pg 147 Charts & Figures 158)

Love Is The Key
Matthew 22:34-40 & Mark 12:28-31
"On these two commandments hang all the laws and the prophets"
(Matthew 22:40)

Old Testament	Old Testament
Thou Shalt Love The Lord Thy God With All Thy Heart And All Of Thy Soul, And All Thy Mind (Deuteronomy 6:5) Deut. book of the second law.	Love Thy Neighbor As Thyself (Leviticus 19:18) Leviticus book of the first law.
Matthew 22:40 On these two Commandments hang all of the law and the prophets.	Mark 12:31 There is no other Commandment greater than these.

Charts & Figures 9.1

Perceptions Vs. Realties (Chapter 10, Pg 172 Charts & Figures 10.1)

PERCEPTIONS Vs. REALTIES		
Heterosexual	Black on Black	LBGT/SGL
Based on commitment to God **** Let nothing come between them **** Friendship grew after being tested **** Friendship never died	Homeboy is the only one that stuck with me **** When I did not have the money my friend help me	Secret love affair, Down low couple **** Best friend stuck with me when my family did not. **** Heterosexual friend has always been understanding

Charts & Figures 10.1

Appendix

1Timothy 1:10 Bible Comparison
(Chapter 12, Pg 257 Charts & Figures 12.1)

1Timothy 1:10 Bible Comparison	
✓ For them that defile themselves with mankind (King James Version)	✓ These laws are for people who are sexually immoral, for homosexuals (New Living Translation)
✓ For adulterers and perverts (New International Version)	✓ Immoral men and homosexuals (New American Standard Bible)
✓ And immoral men and homosexuals and kidnappers and liars and perjurers, and whatever else is contrary to sound teaching, (New American Standard Bible)	✓ [For] impure and immoral persons, those who abuse themselves with men (Amplified Bible)

Charts & Figures 12.1

The Mis-Education Against Homosexuality In The Bible

Appendix C

Canada Civil Marriage Act
(Refer Gay Marriage Chapter 6, pg 81)

Bill C-38. The Civil Marriage Act. "An Act respecting certain aspects of legal capacity for marriage for civil purposes" Feb.1, 2005.

The Preamble and Sections 1-4.

"WHEREAS the Parliament of Canada is committed to upholding the Constitution of Canada , and section 15 of the *Canadian Charter of Rights and Freedoms* guarantees that every individual is equal before and under the law and has the right to equal protection and equal benefit of the law without discrimination;

"WHEREAS the courts in a majority of the provinces and in one territory have recognized that the right to equality without discrimination requires that couples of the same sex and couples of the opposite sex have equal access to marriage for civil purposes;

"WHEREAS the Supreme Court of Canada has recognized that many Canadian couples of the same sex have married in reliance on those court decisions;

"WHEREAS only equal access to marriage for civil purposes would respect the right of couples of the same sex to equality without discrimination, and civil union, as an institution other than marriage, would not offer them that equal access and would violate their human dignity, in breach of the *Canadian Charter of Rights and Freedoms* ;

"WHEREAS the Supreme Court of Canada has determined that the Parliament of Canada has legislative jurisdiction over marriage but does not have the jurisdiction to establish an institution other than marriage for couples of the same sex;

"WHEREAS everyone has the freedom of conscience and religion under section 2 of the *Canadian Charter of Rights and Freedoms;*

"WHEREAS nothing in this Act affects the guarantee of freedom of conscience and religion and, in particular, the freedom of members of religious groups to hold and declare their religious beliefs and the freedom of officials of religious groups to refuse to perform marriages that are not in accordance with their religious beliefs;

"WHEREAS, in light of those considerations, the Parliament of Canada's commitment to uphold the right to equality without discrimination precludes the use of section 33 of the *Canadian Charter of Rights and Freedoms* to deny the right of couples of the same sex to equal access to marriage for civil purposes;

"WHEREAS marriage is a fundamental institution in Canadian society and the Parliament of Canada has a responsibility to support that institution because it strengthens commitment in relationships and represents the foundation of family life for many Canadians;

"AND WHEREAS, in order to reflect values of tolerance, respect and equality consistent with the *Canadian Charter of Rights and Freedoms* , access to marriage for civil purposes should be extended by legislation to couples of the same sex;

"NOW, THEREFORE, Her Majesty, by and with the advice and consent of the Senate and House of Commons of Canada, enacts as follows:

Appendix

1. This Act may be cited as the *Civil Marriage Act*
2. Marriage, for civil purposes, is the lawful union of two persons to the exclusion of all others.
3. It is recognized that officials of religious groups are free to refuse to perform marriages that are not in accordance with their religious beliefs.
4. For greater certainty, a marriage is not void or voidable by reason only that the spouses are of the same sex..."

Sections 5-15 deal with "Consequential Amendments" (Income Tax Act, Divorce Act, Prohibited Degrees, etc.). In these amendments the terms "natural parent" and "blood relationship" are replaced by "legal parent" and "legal parent-child relationship."

The Mis-Education Against Homosexuality In The Bible

APPENDIX D

BLACK SGL SURVEY

Black SGL Survey

This was an online survey of 167 Black SGL's. The goal of the survey was used to give me some guidance about what and how I should be writing or informing my community. This is not about any group, person or project being bad or good.

Which from the list provided you feel the most negative perception about your same-sex attraction?	
a. Parents	33.70%
b. Brother/Sister	21.40%
c. Friend	0%
d. In-Laws	0%
e. Clergy (Bishop/Pastor)	50%
f. Church Members	35.70%
g. Television Evangelist	14.30
h. Other -- Aunts/Uncles	7.10%

Which one of the following areas listed was a major factor with you becoming same-sex attracted?	
Born Gay	53.3%
Living environment gave you the opportunity to explore your sexuality	40%
Molested or Raped	33.3%
None of the above	6.7%

Do you believe Ruth & Naomi or Jonathan & David were in a same sex relationship?	
Yes	37.5%
No	18.8%
First time hearing that point of view	13.3%
Do not care	12.5%

Let Us Know What You Think?

a. Do you believe the bible is without error?

Yes – 35.7%   No – 63.3%

b. Do you believe it is okay to question the bible?

Yes – 80%   No – 20%

c. Would you consider yourself knowledgeable in the bible?

Yes – 80%   No – 20%

d. Do you believe you are going to hell because of your same sex attraction?

Yes – 7%   No – 93%

e. Do you know where in the bible it speaks about homosexuality in the bible?

Yes – 46%   No – 54%

f. Have you ever heard the word homosexual or effeminate in the bible was a mistranslation?

Yes – 33%   No – 67%

Appendix

Your Thoughts About Same Sex Marriage				
	Yes	No	Maybe	Need more info
(a) Do you believe in Same Sex Marriage?	70%	10%	20%	0%
(b) Do you believe in Same Sex Civil Unions?	61.5%	7.7%	30.8%	0%
(c) Do you believe the bible specifically speaks against Same Sex Marriage?	13.3%	73.3%	6.7%	6.7%

What are top three words from the list below, you feel have had the largest negative impact on people that are same sex attracted?

Abomination	68.8%
Anti-Christ	0.8%
Devil	0.9%
Evil	12.5%
Hell/Damnation	62.5%
Sexuality Immorality (religion and sexuality)	43.8%
Pervert/Perversion	37.5%
Repentance	25.0%
Satan	0.9%
Sinner	56.3%

Have you read or heard about any of the following books?	Read this book	Heard of this book	Have not heard of this book
Steps to recovery from bible abuse	0%	6.70	93.30%
The Church and the Homosexual	6.70%	26.70%	73.30%
The Good Book	6.70%	46.70%	46.70%
The invention of Sodomy in Christian Theology	0.%	0%	100%
New Testament & Homosexuality	0.%	13.30%	86.70
What the bible really says about homosexuality	33.30%	4%	33.30%

Bibliography

What The Bible Really Says About Homosexuality & The Bible,
Dr. Daniel A. Helminiak, Ph.D, Alamo Square Press Tajique, NM
ISBN 1-886360-09-X

Our Tribe: Queer Folks, God, Jesus, and the Bible. Rev. Nancy Wilson 1995 Harper Collins Publishers ISBN 0-06-0693967-7

The Good Book "Reading The Bible With Mind And Heart", Peter J Gomes, Harper Collins Publishers ISBN 0-06-008830-3

God of the Oppressed, James Cones 1975 Harper Collins Publishers, San Francisco
ISBN 0-0864-2607-4

The New Testament and Homosexuality: Contextual Background for Contemporary Debate, Robin Scroggs 1983 Fortress Press
ISBN 0-8006-0699-X

The Invention of Sodomy in Christian Theology, Prof. Mark D. Jordan, 1997 The University of Chicago Press ISBN 0-226-41039-0

Bible Almanac, 1980 Thomas Nelson Publishers, Nashville Tennessee
ISBN 0-8407-5162-1

The IVP Bible Background Commentary New Testament, John H. Walton, Victor Matthews, Mark Chavalas, Inter Varsity Press, Downers Grove, Illinois 60515   ISBN 0-8308-1419-1

The IVP Bible Background Commentary New Testament, Craig S. Keener, Inter Varsity Press, Downers Grove, Illinois 60515 ISBN 0-8308-1405-1

King James Homosexual, Croft, Pauline (2003). *King James*. Basingstoke and New York: Palgrave Macmillan. ISBN 0-333-61395-3. Page(s) 11-15

Davies, Godfrey ([1937] 1959). *The Early Stuarts*. Oxford: Clarendon Press. ISBN 0198217048.
Guy, John (2004). *My Heart is My Own: The Life of Mary Queen of Scots*. London and New York: Fourth Estate. ISBN 1-84115-752-X.

Lindley, David (1993). *The Trials of Frances Howard: Fact and Fiction at the Court of King James*. Routledge. ISBN 0415052068. .

Rhodes, Neil; Jennifer Richards; and Joseph Marshall (2003). *King James VI and I: Selected Writings.* Ashgate Publishing, Ltd. ISBN 0754604829.

Stewart, Alan (2003). *The Cradle King: A Life of James VI & I.* London: Chatto and Windus. ISBN 0-7011-6984-2. Page(s) 33,45,51-63

Stroud, Angus (1999). *Stuart England.* Routledge ISBN 0415206529.
Williams, Ethel Carleton (1970). *Anne of Denmark.* London: Longman. ISBN 0 582 12783 1.

Willson, David Harris ([1956] 1963 ed). *King James VI & I.* London: Jonathan Cape Ltd. ISBN 0-224-60572-0. Page(s) 18,28-29,35

Friedan, Betty. *It Changed My Life: Writings on the Women's Movement*, Hardcover Edition, Random House Inc. 1978 ISBN 0-394-46398-6

Friedan, Betty. *Life So Far*, Paperback Edition, Simon and Schuster 2000 ISBN 0-684-80789-0

Friedan, Betty. *The Feminine Mystique*, Hardcover Edition, W.W. Norton and Company Inc. 1963 ISBN 0-393-08436-1

Bergeron, David M. King James and Letters of Homoerotic Desire, Iowa City: University of Iowa P, 1999 "Esme Stuart".

Otto Scott's "James I: The Fool As King" (Ross House: 1976), pp. 108, 111, 120, 194, 200, 224, 311, 353, 382; King James-VI of Scotland/I of England by Antonia Fraser (Alfred A. Knopf, New York 1975)pp. 36, 37, 38;

King James VI and I by David Harris Wilson, pp.36, 99;

James I by his Contemporaries by Robert Ashton, p114; and
A History of England by Samuel Rawson Gardiner, Vol. 4, p.112.

Jonathan Loved David: Homosexuality in Biblical Times: Tom Horner, (1978) Westminster Press

A Literary History Of The Bible by Geddes MacGregor who has devoted a whole chapter entitled "QUEEN" JAMES.

The Mammoth Book of Private Lives by Jon E. Lewis, pp. 62,65,66
James White also makes mention of it in his book, THE KING JAMES ONLY.

A poem written by King James to his homosexual love interest King James-VI of Scotland/I of England, by Antonia Fraser, New York 1975

Today's Handbook of Bible Times & Customs, William L. Coleman, author Bethany House Publishers, Minneapolis, Minnesota 55458

Paul, Gregory S. (2005). "Cross-National Correlations of Quantifiable Societal Health with Popular Religiosity and Secularism in the Prosperous Democracies: A First Look". Journal of Religion and Society 7.

Gerson Moreno-Riaño; Mark Caleb Smith, Thomas Mach (2006). "Religiosity, Secularism, and Social Health". Journal of Religion and Society 8.

CONTROVERSY. King James and the History of Homosexuality by Michael B. Young

"He disdained women and fawned unconscionably on his favorite men." ENCYCLOPEDIA AMERICANA-pp. 674,675

Origins of the word Homosexual Feray, Jean-Claude; Herzer, Manfred (1990). "Homosexual Studies and Politics in the 19th Century: Karl Maria Kertbeny". Journal of Homosexuality, Vol. 19, No. 1

The Handbook On Biblical Personalities, George M. Alexander The Seabury Press Greenwich, Connecticut 1962

Slaves who dared : the stories of ten African-American heroes / by Mary Garrison. ISBN 1572492724   viii, 142 p. : ill. ; 27 cm. Includes bibliographical references (p. 131-135) and index.

Frederick Douglass and the fight for freedom / Douglas T.Miller. New York, N.Y. : Facts on File, c1988. ISBN: 0816016178

A woman called Moses : a novel based on the life of Harriet Tubman/ Marcy Heidish. Boston Houghton Mifflin, 1976. ISBN: 0395215358

Index

1

1 Corinthians 15:47 · 26

2

2 Kings 17:24-41 · 62
2 Timothy 3
16-17 · 4

A

A Point of View on the Ham Scenario · 47
Abomination
Adultery
  (Lev. 18:20) 180
Charging or paying interest
  (Psalm 15:5) · 181
Cheating weights and measures - i.e. Wall Street Greed Dishonesty in business.
  (Deut. 25:13-16,
  Prov. 11:1, 20:10, 20:23) · 181
Christian and Jewish Old Testament scriptures refer to homosexuality
  (Lev. 18:22, 20:13) · 180
Cross-dressing or women wearing pants (Deut. 22:5) · 180
Do not mix fabrics- i.e linen, silk (Lev 19:19, Deut. 22:11) · 180
No Blood – i.e. Medium rare food (Lev. 17:10 &19:26) · 180
No Haircut - i.e. trims, shaving (Lev. 19:27) · 180
No scales or fins –i.e. Lobster and crab (Lev. 11:10-12) · 180
No tattoos (Lev. 19:28) · 180
Pork i.e. ribs, chitterlings, bacon (Lev. 11:7) · 180
Thou shalt not hate thy brother and bear evil against him (Lev. 19:17) · 180
Wages shall not be kept overnight (Lev. 19:13) · 180
ABOMINATION · 179
Abominations
Do Not Mix Materials · 78
Love Thy Neighbor · 77
No Rare Steaks · 78
Sabbath Laws · 80
Abraham · iv, 32, 54, 55, 56, 59, 68, 86, 89, 151, 158, 205, 289, 319
Adam and Eve · 15, 21, 23, 25, 33, 34, 85, 214

Adversity
James 1:11 · 288
African-American · viii, x, 11, 90, 103, 125
Aging
Psalms 92:14 · 289
AIDS · 117, 187, 217, 221, 223, 329, 350
Angels · 52, 55, 56, 59, 60, 61, 86, 87, 149, 198, 257, 259, 260
Anger
Matthew 18:15-20 · 290
Anti-Christ
Jesus will not come with signs and symbols · 185
John 4:43-54 · 185
ANTI-CHRIST · 183
Are There Ten Righteous In The City? · 52, 59
Assurance
John 10:27-30 · 292
authorities · 2, 52, 53, 56
Avoiding Morality Utterances · 276

365

B

Bailey and Pillard · 36
Ballot Initiatives · 98, 356
Beginnings
2Corinthians 5:17 · 293
Betrayal
Romans 12:19-21 · 294
Bible
2Timothy 3:16-17 · 295
bisexual · 36, 60, 72, 75, 219, 264, 288
Blessings
Proverbs 19:17 · 296
blood line · 124
Blumendbach, Johann Friedrich
Almighty God created the races... ·
See Interracial Relationships
Booker T. Washington · 90
But every man is tempted,...
(James 1:14-15) · 243

C

Cain & Abel: Who "Dat" Woman? · 33
Calvin, John · 243
Caputo, Dr. John · 62
Caucasian Christians. · 125
Challenges
James 1:2-4 · 298
Character
Galatians 5:22-23 · 299
City of Samaria Rejects Jesus · 62
Civil Rights Act ·
See Gay Marriage
Civil Unions · 93
Communion
1Corinthians 11:23-26 · 300
Jeremiah 31:34-34 · 301
Matthew 26:26-29, Mark 14:22-25, Luke 22:19, 20 · 300
Concern with Homosexuality · 75
concubine · 257
concubines · 225
Conflict
Christian principles of paradox · 302
Psalms 27:1-3 · 301
Courage
Philippians 4:13 · 303
Creation · iv, 17, 18, 19, 20, 21, 22, 26, 32
Creation Story Challenges · 20
Cross Dressing · v, 217, 218, 350
Deuteronomy 22:5 · 218
Cultural Perceptions vs. Reality · See Chapter 10 Love In The Bible
Curse
1 Corinthians 6:10 · 187
Galatians 3:10-14 · 188
Judgment of the Gentiles Matthew 25:31-46 · 187
Luke 6:28 · 187
CURSE · 187
Cursing Of Ham Linked To Slavery · 45
Customary Marriages Act · See Gay Marriage/South Africa

D

Dealing With Emotions · 273, See Chapter 13
Depression
Matthew 11:28 · 304
Desodomizing
Desodomozing · See Chapter 4 Sodom & Gomorrah
Desodomizing\ Your Minds · 66
Deuteronomy 24:16 · 33
DEVIL/SATAN · 189
Did Noah's son really have relations with him? · 46
Discernment
Hebrews 5:12-14 · 305
DNA · 35

Index

Does The Church Not Know The Scriptures? · 85
dominions · 56
Doubt
James 1:6 · 306
Dr. John Caputo
Deconstuction · 62

E

Effeminate · v, xxiii, 70, 132, 139
Wanton · See Chapter 8
EGO (Edging God Out). · 151
Elisabeth Anne Kellogg, · 180
Elizabeth was King; Now James Is Queen!
King James · 6
Elizabeth, Queen
'Rex fuit Elizabeth nunc est regina Jacobas. · 7
Emancipation Proclamation · See No State Elections
Endurance
Mark 13:13 · 307
Romans 8:39 · 308
Esmé Stewart · See
Eunuch
Phillip & The Eunuch · 255
Eunuchs
Acts 8:26-38 · 253
Daniel 1:9 · 253
Matthew 19:12 KJV · 153
mis-education of eunuchs · 153, 217, 253, 254, 351
EVIL · 193

F

Failure
Luke 22:33, 34 · 310
Faith
Mark 11:22,24,
Matthew 21:20-22,
Hebrews 11:1,
Matthew 17:20 · 308
False Teachers · See Gay Clergy
Fear · 313
Exodus 46:3-4 · 313
Romans 8:31 · 314
Female prostitutes · 53
Feminist · 8
Feminist Interpretation of the Bible · 8
Forgiveness · 314
how many times should thy forgive · 315
Matthew 11:25-26 · 314
Matthew 18:22 · 314
fornication · 202
sexual immorality · 260
Fourteenth Amendment · 89, 355
Free · xiii
Freedom · 24, 125, 127, 357

G

Galatians 2:11-20 · *See* Gay Marriage
Gay Clergy · v, 217, 235, 351
1Tim 1:7-10 · 236
1Timothy 1:7-10 · 235
2Timothy 3:16-17 · 235
ecumenical · 237
Gay Marriage
Black LGBT/SGL "Blood Line" Connected To Civil Rights History. · 124
Canada Civil Marriage Act · 361
Canada Legalized Marriage · 99
Civil Unions · 93
Conservation Christian Coalitions · 93
Deuteronomy 7:3 · 97
Gentile Mentalities · *See*
Inclusive Definition of Marriage · 85
Interracial Marriages · 101

Matthew 15:1-3 · 118
Matthew 22:23-33 · 86
Matthew 7:1-3 · 121
New Understanding of Jumping The Broom · 105
Pat Roberson · 94
Practice What We Preach · 118
Re-Addressing The Marriage Definition · 96
Romans 3:8-9 · 12:9-10 · 122
Romans 3:21 · 122
Slave Marriages · 103
South Africa Legalized Same Sex Marriage · 100
The Definition of Marriage · 96
We Are All Guilty · 121
Genesis
Gen. 1:31-2:3 · 17
Genesis 1:2 , 27 ·
19:31, · 20
Genesis 6:8-9, 29, 40
Genesis 9:22 · 40
Genesis 1:1-2:3 · 35
Genesis 1:26 · 21
Genesis 1:27 · 15
Genesis 1:27-28 · 29
Genesis 1:28-29; 2:15 · 29
Genesis 12 · 32
Genesis 18 · *See*
Genesis 19 · 52, 257
Genesis 19:2- · 57
Genesis 19:4-7 · 57
Genesis 19:5 · 58
Genesis 2:15 · 23
Genesis 2:17 · 24
Genesis 2:21 · 15
Genesis 2:22 · 21
Genesis 2:23 · 23
Genesis 2:24 · 27
Genesis 2:25; 3:7 · 27
Genesis 2:7 · 21
Genesis 2:8 · 21
Genesis 2:8-15 · 26
Genesis 2:9 · 23
Genesis 3:1 · 27

Genesis 3:10 · 28
Genesis 3:12-13 · 28
Genesis 3:14-15 · 28
Genesis 3:16 · 29
Genesis 3:18 · 31
Genesis 3:20 · 31
Genesis 3:21 · 21, 31
Genesis 3:22 · 31
Genesis 3:24 · 31
Genesis 3:2-5 · 27
Genesis 3:5 · 24
Genesis 3:8 · 21
Genesis 4:16-17 · 34
Genesis 4:9 · 34
Genesis 6:5 · 46
Genesis 7:7 · 46
Genesis 9:22 · 46
Genesis 9:23 · 44
Genesis 9:24 · 44
Genesis 9:25 · 45
Genesis. 1:3 · 21
gentile mentalities · 118
Giving · 316
2 Corinthians 9:6-7 · 316
Gnostic · 249
Going After Strange Flesh · 260
Going After The Flesh
Genesis 6:1-4 · 261
Gnostics · 249, 261
John 1:14 · 261
Jude 7 · 260
Mark 6:3 · 260
Matthew 15:2 · 262
Gomes, Peter
Peter Gomes: The Good Book, pgs 155-162 ·
See Chap. 8 The Word Homosexual
Grace · 317
Ephesians 1:7-8 · 317
Greek Words For Love
See Chapter 10 Love In The Bible
Guilt · 317
Romans 2:11 · 318
Romans 3:9-10 · 318

Index

H

Ham · iv, 40, 41, 42, 43, 44, 45, 46, 47, 213
Heaven · 319
  Corinthians 5:1 · 320
  Matthew 22:29-33,
  Luke 27, 40, Mark 12:24-25 · 319
Hebrews
Hebrews 11:1-2 · 19
Hell · 11, 60, 68, 121, 149, 151, 163, 183, 197, 198, 199, 250, 251, 268
Helminiak, Dr. Daniel · 131, 169, 254, 255, 369
Dr. Daniel Helminiak pgs 117-130 · See Chapter 8 Word Homosexual
Homophobia · 273
Homosexuality
Malakoi (effeminate · See
Homosexuality
Deuteronomy 28:54 ·
See Isaiah 3:15-24 · 134
Rev. MLK. Jr · 138
Romans 5:1-2 · 135
Temple Homosexuality · 217, 224, 350
The First Appearance of the Word Homosexual · See
The Primary Issue Was Politics Not About Homosexuality · See
Homosexuality Is Not Unnatural · 87
See Mary Miraculously Conceives
Homoxsexuality
Jude 1:4 · 134
Hope
Matthew 10:22 · 321
Philippians 3:13-14 · 320
Hospitality not homosexuality · 54
Hospitality Not Homosexuality Appeared To Be The Issue But It Really Is Not · 56
Human Rights · 85, 99, 166
Humility · 321
John 13:8 · 322

Matthew 18:1-5 · 321
Hunger for God
Matthew 6:33 · 323

I

I am not ashamed of the gospel
Luke 14:7-14 · 115
Romans 1:16-17 · 114
I Am Not Ashamed of the Gospel · 113
Immoral
fornication · 202
Matthew 7:1-2 · 203
Romans 2:11-16 · 204
tionary of Philosophy · 202
IMMORAL · 201
Immorality
Morality · v, 56, 201, 276
Inclusive · 9, 11, 85
Inclusive Bible Language · 9
Integrity
Psalms 25:21 · 324
Psalms 25:3 · 324
internalized homophobia · xxii, 66, 273
Is Abraham Advocating To Save The Homosexuals? · 54

J

Jehovah
Elohist · 22
Jahweh · 22
Jahwist · 22
Jeremiah 1:5 · 47
Jesus & Eunuchs · 153
Jesus & Homosexuality
See Jesus & Eunuchs
See Love Is The Key Ch.9
Jesus Accused of Blasphemy · 82
Matthew 12:9-13 · 82
Jesus Challenges Religious Traditions · 80

Matthew 12:1-8 · 81
Jewish Christians · 109, 115, 123, 206, 207
John
John 1:14 · 19
John 10:30 · 64
John 17:23 · 64
John 3:16-17 · 5
John F. Kennedy · *See* No State Elections
John Wesley's · 133
Jonatha and David
1Samuel 20:41 NIV · 170
Jonathan and David
1Samuel 18:1-4 · 168
1Samuel 18:5-30:31 · 168
2Samuel 1:26 · *See*
The Love of Jonathan & David · *See* Helminiak, Dr. Daniel
Judaizers · 110, 115, 207
Jude 7 · 260
Judges 19:11-30 · 257
Judges 19:11-30 · 257
Judging · 325
Matthew 7:1-6 · 325
judgment · 30, 31, 32, 39, 40, 55, 99, 121, 197, 202, 203, 205, 206, 207, 208, 231, 233, 255, 276

K

Karl-Maria Kertbeny · 136
King James Male Relationships
King James · 7
King, Dr. Martin Luther · 72, 92
King, Dr. Martin Luther Jr. · 127

L

Laws of Sexual sin
Leviticus 18:20 · 76
Laws of Sexual Sin · 76
Leviticus 18:19 · 76
22, 20:13-14 · 76
23 · 76
6-17 · 76
Laws of Sexual sins
Leviticus 18:19 · 76
Lesbianism In The Bible · 115
John 3:17 · 118
Romans 1:26-17 · 116
Leviticus 18:22 · 71
Leviticus 20:1-5 · 73
liberation · xix, 8, 9, 124, 126
Lords Prayer
Matthew 5:9-15 · 326
Lot · 52, 55, 56, 57, 58, 59, 60, 64, 152, 353
Love · v, xxii, 71, 75, 77, 83, 112, 118, 122, 127, 146, 147, 149, 157, 158, 159, 161, 164, 167, 175, 213, 215, 227, 246, 268, 282, 291, 328, 329, 340, 350, 352, 357, 358
1John 4:20 · 146
1John 4:20-21 · 329
1John 4:8 · 328
John 15:13 · 329
John 3:16 · 329
Mark 12:28-34 · 146
Romans 13:10 · 328
Witness of the Scriptures John 15:12-17 · 158
Love (greek) · 160
Agapē · 159
Eros · 160
Philia/os · 160
love the sinner but hate the sin · 55
Loving v. Virginia, landmark case, · *See* Interracial Marriages
Luke 1:34-37 · 88
Luke 20:1-8
But and if we say, Of men; · xviii
Luke 9:5 · 63
Luke 9:51-56 · *See* City of Samaria Rejects Jesus
Luke 9:54 · *See* City of Samaria Rejects Jesus

Index

Lust · 146, 217, 243, 351
epithemuo · 243
James 4:2-6 · 243
Matthew 6:24 · 244
Matthew 6:33 · 244
Lynn Lavner · 77

M

Managing Emotions · See Chapter 13
Mark 10:2-12 · 27
Marriage Vs. Civil Union · 92
Matthew
Matthew 7:1-2 · 40
Matthew 15:2
Why do your disciples transgress the tradition of the elders? For they do not wash their hands when they eat bread." · xviii
Matthew 15:21-29 · 73
Matthew 15:26 · 74
Matthew 22:23-33 · See Gay Marriage
Matthew 5:11 · 39
Matthew 7:1-2 · 42
Matthew Shepherd · 83
Ministry · 330
Corinithians 3:6 · 330
Apostle Paul · 330
Ephesians 3:8 · 330
Mission · iii, xii, 4, 47, 81, 95, 114, 138, 146, 149, 150, 173, 228, 249
Molech · 74
Moving Yourself To The Next Level · 13, 37, 49, 70, 84, 107, 129, 139, 155, 175, 278

N

Nakedness · 27
New International Version · 41, 58, 65, 237, 246, 354, 359
Nicoloff & Stigliz, 1987
As a minority group; same gender loving folks are victims of systemic and ongoing oppression. It can lead to feelings of alienation, despair, low self-esteem, self-destructive behaviors, and substance abuse ·
See No State Elections For Some Marriages ·
See Gay Marriage
Noah · 46, *See* Chapter 3
Noah's Drunken Decision · 44
Noah's Task · 42

O

Obedience · 332
Matthew 23:23-24 · 332
omnipotent · 48
omnipresent · 48
omniscient · 48
Orpah · 161

P

Pagan rituals · 56
Parents Don't Sacrifice Your Children · 73
Pat Robertson, Rev · 94
Pervert
Acts 13:10 · 206
Galatians 1:7 · 206
Perversion - Philippians 2:15 · 207
PERVERT · See Perversion
Physical Creation · 15
Planning · 333
Matthew 6:34 · 333
Plato · 75
Power of God · 334
Ephesians 6:12-13 · 335
Exodus 4:2-4 · 334
Powers · 56, 149

Presence of God · 336
Psalms 27:5 · 336
principalities · 56, 149
Progressive National Baptist Convention · 128
proselytizing · xiii, 10, 113
prostitution · 53, 54, 56, 136, 137, 225, 226, 227, 276
Protection
Psalms 17:8 · 337
Proverbs 6:23 · See
Psalms 36:1 · 3
Punishment · 217, 232, 351
Ezekiel 16:15-19 · 233
Ezekiel 16:20-22 · 233
Ezekiel 16:35-39 · 233
Ezekiel 16:40-43 · 233
Ezekiel 16:44-52 · 233
Ezekiel 16:4-6 · 232
Ezekiel 16:49-50 · 232
Ezekiel 16:53-58 · 233
Ezekiel 16:59-63 · 233
Ezekiel 16:7-8 · 232
Ezekiel 16:9-14 · 232
fertility cults (1Kings 15:12, 22:46; 2Kings 23:7) · 233
Purpose/Mission
1Samuel 17:47 · 339
Esther 4:14 · 339
Matthew 6:33 · 339
Romans 8
29 · 338

Q

Qoutes

"Homosexuality is assuredly no advantage, but it is nothing to be ashamed of, no vice, no degradation, it cannot be classified as an illness." Sigmund Freud · 87

Almighty God created the races white, black, yellow, Malay and red, and He placed them on separate continents. And but for the interference with His arrangement there would be no cause for such marriages. The fact that He separated the races shows that He did not intend for the races to mix. · *See* Interracial Marriages

As interpreted by Augustine (d. 430) a Christian theologian, love is directed first toward God. And human being is so structured as to find lasting happiness only in God, the highest good. Human pursuit of happiness by loving what is less than God is futile; the chief purpose of love is to bring one's neighbor into communion with God. True self-love and love for God are synchronized or coextensive. Augustine held that the solid rock for Christian love is the spirit, rather than the body, the urges of which lead thy self from God. Harper Collins The Bible of Religion "Christian Love" First Edition · 159

Dr. Martin Luther King Jr in an interview responded to question presented by the reporter. In your statement you assert that our actions, · 72

I realize that gay people have put me on a pedestal, and I love it. Of all the oppressed minorities, they have to be the most oppressed. Sylvester · 45

Sometimes you need to cry; · *See*

The Bible contains 6 admonishments to homosexuals and 362 to heterosexuals. This

Index

doesn't mean that God doesn't love heterosexuals; it's just that they need more supervision. (Lynn Lavne · 77

Wherever it has been established that it is shameful to be involved with sexual relationships with men, that is due to evil on the part of the rulers, and to cowardice on the part of the governed." Plato · 75

While some will point out that homosexuality and cross-dressing are in the same category as incest and bestiality, it should be noted that so are divorced people who remarry, those who have sex during menstruation and children who fight with their parents. In fact it seems that any uncleanness, any violation of Jewish Law, can be considered to'ba... · 180

Queen Elizabeth · 6

Quotes

We come out of our mothers naked; everything else is just drag!" Rupual in her book "Letting It All Hang Out" · 35

R

Racial Equality · 91
Racial Equality In The Military · 91
Rainbow · *See* Chapter 3
Relationships · 339
Mark 3:31-35, Matt 12:46-50, Luke 8:19-21 · 339
Religious · ii, iv, xii, xiii, xvi, 2, 3, 4, 9, 11, 15, 35, 51, 52, 53, 55, 56, 60, 61, 63, 67, 72, 73, 75, 78, 80, 81, 82, 83, 86, 87, 93, 95, 96, 97, 109, 112, 113, 114, 115, 116, 117, 119, 120, 132, 135, 136, 137, 146, 148, 151, 152, 153, 154, 158, 159, 167, 169, 171, 177, 183, 187, 188, 190, 194, 198, 202, 203, 204, 207, 208, 214, 215, 218, 219, 221, 226, 227, 228, 229, 230, 231, 234, 235, 236, 237, 248, 249, 253, 261, 262, 266, 274, 362, 363

Repentance
2Corinthians 12:10 · 211
Change of heart and mind · 210, 211
Gen 32:26 · 210
Job 2:4-7 · 211
Luke 10:13 · 210
Matthew 27:3 · 210
Metanoia · 209
Psalms 51:10 · 210
Second Corinthians 12:7-10 · 211
REPENTANCE · 209
Romans 3
18 · 3
Romans 8:22 · 28
RuPaul · 35
Ruth & Naomi · v, 76. *See* Chapter 10 Love In The Bible
Beauty That Comes Out Of The Story · 165
Robert Woods Theory · 162
Romans 12:2 · 166
Ruth 1:16-17, 2:10-11 · 161

S

Sacrificing · 52, 53
Salvation
Ephesians 2
8 · 341
Samaritan · 63, 234
Same Gender Loving
"Brotha-z or Sista-z" - This is a phrase I established as a means to include all in our community

373

regardless of how they self identify. Everyone is covered from "a-z" sista-z or brotha-z. "BriSta-z" is just a compound of the Brotha-z and Sista-z. This term is listed in alphabetical order not to imply the male takes precedence before female. The word Brista-z has its own evolution process evolving from "effeminate male or masculine · xvii

"Same Gender Loving" is a phrase used instead of Lesbian, Gay, Bisexual and Transgender by some African Americans in the homosexual lifestyle. You will find many Africans Americans in the life that prefer this reference over Lesbian, Gay or queer (you will not find queer used anywhere in this book). The phrase was originally introduced to the community by Mr. Cleo Manago, Founder of the AMASSI Centers. This term in some areas of the community is the politically correct reference for black homosexuals. · xvii

Satan · v, 27, 28, 184, 189, 190, 191, 194, 198, 211, 214, 217, 222, 228, 229, 230, 350, 351

1Chronicles 21:1-4 · 228
Bildad · 230
Elihu · 230
Eliphaz · 230
Zophar · 230
See Gay Marriage · 120·
Sexual Orientation
Born Gay · 265
Coming Out · 269
Dealing With Emotions · 273
Developing A Healthy Sexuality · 267
Empowerment Networks · 271
Managing Emotions · 274
Supplementary Support · 277
Sexual relationships · 53, 75, 279
Sigmund Freud · 87
SIN
hamartia · 213
SINNER · 213
Human sin · 214
The religious community has different ideas of sin · 214
"cast first stone" John 8:7 · 215
"Christ died for us" Romans 5:6-8 · 216
"gift of god" Romans 6:23 · 216
"none but the woman" John 8:11 · 215
Ephesians 2:1-3 · 214
Ezekiel 28:6-9 · 214
Forgivable sin · 214
Isaiah 53:6 · 214
Original Sin - Genesis 2:4-3:24 · 214
Romans 3:23 · 214
Unforgivable sin · 215
Sins
Matthew 11:28 · 344
Matthew 11:30 · 344
Romans 3:23, Galatians 3:22 · 342
Slavery · iv, xiii, 13, 39, 45, 46, 89, 90, 91, 104, 105, 124, 125, 126, 127, 151, 179, 264
Slave Marriages · 103
1
Sodom · iv, v, 51, 52, 53, 54, 55, 56, 57, 59, 61, 62, 64, 66, 70, 146, 149, 150, 151, 152, 217, 228, 232, 233, 234, 248, 250, 252, 349, 351, 353
Matthew 10:5-42 · 150
Matthew 11:23 · 151
2Peter 2:6 · 248
Revelations 11:8 · 250
Revelations 20:10 · 250
Sodom & Gomorrah · iv, 51, 55,59, 61, 64, 70, 150, 217, 232, 248, 257, 260, 349, 351, 353

Index

odomites · xxiii, 53, 224, 234, 260
Southern Christian Leadership Conference · 128
Spiritual Creation · 15
Strength
1Corinthians 1:27 · 345
Isaiah 40:29-31 · 344
Sylvester · 45
Syro-Phoenician · 73

T

Temple Homosexuality
1King 15:12 · 224
1Kings 14:21-24 · 224
1Kings 14:24 · 224
Temple Prostitues
1Kings 15:9-15 · *See*
Temple Prostitutes · v, 217, 227, 350
1Kings 15:16-24 · 227
Temptation · 228
Temptations · 243
The Civil Rights Act of 1964 · 90
There Is Neither Male nor Female In Heaven · 86
Thou shall feareth the Lord · See Psalms 36:1
Transgender
Transvestism · 218
Transvestite · See Cross Dressing, See Cross Dressing
Transsexual · 60
Transvestism · *See* Cross Dressing
Tribal Immorality
Genesis 19 ·
Genesis 19:1 · 257
Hospitality not homosexuality · 258
Judges 19:11-30 · 257
Judges 19:15 · 257
Judges 19:22 · 258
Judges 19:25 · 258
Judges 20:5 · 258
Leviticus 21:7 · 258

St. Augustine · 259
Truman, President Harry S. · 91
Tubman, Harriet
(Modernization) "Harriet, you freed so many slaves. · xiii
TV Evangelist · 217
unfeigned · 246

U

Upper Room · 119

V

vengeance · 260

W

Wanton · *See* effeminate
Wealth
John Calvin · 347
Matthew 6:33, Luke 12:34 · 346
What is the greatest commandment?" · 147
What Would Jesus Do? · 61
Who "dat" woman? · 34
Why are we being punished for the sin of Adam? · 33
Wisdom of Solomon 2:24 · 27
Witnessing
Luke 15:2 · 348
Matthew 28:18-20, James 2:26 · 347
Women Being Silent
1Cor 14:34-35 · 240
1Peter 2:15 · 240
Acts 18:24 · 241
Acts 21:9 · 241
Women Silent · 217, 351
Wood, Robert

375

The Robert Wood Theory · 162
worship · 16, 52, 53, 54, 64, 70, 111, 115, 116, 117, 120, 204, 225, 227, 233, 235, 239, 249, 253, 353

Y

You Are Not An Abomination · 83

You Have God's DNA · 35

Z

Order Today

Check Amazon.com, Barnes & Nobles, Local Bookstores or Order Here

☐ Yes, I want _____ copies of the book The Mis-Education Against Homosexuality In The Bible, First Edition (#MH1000) for $17.99 each.

☐ Yes, I want _____ copies of the Audio CD version of "The Mis-Education Against Homosexuality In The Bible, First Edition (#AV1000) for $17.99 each. *(Available April 2010)*

☐ Yes, I am interested in having Rev. Greg Smith speak or give a seminar to my group, association, faith center or academic institution. Please send me information. *(To receive a faster response we recommend you send an email to requests@pointofviewpublishing.com)*

My check or money order for $_____ enclosed.
If you are using online bill pay include the following in the memo #BK or AV, # of items request. If using a debit/credit card recommend for security reasons using Amazon.com for your order. Include $4.95 shipping and handling for up to five books. Canadian orders must include payment in US funds, with 7% GST added. Payment must accompany orders. Allow ten days for delivery.

Name_____

Organization (if applicable)_____

Address_____

City/State/Zip_____

Email_____

Phone_____

Make your check payable and return to
NPOV Publishing   P.O. Box 181754 Atlanta, GA 31119-1754
requests@pointofviewpublishing.com